Praise for *Women, Spirituality and Transformative Leadership: Where Grace Meets Power*

"Many religious institutions still hold to explicit glass ceilings that keep women from formal leadership. This obscures women's extraordinary spiritual roles, their potential to change what we mean by religion and spirituality, and what a spiritual lens can offer to the world's leading problems. Exploring vital and complex themes like communication and leadership with freshly defined terms, the editors and contributors look to a world governed by new conceptions of power and success. The personal spiritual journeys of a diverse group of women offer glimpses of the types of transformations that women spiritual and religious leaders might bring to society."
—**Katherine Marshall**, Berkley Center for Religion, Peace, and World Affairs, Georgetown University; executive director, World Faiths Development Dialogue

"We all long for inspiration and guidance. With enormous sensitivity, *Women, Spirituality, and Transformative Leadership* gives us gems that are both joyous and poignant. Prepare to be uplifted and transformed!"
—**Susannah Heschel**, Eli Black Professor of Jewish Studies, Dartmouth College

"Call[s] us as women to the urgent task of developing a deep spiritual identity, not for our own good but to better equip us to be agents of transformation in a deeply divided world. Rejoice as you read this inspiring book and ready yourself for transformation."
—**The Rev. Dr. Joan Brown Cambell**, Department of Religion, Chautauqua Institution, Chautauqua, New York; author, *Living into Hope: A Call to Spiritual Action for Such a Time as This*

"This carefully crafted collection of women's insights into leadership from a spiritual root goes a long way in connecting the concept of power with the concept of love. Such a linkage stimulates moral courage, encourages social justice and opens one to deeper, more authentic, spiritually grounded relationships."
—**Helen LaKelly Hunt, PhD**, author, *Faith & Feminism: A Holy Alliance*; president, The Sister Fund

"An important book for this pivotal moment. Its collection of voices embody a non-denominational, invitational and inclusive approach to spirituality, while also addressing the nitty-gritty practicalities and challenges that leadership in this transformative time requires of us. It offers a systemic overview of a landscape we'd all be advised to visit, frequently— that of the intersection of diverse women (and men), reinventing leadership to address a pivotal moment of change in ourselves, our communities and the world, while staying connected to the mystery, or sacred, within and surrounding us all. It offers useful practices and perspectives for how we may cultivate ourselves to return to right relationship with ourselves, each other and the Earth."

—**Nina Simons**, cofounder/co-CEO, Bioneers

"If human civilization is to not only survive but thrive, it will be because of women: radical, gutsy, revolutionary women; women who don't simply become leaders, but who reinvent leadership; women who don't simply become clergy, but who reinvent religion and spirituality. We don't need women taking their place in a man's world—we need women to topple that world and lead us to a new and better one. The wisdom in *Women, Spirituality and Transformative Leadership* points us in the direction of a new world with a new heart and a new mind. This book gives me hope."

—**Rabbi Rami Shapiro**, translator/annotator,
*The Divine Feminine in Biblical Wisdom Literature:
Selections Annotated and Explained*

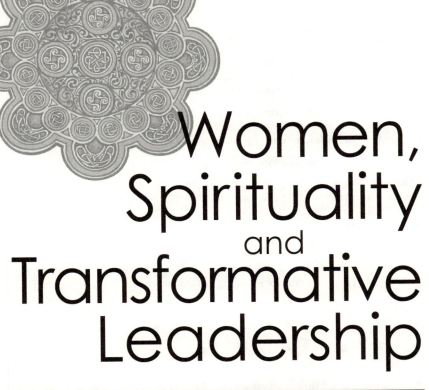

Women, Spirituality and Transformative Leadership

Where *Grace* Meets *Power*

EDITED BY
Kathe Schaaf, Kay Lindahl,
Kathleen S. Hurty, PhD, and Reverend Guo Cheen

Walking Together, Finding the Way ®
SKYLIGHT PATHS ®
PUBLISHING
Woodstock, Vermont

Women, Spirituality and Transformative Leadership: Where Grace Meets Power

2012 Hardcover, First printing

Library of Congress Cataloging-in-Publication Data
Women, spirituality, and transformative leadership : where grace meets power / edited by Kathe Schaaf ... [et al.].
p. cm.
Includes bibliographical references.
ISBN 978-1-59473-313-0 (hardcover)
1. Women—Religious life. 2. Leadership—Religious aspects. 3. Religion and social problems. 4. Leadership in women. I. Schaaf, Kathe.
BL625.7.W645 2011
204.082—dc23
2011037759

10 9 8 7 6 5 4 3 2 1

Manufactured in the United States of America
Jacket Design: Heather Pelham
Text Design: Tim Holtz

SkyLight Paths Publishing is creating a place where people of different spiritual traditions come together for challenge and inspiration, a place where we can help each other understand the mystery that lies at the heart of our existence.

SkyLight Paths sees both believers and seekers as a community that increasingly transcends traditional boundaries of religion and denomination—people wanting to learn from each other, *walking together, finding the way*.

SkyLight Paths, "Walking Together, Finding the Way" and colophon are trademarks of LongHill Partners, Inc., registered in the U.S. Patent and Trademark Office.

Walking Together, Finding the Way®
Published by SkyLight Paths Publishing
A Division of LongHill Partners, Inc.
Sunset Farm Offices, Route 4, P.O. Box 237
Woodstock, VT 05091
Tel: (802) 457-4000 Fax: (802) 457-4004
www.skylightpaths.com

To the Divine Feminine
as She manifests through us
individually and collectively

CONTENTS

A Blessing and an Invitation

Pire kan`ama, sii kanpattan, hittew kannossow, sottow kannossow.

Ancestors, on whose land we are on, I humbly ask you to guide us, so our actions and words that are shared will honor you, the ancestors on whose land we are on.

May these teachings go out in all four directions, father sky, mother Earth and the universe.

Noso-n (In breath, so it is in spirit).

> —Ann Marie Sayers, tribal chair of Indian Canyon Nation in
> Hollister, California; founder, Costanoan Indian Research, Inc.

A nation is not conquered until the hearts of its women are on the ground. Then it is done, no matter how brave its warriors nor how strong their weapons.

> —Cheyenne proverb

My name is Rachelle Figueroa and I am of the Tarascan and Arapaho Nations. I write this from my heart and offer you my hand in friendship and peace. With the utmost respect for my ancestors, Elders, and spiritual teachers that have gone before me, I would like to share with you some words of encouragement and hope. This is remarkable time on Mother Earth, offering an incredible opportunity that has never taken place on this planet. This is an opportunity to shift the consciousness of sharing, peace, and love into the Fifth World; to birth a new planet of compassion, generosity, and joy. The Indigenous/Native people of the world have been holding earth, air, fire, and water ceremonies and following their prophecies for hundreds of years for this moment in time.

We, as women, have been given the responsibility of birthing this new, balanced, unified world. We have within us a most incredible power that no man has ever experienced. The time is unfolding for each of us to take our place in the Circle of Light, the Sacred Hoop of the Woman Nation. Our connection with Spirit is growing exponentially, our hearts healing with sincere surrender. Do not be afraid of your power, of your light. This is our destiny. Hope belongs to the next generations that are arriving on our Mother Earth: As Mayan Shaman Elder Mitakuye Oyasin told me, "The new leadership of our Nations has a Female face." Together with all the women who have put their pen to paper for this book, we pray with uplifted hearts, to the Six Sacred Directions, for help and courage.

To all my relations. May you always walk in beauty.

—RACHELLE FIGUEROA, Sundancer, founder,
Morning Star Foundation

INTRODUCTION

As a woman of spirit and faith, you know something important
about this moment in human history.
You know it from your rich experiences in the world,
and you know it from a place of deep wisdom within.
Your unique pattern of knowing is part of a larger pattern
of feminine wisdom
being called forth at this time in service of this Earth
and of humanity.

We invite you to join us on this journey as we explore the creative connections between women, spirituality, and transformative leadership. We invite you to come with curiosity into this living community of spiritual women, listening deeply as they share their personal stories of how their spiritual journeys have shaped and honed them as leaders, stories about breakdowns that were actually breakthroughs, stories of relationships with other women that were both affirming and challenging, and stories about local and global challenges that were faced with integrity and collaboration, candor and compassion. We do not offer answers to all of the complex questions facing us as a human family, but we invite you to join us as we surrender to the mystery of being open, present, and engaged together in these uncertain times.

Many of us are feeling called into this fluid and dynamic community of women guided by an inner knowing that it's time, discovering our shared passion for service to others and to this Earth, and inspired by our diverse spiritual practices and beliefs. We are finding our individual voices and we are weaving communities of connection so that we can listen to and learn from one another. This self-organizing community—women of spirit and faith—is supported and sustained by a few simple shared understandings:

- We come together as women from diverse faith traditions and spiritual perspectives.
- All forms of spiritual expression are welcomed in this sacred space—prayers and songs, poetry and prose, words and silence, meditation and movement, reflection and action, solitude and community.
- We come with curiosity and deep respect for the values, voices, and beliefs of every woman.
- We are all leaders with valuable gifts that are urgently needed at this time.
- We are all invited to speak from our hearts and listen deeply when others speak.
- We individually make a commitment to self-care—to nurture ourselves with rest, nourishment, silence, movement, music, nature, laughter, or whatever else we need to feel fully present and prepared for the opportunities before us.
- We acknowledge that it may require courage to face our fears and show up fully for our Divine assignments at this crucial time ... and we surrender ourselves to this service.

We invite you to bring your leadership skills and deep spiritual wisdom to this community. We invite you to take a deep breath and simply *be* here as your authentic and full self.

In the Beginning

This book was born out of a deep curiosity about the current pattern of women's spiritual leadership in North America and profound excitement about the possibilities that lie before us as women of faith and spirit. It is our intention to offer a sacred space where the spiritual and faith-informed voices of diverse women can be heard and where the power of women's spiritual leadership can be explored, nurtured, and celebrated.

The four editors of this book— Kathe Schaaf, Kay Lindahl, Kathleen Hurty, and Reverend Guo Cheen—met at the Parliament of the World's

Religions in Melbourne, Australia, in December 2009. This Parliament was buzzing with feminine energy. People everywhere were talking about Earth-based spirituality, the Sacred Feminine, feminine principles, the full inclusion of women, women's leadership, and the critical global issues facing women and their children. Sprinkled liberally among the more than six thousand attendees were little pink buttons with the question, "What happens when women lead?" There was a full page of workshops listed under the program cluster "Women in Leadership." One woman observed with surprise and delight, "The Sacred Feminine is the rock star of this Parliament!"

> "It seems to me that whereas power usually means power-over, the power of some person or group over some other person or group, it is possible to develop the conception of power-with, a jointly developed power, a co-active, not a coercive power."
>
> **—Mary Parker Follett.** Follett (1868–1933) was an American social worker, management consultant, and pioneer in the fields of organizational theory and organizational behavior. She was one of two great female management gurus in the early days of classical management theory.

We four came from diverse segments of the spiritual community. Kathleen Hurty is the daughter of a Lutheran pastor, the wife of a Lutheran pastor, and a teaching fellow at Pacific Lutheran Theological Seminary. She also worked with the National Council of Churches and the Parliament of the World's Religions. Reverend Guo Cheen is an ordained Buddhist nun in the Mahayana Chan tradition and the founder of the Compassion Network. She has an interest in delivering inspiration via technology and a background in public administration and civil rights. Kay Lindahl is a pioneer in the interfaith movement and the founder of The Listening Center who describes herself as an "interfaith Christian" and teaches the sacred art of listening. Kathe Schaaf is a woman of spirit not currently affiliated with any religion, a follower of the Sacred Feminine. She has worked with numerous women's organizations using circle process and shared leadership models.

Our global experiences at the Parliament inspired us to learn more about women's spiritual leadership in our part of the world—North America. As we came together, we discovered:

- Although there are currently many initiatives focusing on women's leadership, most do not put an emphasis on the spiritual needs and issues that are unique to women and that may indeed represent some of the most significant barriers to activating authentic leadership.
- The community of spiritual women in North America is a complex pattern of overlapping networks, initiatives, and impulses. Individual women are often strongly identified with a particular segment of the larger community: secular feminists, feminist theologians, spiritual activists, subtle activists, religious women, interfaith women, women of spirit not affiliated with religion, Earth-based spirituality, spiritual seekers, and others.
- Many women's organizations and networks are structured in traditional "masculine" ways using hierarchical leadership models and processes that may not invite the deepest feminine wisdom or effectively catalyze social change.
- Although there are many diverse initiatives and networks for spiritual and faith-oriented women, there exists at this moment a powerful opportunity to build a larger field of collaboration, passion, and action by building bridges of understanding to connect these diverse networks in a web of spiritual presence and active leadership toward global transformation.

The four of us created a new organization in 2010—Women of Spirit and Faith—with a commitment to core principles that model a different way of working: shared leadership, collaborative practices, circle processes, deep listening, mindfulness, and compassionate action. The organization exists to invite the many brilliant threads of feminine spiritual leadership into relationship and to support emerging patterns for transformation. Over a four-month period in 2010, we began by listening deeply to the voices of many women representing diverse spiritual perspectives through a series of conversations held as teleconference calls. The calls explored a series of questions, and the resulting conversations guided the emerging organization.

The next step was holding a retreat later that year for twenty-five women spiritual leaders from the United States and Canada. Leaders representing diversity of age, geography, ethnicity, spiritual orientation, and communities of passion came together for three days of dialogue and inquiry focused on the potential for collaboration among the many organizations and networks represented. Questions were explored: What is it that wants to be birthed now? What are the possibilities that can flow from our shared wisdom?

This conversation expanded in April 2011 with a larger gathering, "The Alchemy of Our Spiritual Leadership: Women Redefining Power." Our choice of the word *alchemy* was a bold acknowledgment of the mystery inherent in faith. We've discovered there are many layers of meaning in this word. The original meaning (a chemical process to turn lead into gold) has expanded and evolved over the course of history. The Swiss psychoanalyst Carl Jung used the concept of alchemy in a psychological framework related to the process of individuation. Some religions use the word to describe a process of transformation and the acquiring of wisdom. Dictionary.com offers this definition: "any magical power or process of transmuting a common substance, usually of little value, into a substance of great value." There is a sense of mystery wrapped around the word *alchemy*, an invitation to surrender to the unknown together and be changed.

More than 150 women from across the United States and Canada came together in San Francisco to experience many diverse expressions of spiritual leadership. A series of questions explored through circle dialogues invited the wisdom and experience of every woman present. As we inquired into our diversity, we discovered something powerful about our unity. Catholic and Buddhist nuns, indigenous wisdom keepers, Episcopal priests, Jewish and Muslim activists, Pagan priestesses, young feminists, Lutheran theologians, Hindu practitioners, Urantia Readers, Christian Scientists, New Thought ministers, lesbian clergy, Sikh filmmakers, interfaith leaders, and unaffiliated spiritual seekers came together to share their stories and to listen deeply to the stories of their sisters. Some of them were women of faith affiliated with a particular religion; others of them were women of spirit who live their spiritual lives in the spaces between organized religions, often blending spiritual traditions.

Through a series of honest conversations, they began to glimpse their common ground: Many women shared a sense of urgency about being of service to the planet at this time of uncertainty and transition. Many contributed creative ideas of ways to encourage the flourishing of the human family. Many described feeling marginalized and undervalued as leaders in their workplace, churches, organizations, and communities. Many sought new models for leadership and success that valued the "softer" qualities of collaboration, cooperation, compassion, intuition, and emotional intelligence. The Alchemy gathering offered a lived experience of the Sacred Feminine as the grace and power of our collective feminine wisdom and passion transcended the boundaries of culture, ethnicity, religion, or age. This is a potent moment for women, a portal that has been opened by the turbulence of the world. The author John Shea writes in *Stories of God*, "When order crumbles, mystery rises."[1] We welcome you, the reader, on a journey into the mystery and potential at the intersection of women, spirituality, and transformative leadership.

Words Matter

As we begin this journey, we acknowledge that this book is created with words. Most words used to describe leadership, power, and even the Divine are distorted by the patriarchal, dominator culture. We know that as women, we have a distinct way of relating in the world that is different from the way men relate. Current definitions of these concepts are often based on male relationship models. As women, we have spent a great deal of time and energy trying to fit into—or even to master—that male model. But this has ultimately not served us as women, nor has it served the greater good. It has not helped us to bring forth our deepest feminine wisdom, and it has failed to create lasting change in the hierarchal systems and structures that threaten our future on this planet.

Words are powerful indeed, and it is important for women

"If the first woman God ever made was strong enough to turn the world upside down all alone, these women together ought to be able to turn it back, and get it right side up again! And now they is asking to do it, the men better let them."

—**Sojourner Truth.** This was the self-given name of Isabella Baumfree, an African American abolitionist and women's rights activist. She was born into slavery, escaped, and became known for her extemporaneous speech on racial inequalities, "Ain't I a Woman?" The speech was delivered in 1851 at the Ohio Women's Rights Convention in Akron.

to reclaim the language of spiritual power, once again breathing balance, mutuality, and a respect for all of life into our human vocabulary. Let's begin with some fresh definitions of these terms.

> **Leadership.** One of our favorite definitions of leadership comes from contemporary management philosopher Meg Wheatley: "A leader is anyone who is willing to help."[2] Women have been leaders in their families and communities throughout human history as they have done the often unpaid work of raising children, taking care of the elderly and sick, hospicing the dying, and sustaining their communities. Though their leadership skills have seldom been recognized, rewarded, or perceived as valuable by the dominator culture, these are precisely the skills the world needs today. Frances Hesselbein, president of the Leader to Leader Institute, defines leadership in her own terms and from her own experience: "Leadership is a matter of how to be, not how to do it."[3] Women's ways of being in the world are honored as authentic approaches to leadership for transformation.

> **Power.** We have observed that women are acutely uncomfortable with the word *power*, which has come to mean "power over" others, to subjugate, to manipulate, and to control. As we move into a new paradigm of "power with," imagine what might be different in the world if we could each become truly powerful on behalf of the greater good for all, if we understood the power to create change through cooperative action with others in partnership with Spirit, if we experienced power as the capacity to get the job done, in collaboration with others, for mutual benefit and the common good.

> **Success.** The *Wall Street Journal* recently featured an article exposing the lack of "success" for women-owned businesses.[4] The piece, titled "What's Holding Back Women Entrepreneurs?" defined success based only on fiscal measurements of growth and profit, even though the article quoted research showing that men and women have very different ideas of what it means to be successful. Men start businesses so they can be the "boss" and grow as big as possible, while women start their own businesses

so they can have a better balance of time with family and personal challenge in their work. A recent *New York Times* article found similar differences in the reasons why men and women run for public office; men want to win and see politics as a career move, while women are motivated to serve and make a difference on the issues.[5] The bottom line: Women have a completely different bottom line. We argue that this is not a lack of success—just a different definition of it, one that may actually point us toward a more sustainable paradigm for the human family than the old "profit at all costs" definition.

Collaboration. Right now we are poised at an exciting moment of opportunity for discovering new models of collaboration and collective action—even though we may not yet know exactly what these words mean. Along the way we have learned some things about what collaboration is *not*. It is *not* consensus—which often takes the passionate, brilliant ideas of the individuals in the group and runs them through some kind of homogenizing process to achieve an outcome that is not offensive to anyone (and no longer passionately alive for anyone either). Collaboration is *not* an exercise in subtle domination, wearing down the resistance of one's peers with a stubborn refusal to adjust one's ideas or agenda. Rather, collaboration is a fluid process, open to synchronicity, collective wisdom, and divine guidance with no attachment to outcomes. Somehow collabo-

"My memory runs easily back to the time when, in all the modern world, there was not one well-equipped college or university open to women students, and when, in all the modern world, no woman had been ordained, or even acknowledged, as a preacher outside the denomination of Friends."

—Augusta Jane Chapin. She was the second woman to be ordained as a Universalist minister, the first woman to serve on the Council of the Universalist General Convention, and the first woman ever to receive an honorary Doctor of Divinity degree. She was an organizer of the 1893 Parliament of the World's Religions in Chicago and the only woman to present a session at the Parliament.

ration needs to keep all the brilliance and passion alive, to value the unique function of each cell of the organism, and to experiment with new ways the cells can function together more effectively, gracefully, and joyfully. Jeanie DeRousseau, founder of the Women's Learning Exchange, poses this excellent question in her collaborative newsletter *Allies for the Greater Good*: If we are one humanity evolving, how can we adjust our thinking and our projects just a little to be more precisely together?

Mentoring. An old model of mentoring is a one-way flow of experience and guidance from one more experienced person (the mentor) to another less-experienced person (the mentee). The new paradigm of mentoring recognizes that we all possess wisdom and unique life experiences, and we can all grow as leaders when we are in authentic relationships where there is mutuality and a two-way exchange of wisdom. Mentoring, as we see it, therefore is a reciprocal process of listening to and learning from each other. Mentoring happens in one-on-one relationships, but it also happens in women's circles and at potluck suppers and around the kitchen table whenever two or more are gathered. We all need support, validation, mirroring, and reflective listening to build confidence and stretch our leadership muscles; mentoring is any opportunity to offer and receive that nurturing.

Faith. Nothing is more important in these turbulent times than faith, we believe, and yet the current divisive public discourse seems to have hijacked this word too. The meaning of *faith* has been narrowed and given sharp edges, often used as a wedge to divide those who have the "right" kind of faith from those who do not. We have a more inclusive view, however. It is both traditional and progressive. Many women consider faith to be centered in community—a congregation, synagogue, mosque, or temple where people share a vision of the way God works in the world. Some women focus their religious practice within a specific faith community that is defined in part by creeds or sets of beliefs—that is, Christian, Jewish, Muslim, Buddhist—and within each of these communities, there is diversity as well. For example, within Christianity there are Roman Catholics,

Lutherans, Methodists Presbyterians, Episcopalians, and others. But shared faith in God's divine presence, along with common rituals and practices, are at the core of communities of faith. We see faith as an amazing inclusive resource, available to everyone and absolutely essential for the tasks ahead. Faith is our assurance that there is a Divine plan of infinite love at work even in the most challenging moments, and that we are a part of that plan. Faith gives us the confidence to move ahead with vast visions in the face of enormous odds; it is an invitation to work in active partnership with the Divine in service of a better world.

Interfaith. At one time it was a radical idea to sit in dialogue with other people of diverse faiths, to learn about their spiritual traditions, and to develop personal relationships that transcended religious boundaries. In some parts of the world, it is still forbidden by law to do such a thing. This important work has unfolded over the past century and has yet to fully realize its enormous potential to transform the world. Since the Parliament gathering, we have witnessed an expansion of the concept of *interfaith*, as we intentionally began inviting women who don't define their beliefs by the word *faith* into the interfaith conversation. These women are deeply spiritual, although they may no longer be affiliated with a specific religion. The arms of the interfaith community have been opened wider, and the conversation is both richer and deeper as a result.

Names for the Divine. At the center of almost all spiritual paradigms is the concept of the Divine—whether it is called God, Creator, Allah, Jesus, Source, Holy Spirit, or any number of other names. We acknowledge that the dominant culture has defined God as masculine for centuries; many generations of our female ancestors have lived and died in a world where God is described entirely with masculine nouns and pronouns—Father, Son, He, His, and Him. How has this masculine language impacted women individually and collectively? Has it contributed to the subjugation and marginalization of women around the world? Feminist theorist Mary Daly said, "If God is male, then the male is God."[6] Educator and author Jeanette Clancy has challenged this language directly with a slim volume titled *God Is Not Three Guys in the Sky.*[7] Some of the women in this community challenge us to balance our language to make room in our spiritual paradigms for Mother, Daughter, She, and Her.

Grace. We have saved the definition of "grace" until last because it is both important and challenging. In a secular way, grace is often associated with certain qualities of the feminine; it communicates attributes of flowing movement, delicate features, and fragile beauty. In this context, "grace" has sometimes been used to confine women to stereotypically weak roles with an emphasis on physical attractiveness and less access to legitimate power and authority. When we explore "grace" in a spiritual dimension, it becomes a very strong word describing a direct personal experience with the power and love of the Divine. For some traditions, grace has always been there—within, without, and all about us—waiting for us to recover it in life's simple, delightful moments. For others, grace means God's love given generously with wild and wondrous abandon—to all. It isn't earned; we may not feel it is always deserved. It is in the mystery of God's amazing grace that strength and power are generated for justice. Openness to receiving that grace empowers women's leadership. Divine grace can be the powerful spiritual wind beneath one's wings. We are intrigued and excited by the intersection of these nuances of meaning: What leadership and service might women be inspired to bring to the world when they feel fully supported and connected with divine grace?

"When you have come to the edge of the light you know and are about to set off into the darkness of the unknown, faith is knowing that one of two things will happen—there will be something solid to stand on, or you will be taught how to fly."

—Barbara J. Winter

Where We Are Headed

This book is divided into four main explorations—questions that have made us pause and reflect, which have led us forward into new discoveries about women, spirituality, and transformative leadership. Each exploration has a short introduction followed by reflections from five or six women from diverse backgrounds, ages, ethnicities, religions, spiritual practices, and geographic locations. After each exploration is a "Living Our Leadership" section, which offers additional ways to continue your discovery:

Questions. We have generated a few questions that you might wish to use in conversations with other women, whether one-on-one, with two or three friends, or within a circle group or larger gathering. They are designed to support you in exploring new territory in all of your relationships.

Circle practices. We offer information about how to start a circle, what works, various types of circles, and some personal stories from women who participate in circles.

Blessings. This may be a poem, a prayer, a ceremony, or a simple quotation. We know the value of tuning in to the Divine, and these are some offerings for you to use and explore.

How women are leading. In these sections we offer examples of organizations where women have taken the initiative and are creating new ways of being leaders in their communities and in the world. This is a highly personal list and is not intended to be comprehensive in any way. We know there are many others also doing exemplary work. We invite you to send descriptions of them to us at womenofspiritandfaith@gmail.com to be posted on the resource list on our website, www.womenofspiritandfaith.org.

Leadership tools. Here is where we provide practices to support your leadership, ideas from women in leadership, as well as sources for further growth and development.

Between the four explorations are longer essays, drawn from keynote presentations at the Alchemy conference. Each one digs deeper into these questions and provides food for thought. There is also a rich resource section at the end of the book, including a selected bibliography and lists of networks, organizations, and websites. We invite you to view this book as part of an ongoing conversation, where each of us is encouraged to contribute. Imagine that we are all in the same room, sitting in a circle, listening to each other's stories. There is a welcoming and sacred feeling to this space. We are excited about what we will hear from each other, and what we will learn about ourselves. We know we are already connected. Be prepared to be surprised, and let us know what you discover!

SOME THINGS I KNOW TO BE TRUE

There is something here
that feels like
a lovely gravity,
And it is pulling me.

Into alignment,
into resonance,
into a pattern,
whose complexity
I cannot begin to grasp
except in moments,
in lovely
holographic
bits.

And there are others
who have been pulled
into this stream of grace,
swimming with me.
Sweet arms,
strong against the current.
Some of them such familiar souls
from the ancient future sisterhood,
that my soul relaxes at the sight of them
and sings in Her earthy voice
"Oh my darling,
finally I have found you."

The rules here are as complex
and as simple
as the pattern.

We must not merely survive,
but learn to celebrate,
the paradox,

the Both
and the And,
as it shows up moment to moment.

We come to serve, yet each to shine brilliantly.
We come to lead, yet no one of us leads.
We come to lead
by following.

(The clues have been left everywhere
for Her children
by the most compelling,
intelligent,
compassionate
Mother.)

This is what I know to be true:

We solve the mysteries
as we remember the code
as we laugh and stay in gratitude
as we surrender to the relationship
with the other
whose piece of the puzzle
perfectly fits
snuggled
against our own.

We must remember.
I must remember.

It has already been accomplished.

Though it will not
become visible
in a lived dimension
on this round planet
until the last seed has been planted,
until the final drops fill the wine sac,
until some magic number has been reached.

Until some magic number
of us
remember.
(We do not remember that number
exactly
but we know it in our bones.)

Our bones know
it has already been accomplished
in beauty.

Another paradox:
Each of us is profoundly important
yet I have no meaning
outside the context of the Whole.
Each of us is called to be
big
bold
beautiful
bountiful
bodacious
as smart as we can be
and only when we rise up
our fullest Self
can we fully surrender to the Whole.

And then there's life:
the children and the births,

the deaths,
the loved one ill,
the community fractured.
I must risk
leaving home,
to venture into a new land.

We must understand this:
There will be conversations.

There will be many conversations.
There will be resonant conversations,
fully wired with joy and recognition,
and there will be challenging conversations.
There will be times
when fear jumps into the electrical flow
and shorts out the entire system
for a moment.

I know this to be true:
It is all about the conversation.

And finally, there will be grace
wide rivers of it
flowing silver and turquoise,
glistening in the light.

The trick is
to trust the rivers.
I have to trust my bones,
and the story written there
and all the stories.
　　　　—Kathe Schaaf[8]

How Do I Express Being an Empowered Woman of Spirit and Faith?

Willingness

Here we are, Loving One, Mystery, Light,
beginning to quiet ourselves,
beginning to be still;

remembering you created us
to flourish in your love,
remembering an old desire to grow in you.

We long to be more than we are living now,
we long to live all we can become
but, fearful, wonder how we can.

We try to choose the best and truest path
but stumble in our living and in our choosing.
We want to handle things ourselves;

we'd rather make it on our own,
and besides,
trusting you, God, can be very hard.

But we need more light, your Light
to see the ways ahead,
we need more wisdom, yours, to choose
the way that's well for us.

Here we are, beginning willingness,
beginning to trust, to open ourselves,
our lives and our decisions
to your illuminating Light.
Here we are, Loving One, ready to begin.

—Nancy Bieber[1]

Our first exploration takes us on an inward journey. What led us to where we are now, and how has our spiritual growth empowered us (or not)? We wondered about so many things: What does it mean to be a woman of spirit and faith? What is the special role of women in leadership? How does faith hinder us? What happens when you have a crisis of faith, and how do you rebuild it? We became interested in identifying, acknowledging, and validating feminine ways of leadership. This led to the question of how we embody our spiritual expressions when we are in positions of leadership, and how we attend to our own spiritual formation in the midst of the realities of life, including how we balance work and family. Where do we find inspiration, renewal, and encouragement? What are some practices that keep us grounded, centered?

These many questions make for a rich and deep conversation. We encourage you to think about your response to questions that resonate with you and to make note of new questions that arise. We invite you to expand this exploration by sharing these questions with one or two women friends or by inviting a circle of women into deeper conversation.

Lynda Terry is a writer, meditation teacher, and founder of Vessels of Peace, the international spiritual network for women that, from 2002 to 2010, nurtured and supported women subtle activists in service to humanity and the earth. Subtle activism is the use of spiritual or consciousness-based practices for collective benefit, such as certain forms of meditation, prayer, arts and media, healing practices, or ritual. She also has served as a communications consultant for humanitarian organizations, including the PRASAD Project and Children's Hunger Relief Fund. Terry has offered service to a number of women's spiritual organizations. Her areas of professional interest include nurturing the feminine spirit in women and girls, the evolution of women's spiritual leadership, interspiritual practices and initiatives, peace-making, and subtle activism. She is author of *The 11 Intentions: Invoking the Sacred Feminine as a Pathway to Inner Peace*.

Becoming a Vessel of Peace

Lynda Terry

Acquire inward peace, and a multitude around you will find their salvation.

—Saint Seraphim of Serov

On an early spring day in 1984, this quotation by Saint Seraphim, hand-painted on a small, shades-of-sea-blue canvas, stopped my mind and stopped me in my tracks. I was standing in an art gallery on the campus of a Catholic women's college, where I worked as both writing instructor and public relations director. Three months earlier, I had felt so lost, confused, and conflicted about what kind of woman I wanted to be that I had a "nervous breakdown"—the medical world's catch-all term for what happens

19

when a woman exhausts herself trying to juggle and/or choose between the many roles that society's (and her own) expectations compel her to take on.

In my mid-thirties and in a stressful marriage (my third!), mother to both a toddler and a teenager, and newly committed to an exciting but demanding dual professional role, I had been barely holding it together at work, then crying my way through the evenings and weekends. After I fell apart in her office, my family physician (sensitive to my husband's prominent position in the community) put me in the hospital "for tests" rather than in the mental health unit. An extensive physical and psychiatric evaluation revealed that I was suffering from extended postpartum depression. The treatment, a low-dose antidepressant, was just enough to help me stop crying and be able to sleep, but not enough to cure the unremitting hunger for something I could not name. Standing in that art gallery, however, for the first time in my life I could name it. Every cell in my body longed for peace. Reflecting on that experience almost three decades later, I can understand it as the moment that set me on the journey to find my spiritual true north as a woman.

What was it about the words of an eighteenth-century Russian Orthodox hermit and mystic that so rocked my world back then? Recently I felt guided to revisit this catalyst for my awakening. I chose a form of reflection that I had learned in my study of yoga, where the key words of a written teaching are researched for their meanings, then contemplated in meditation. Although there are other variations on the quotation to be found, it's interesting to me that the one I was meant to discover begins with the word *acquire*. *The Free Dictionary* defines *acquire* in four ways: "(1) to gain possession of; (2) to get by one's own efforts; (3) to gain through experience; and (4) to locate." To gain possession of inward peace, we must first locate it within us. I once heard a great saint of India speak about how we look everywhere outside of ourselves for peace, when the secret to its location is in looking beyond the obstacles of our own ego and desires. To get around those boulders in our path, however, we have to be willing to change our course.

In my case it took more than six years and another emotional breakdown before I finally could see that acquiring inward peace was going to require me to change, to make an effort! So I signed up for a five-day meditation class. In my first twenty-minute sitting, my mind did its best to distract me with everything from barking dogs, to thinking I'd left the iron on at home, to wondering if my meditation instructor was single, to fearing the incense would trigger an asthma attack. But there was one minute, toward the end, where all of that chatter receded … where I experienced an inner stillness and peace I'd never known before. And in that moment something switched on inside me—as if an ancient code had been activated—and I was determined not to lose sight of this place of peace I'd discovered. I made the commitment, then and there, to meditate every day for the rest of my life, no excuses, no exceptions.

From the vantage point of more than twenty years of daily meditation practice, I can report that my capacity to re-locate that sense of inner peace while meditating gradually increased and then, over time, began to show up more and more in my life "off the cushion." Through the ongoing effort to fulfill my vow to meditate daily, I made many other changes in my life, inner and outer—especially in those early years. The details of my practice also evolved as meditation took me into deeper and more difficult areas of self-inquiry, healing, witnessing. I expanded from my original meditation technique into other forms, engaging in extensive self-study as well as studying with different meditation teachers. Through it all, my resolve to bring about greater congruence in my thoughts, words, and actions strengthened and matured my moral framework while simultaneously deepening my capacity for empathy and compassion. It was hard, humbling work, confronting my inconsistencies and hypocrisies. It *still* is; I struggle with it daily. Yet it also can be an exalted endeavor.

When I gaze out on the landscape of these twenty-plus years, I am rendered breathless at the terrain I have traveled, the progress made … and so very grateful. Through a combination of earnest self-effort and a great deal of grace, the periodic emotional breakdowns ceased, and I gradually regained my physical, mental, and spiritual health. I believe now that my ability to make the other positive changes of those early years—such as improving my diet, giving up alcohol, and letting go of unhealthy relationships—arose from the inner steadiness and grounding that daily meditation provided me. Meditation gave me a felt experience of peace, the courage and discipline to keep negotiating around the boulders my ego placed in my way, and a spiritual container—a sacred vessel—in which to hold it all.

The latter part of Saint Seraphim's quotation—"and a multitude around you shall find their salvation"—played out in my life in ways I never could have predicted that day in the gallery. Early on in my meditation practice, I was surprised to find people asking me to teach them to meditate. Though still, by my definition, a newbie to meditation and to the experience of inner peace, I realized that the fruits of my practice were beginning to show up in my interpersonal world. I could see that I had become more tactful, slower to anger, less controlling. There was a spaciousness inside me from which graciousness toward others arose. I had acquired a sustained-enough experience of inner peace that others around me could sense it, were drawn to it. I started sharing informally with others what I had learned from my personal study and practice. Gradually I began to teach meditation classes and workshops, to write about meditation, and to mentor students in their practice. I found this work personally fulfilling and felt I was making a positive contribution by inspiring more people to find peace and healing through meditation.

Then, a few months before 9/11, I began having dramatic visions and recurring dreams about bringing together groups of women for spiritual service. I resisted these inner promptings for many months, questioning their validity, until the memory of two incidents from my past helped transform my ambivalence to acceptance. The initial incident I recalled was from the 1980s, when I first visited the campus of that Catholic women's college where I eventually was employed. As I walked the grounds and halls, I could feel a kind of pulsating, loving presence. When I met with the wonderful faculty and staff, tenderness and longing began to arise in my heart, to the point that I could barely keep from weeping. I was not a Catholic, but I envied the nuns who operated the college; their joy of service and bonds of community stirred something deep within me. There was a part of me that wished I were free to live in a community of women devoted to God—for what else could explain this feeling taking over my heart? The intense confusion this experience brought—especially because I already was so conflicted about marriage, motherhood, and career—played a key role in the breakdown that resulted in my hospitalization. As I recovered, however, and in the years that followed, I pushed that longing away, buried it deep under other ideas of what kind of woman I should be and what kind of work I should do.

The second incident occurred about nine months before the dreams and visions began. I was at a day retreat where those present were asked to go out in nature with the following questions to contemplate: Who is my community? What is my service? By this time I'd been meditating for eleven years, was divorced and remarried (happily so, finally), and my children were grown. I was steady emotionally and spiritually, deeply involved in a spiritual path, and loved my work as a meditation teacher. I assumed the answers to those questions would confirm what I already was doing, but what I heard instead was that I belonged to the community of women and my service was to that community and their—*our*—spiritual service to the world.

Recalling these two incidents as foreshadowings, I saw that the resistance I had been feeling actually confirmed that the dreams and visions were credible. In the archetypical hero/heroine's journey, there always is a first refusal—a buying of time, so to speak, to both test our faith and inwardly prepare for the transformation about to take place. With this shift in understanding, I was able to surrender to the Yes in my heart and, in late 2002, founded Vessels of Peace, an international spiritual development and service network for women.

I was deeply involved in guiding Vessels of Peace for eight years and came to be perceived by some as a visionary—a "vessel of peace"—which made me even more motivated to be sure I walked my talk on every level. I felt a sacred duty to model for other women what being a vessel of peace looks like. Every thought, word, and action was held up for scrutiny. Often, those thoughts, words, and actions fell short of my pictures of what I thought feminine leadership should look like, but I learned so much from leading and falling short, from falling down, then getting up and leading again, from always listening for the guidance, trying to discern what was wanted, how I could best serve. And I learned that this, too, inspired others as much as did the peaceful demeanor and presence. One did not have to be perfect to become a vessel of peace. One could have the intention, and return to that intention over and over again. For it is in that returning again and again—that spiral dance of a woman's inner life—that the secret of feminine empowerment is found.

As I have reflected on Saint Seraphim's quotation and how it has influenced my spiritual "unfoldment" so profoundly, I've struggled with how to hold the word *salvation* in relationship to my journey. Because of its meaning in the religion in which I was raised, salvation in Saint Seraphim's context would seem to be about people being saved *from* themselves. What finally evolved my understanding was to contemplate the words that precede salvation in the quote. "A multitude" (meaning, many), "around you" (meaning, in your vicinity), "shall find their" (meaning, will *themselves* through their *own* seeking and effort).

When I meditated that first time, I saw a pathway to my inner peace and set out on it. I made a commitment and kept it. I learned from my experience and invested that hard-earned wisdom back into my journey. I opened over and over, to grace. In essence, I saved *myself* … first, by accepting that I had to change, then finding the place within me where peace resides, and finally, by living and serving from that place. I can see how people have been inspired by my example o save themselves, whatever that means to them. I can see *salvation* now as a sacred partnership of self-empowerment and grace.

The Saint Seraphim quotation came home with me that day in the gallery; it sits where I can see it daily. The words of many women and men of spirit and faith have inspired me since then, but my heart bows deeply to these words that first stopped my mind and changed my course. I have become a vessel of peace, a woman who has found her spiritual true north and navigates the currents of life constantly attuned to the precious cargo she carries within. A woman who knows she is heading toward a shore with many, many other vessels, a shore where someday the sight of our masts, filling the entire horizon, will bring great rejoicing. *Peace … Om Shanti … Salaam … Shalom.*

Fredelle Brief, who works in public consultation and conflict management, has been a social worker, an environmental planner, and a television executive at Vision TV, the first multifaith television network in Canada. Her passion for peace-building and interfaith dialogue has animated her work. In 1998, Brief was awarded the Canada Peace Medallion from the YMCA. She has contributed to *Stories in My Neighbour's Faith: Narratives from World Religions in Canada,* and *Faith in My Neighbour.*

But I Thought You Knew the Way

Lessons in Leadership

FREDELLE BRIEF

In Jewish folk wisdom there is a saying that for the sake of thirty-six kind and just people, God does not destroy this imperfect world. No one knows who these people are, and they themselves do not know that they are one of them. When one dies, another takes his or her place and the world continues. In Yiddish they are called the *lamed vavnicks,* from the Hebrew letters *lamed* and *vav,* which make up the number thirty-six. When I was a little girl, I heard frightening stories about the Holocaust. I did not know whether it would come to my own family, so I decided to look for people who would save us. Later, I decided to spend my life looking for the *lamed vavnicks* to assure myself that there is always goodness and kindness around us. I began to watch for simple acts of kindness and tried to model myself on this behavior. I also listened to people describe their behavior in difficult situations. I was impressed with the dignity of some people, the heroism of others, and the strength and endurance of many. Most challenges were temporary, and often one person could make a huge difference in turning things around.

As I matured, looking for good and kind people everywhere drew me into interfaith dialogue and peace-building. My empowerment as a woman of faith grew into a wider search for the *lamed vavnicks* while participating in group processes and projects such as these. When I was invited to join these groups, I chose to be an active participant. I decided to undertake only work that I thought was worth doing, whether as a professional or a volunteer. I became the national president of World Conference on Religion and Peace/Canada after the newly appointed president died in office. When other board members asked me to assume this role, I pointed out that I was not the best qualified. However, I agreed to assume the position if others on the board would mentor me and contribute their considerable skills and prestige to the peace-building work ahead of us.

As I became experienced in interfaith dialogue and other peace-building work, I understood that we are all imperfect and I grew more comfortable in leadership positions. One of my first steps in leadership was developing personal insight, including self-knowledge and self-acceptance. I needed to know myself just as I am, and to accept both my personal abilities and limitations. I know that I am brave and dependable, short and chubby, friendly and enthusiastic, artistic and alert. Although I might not be perfect for a particular leadership role, I know what personal tools I have to offer when I work with others.

Respect from Others Begins with Self-Respect

Let me tell you a story about developing relationships with others and how it has empowered me individually, leading to building bridges of understanding and support. After the Oslo Accords had been signed between the Israelis and Palestinians, there was a brief window of opportunity to develop relationships among the adversaries. The Canadian government asked me to attend a conference focused on building better relationships among people of different religions within Canada. We Canadians could be an example for others in the Middle East. Two Christian men, one Muslim man, and one Jewish woman (me) formed our Canadian team of speakers. Scholars and academics from many countries in the Middle East, except for Israel, were invited to this conference. I made it a point to talk with many of the attendees before I gave my speech, so that people in the audience already knew me. When one angry man started shouting at me during my speech, most of the others in the audience rose to my defense. Self-respect had given me the confidence and emotional strength to talk to strangers about my ideas. Others respected me because I had taken the initiative of meeting with and talking to them. Self-respect leads to respect from others.

Risking to Share, Sharing the Risk

Another important step in my leadership development was building trust. We must be prepared to share ourselves with others in interfaith and/or intercultural dialogue. Being open has its risks, but I cannot expect others to take those risks unless I am prepared to take them myself. It takes a long time to develop trust in others. Using my own trusted position wisely was an important step in my peace-building work. In Canada, professional clergy working as chaplains visit and offer comfort to hospital patients and prisoners and soldiers. Most Canadian chaplains historically have been Christians. Therefore the government's method of evaluation for chaplains was based on how Christians become clergy—namely, by graduating from a recognized theological college. Indigenous Elders did not meet these qualifications.

When I was the national president of World Conference on Religion and Peace/Canada, I spoke quietly to leaders of various Christian churches and asked them to quietly urge government officials to change this situation so indigenous Elders could serve as chaplains. This soft approach worked. No one in the government was accused of racism or humiliated publicly. There was no public outcry. The Christian religious leaders were trusted by the government officials, who then made the necessary changes to the law and regulations. From that time on, there have been many indigenous Elders serving as chaplains for indigenous people in hospitals, prisons, and the armed forces.

Commit to Cooperation and Collaboration

Developing collaborative strategies with others is another important aspect of my leadership. Working on a common project demands sensitivity and patience. Our government institutions are imperfect. Sheri Di

Novo, a member of the provincial government of Ontario, was concerned about the high rate of familial abuse of women within many traditional faith communities. Under her leadership this cause of helping abused women was supported by all the political parties in the legislature. Di Novo called together many women leaders from Canadian faith communities for a meeting to ask us to work with her in solving this problem. We all knew that in our own faith communities many women kept secret their terrible situation of being abused. They feared family shame if there were public knowledge of their abuse by family members. Many women even wonder if they are personally to blame for their situation.

In response, the women leaders from various faith communities agreed to form a multifaith group called Ruth's Daughters. Each leader offered to help in a way that fit the needs of abused women in her own faith community. We recognize that all our faith communities share the same dark secret, and we are committed to cooperate together to find solutions. Abused women need not fear shame within their own faith communities.

Responsibility Means Clear Goals and Honest Assessment

Accountability is a final leadership quality I have grown to appreciate. Each one of us is responsible for everything that we do. When we work together in cooperation with others, we are each responsible for the outcome, including working together to find out what went wrong. Several years ago I attended a conference in Amsterdam. I was leaving my hotel for an evening meeting at the same time as a man who was also attending this conference. We decided to walk together to the meeting. I did not know exactly where we were going, so I let him take the lead. On our long and pleasant walk, we were engrossed in sharing our perspectives as a Palestinian Christian academic and a Canadian Jewish social worker.

After about an hour I asked him when we would be arriving at our meeting. He looked at me strangely and told me that he was following me. In his eyes I was a European and should be familiar with European cities. As for me, I tend to follow my husband, who always knows where he is going. We had both made unfounded assumptions. I thought that he would know the way because he is a man (what a sexist I am!), and he thought that I would know the way because he saw me as a European. We laughed together for a long time after we both identified the problem. This experience taught me to set clear goals and expectations at the outset of a project and to evaluate success at the end without finger-pointing.

There is a lovely sequel to the story. Several years later I was invited by the Vatican to facilitate the first conversations between a small group of Palestinian and Israeli academics and clerics. When I was presented to the Palestinian delegation, I heard a man yell out, "Are you going to get us lost again?" My Amsterdam acquaintance was the group leader. It was a wonderful introduction to a rather nervous group of people engaging in dialogue for the first time. Humor is an excellent way to break the tension when people are apprehensive. What does this story have to do with accountability? The Palestinian academic and I chose to discuss what had gone wrong the first time we met each other. Any project, no matter how small, needs people collaborating with each other to set project goals and, later, to evaluate what went right and wrong and why. Accountability is an essential aspect of responsible leadership. The path of religious leadership that I have been following is built on self-acceptance and accommodation of others, willingness to work in collaboration with others who have strengths and weaknesses that are different from my own, using both quiet and open techniques for change, and acting with transparency and accountability.

My leadership journey began when I was a child, hearing stories about the Holocaust from survivors. Their stories focused on suffering, fear, cruelty, the indifference of many, and the courage of some. Some people survived because of the kindness and courage of another person. Hearing one folktale inspired me on my lifelong search for the *lamed vavnicks,* the good and kind people who always look out for the welfare of others. I think that I have partially succeeded in this search, but I will keep looking. It will be my lifelong quest.

Courtney E. Martin—author, blogger, speaker, and "freelance mystic"—is author of *Do It Anyway: The New Generation of Activists* and the award-winning *Perfect Girls, Starving Daughters: How the Quest for Perfection Is Harming Young Women*. A recipient of the Elie Wiesel Prize in Ethics, she is coeditor of the anthology *CLICK: Moments When We Became Feminist*, editor emeritus at Feministing.com, and formerly a senior correspondent for *The American Prospect*. She was a resident with the Rockefeller Foundation's Bellagio Centre and has also been a TED speaker.

Living My Way into Answers

COURTNEY E. MARTIN

I wrote this poem when I was nineteen years old and just beginning to claim my own inner wisdom about the intellectual, the emotional, and the spiritual in my life. It is most profoundly about being the author of your own story of the sacred, falling in love with the ordinary of life, witnessing and being present for the true defining moments. After my upbringing in Colorado Springs—a town dominated by divisive and corrupt religious leaders—and my intellectual hazing at Columbia University, where the brain is privileged over the heart and the soul, I was hungry to articulate my own vision of what the spiritual really meant to me and how it functioned in my life. Plainly, I wanted to name what mattered most. I read this poem in dark bars and crowded coffee shops all over the country in the early aughts as part of the exploding spoken-word poetry movement. It was the most authentically spiritual and communal experience I'd ever had, a place where so many marginalized people were being the authorities on their own lives, experiences, and notions of the Divine.

AMEN

    Momma was looking for God in beautiful brick buildings
someone told her he rested there
but after six years of my restless Mary Janes hitting the Bible
    stands
and my mother forced to tear
my sleeping angel brother and I from
Sunday morning heaven
to uncomforting wooden pew child hell
well
she just decided watching her babies slumber
with sweet half moon eyes
was closer to God than listening to some old man categorize
the saved from the sinners

I guess that makes me a sinner
blood thick and moral thinner
with the freedom to see my own divinity
stereotypical God is invisibility
to me
the ignorant one
blind bliss you might call it
when the preacher asked have you seen God
I responded well call me blind and soulless
but at least my inadequacy is honest
I see god almost exclusively in the smallest
overlooked of things
like a microcosmic spirituality
I don't let the reality
of big churches with big money
turn my 20/20 vision
into a mad scramble for eternal life on commission
like the more cash I throw in the collection plate
the more likely I am to earn a heavenly fate
call it heretical mister preacher man

but I find heaven in the last grain of sand found between
    my toes on the ride home from the beach
not in Sunday commitments or expensive club dues
I find god in warm bread, in a new pen, in a passionate speech

it's like my spirituality is not the big stain glass in the
    church walls
but the light coming through them
the way it falls
on the tip of his smallest eyelash and makes me think of love
light and love
and something not necessarily above
but more in between
the space in between he and I
between beauty and my eye
between the microphone and my lips
between the beat and my hips
between these words and your understanding of them
that is god
just the attempt to listen to someone's story
to feel divine glory
in a simple human connection
understanding
maybe
is the most witnessable resurrection
of this ephemeral projection
of what god really is

god is the smile of a stranger

my version of god is like the blind I guess
the way they always confess to
seeing this constant rainbow of colors in their dark worlds
brilliant blues and greens
though they don't have the names for them
it seems
that's like my god

a brilliant dash of light under my eyelids that I can't label
it's like an ineffable force
that I'm unable
to fit into just one religion
one conviction
that has rules or regulations
the light is bright and free of trepidation
uncharacterized by religions that instill fear
the light is the opposite of fear
it is more near
a naked little girl in a back yard sprinkler
Rodin's thinker
the way my cheeks get pinker
when I kiss
the light, my god
it is endless
and made of something even thicker than hope

and god's not one man
not for me
maybe my god is big-handed momma
maybe just something as small as the comma
that separates his compliments
sweet comma strong
and clearly there are an army of people who'd be happy to
    tell me I'm wrong
but maybe god is the army I find lives inside me waiting to
    deliver salvation
when there is no one else to save me
maybe
god is
butter pecan ice cream and sidewalk chalk
snowballs and waterfalls
and middle of the night calls
painful things too
maybe god abounds in cancer cells

and nursing home smells
and death
and birth
and birth
maybe god lives in the children I will one day bear

the truth for me
god is in the in between
in between the fear and the execution
the question and the solution
the need to express
and the poem that manifests
god is the time it takes between me saying the last word of
    this poem and for you hearing it
amen
    —Courtney E. Martin

It has been almost ten years since I uttered that last "amen" in a crowded poetry reading. My poetics are no longer expressed in bars and coffee shops, but more often integrated into an opinion piece for a national newspaper, an analysis of gender and power at my coedited blog Feminist-ing.com, or in the pages of one of my labored-over books. My sense of the spiritual has also morphed and changed. Although I still find it in the "smallest, most overlooked of things," I have more experience of how those small things function as lifelines when the larger swells of life threaten to overtake and devastate me. A cup of coffee, sipped on a fire escape on a warm morning after a night of anxious dreams or unexpected sadness, is like a prayer to me. A walk with my mom under the giant New Mexico sky after a season of struggle is healing. A reporting trip in which I enter the relationship-rich world of a prison reentry social worker in East L.A., and discover there is so much good underneath all the bad news, is a resurrection of my idealism.

I better understand the ways in which the divine is born from the sheer vulnerability of the human experience. I have suffered since I was an earnest nineteen-year-old writing those audacious words. I have lost people who I loved very dearly. I have been so profoundly disappointed. I have come up against the capacity for cruelty in all of us. And all of this, rather than distancing me from the divine, has tethered me more resolutely to it. My own personal experiences of suffering have given me insight into and empathy for the suffering of others—undeniable evidence of our interconnection. My uncertainty, my failures, my confusion have opened me up even more to the necessity of humility, of admitting what I do not know, of forgiving and being gentle with myself, and at the same time, tuning into my own intuition, my own inviolable sense that there is meaning in this world, in our brief time here, in my one little life.

I thought about going to divinity school to try to understand some of the spiritual questions that I still live with daily—How can we witness such suffering in the world and stay resilient? What does a contemporary, moral life look like? How can I continue to trust the process?—but my intuition tells me that the answers I'm looking for still aren't to be found in "beautiful, brick buildings" handed down by designated male authorities. Instead, I trust that, as the Austrian poet Rainer Maria Rilke advocates, I am living my way into the answers.

Yoland Trevino is principal of Transformative Collaborations International and the former executive director of the Vaughn Family Center, which became a "living lab" for testing out innovations based on spiritual and ancestral values. Involved with international interfaith and intercultural efforts for the past thirty years, she is cocreator, coordinator, and a faculty member of the international program Cities in the 21st Century: People, Planning, and Politics, based in India. Trevino is also founder of the Indigenous Global Initiative and the Women's Global Initiative within the United Religions Initiative.

Reconciling the Blessings and Challenges of Diversity through Ancestral Spiritual Values

YOLAND TREVINO

In Lak'ech Ala K'in. In my Mayan tradition this sacred greeting serves to honor another and means "I am another yourself" or "I am you, and you are me." Another meaning is "I bow to the Divine within you." When this greeting is given, there is always an action of placing the hands over the heart. In the Hindu tradition the greeting *Namaste*, which I learned through my work and connection with spiritual teachers in India, corresponds and is similar to the Mayan greeting. It is a philosophical statement affirming that the doer of everything is not me but the gods. With these greetings I embrace the blessings of diversity.

I was born in Guatemala City, Guatemala, of indigenous Maya lineage. The greatest influence in my life was my paternal grandmother, whom I affectionately called Mama Munda, which means "mother of the world." She was the one who taught me to understand the Maya Cosmo-vision, which views the universe as a dynamic web of ever-changing living energies that constantly flow from invisible to visible living forms, and the Maya holistic understanding of reality. Everything was alive and sentient to my grandmother, who possessed a certain spiritual sight that both guided and informed her. Once she and I were walking in a forested area near our home when she pointed to an elemental being that she alone saw. My grandmother said it was an *enanito*, a small dwarf helper of the rain spirits. Although I did not see it, I will always remember her telling me this. This and other instances where she shared her spiritual worldview instilled in me a sense of wonder and amazement of the worlds both seen and unseen as well as an awareness of the inner lives of all beings.

I experienced my interconnectedness with all creatures, be they human creatures of the air, land, waters, or even the very stones and plants themselves. I learned that we are all part of one vast unchanging network of relationships that can be traced to the Great Spirit Ancestors across many cultures. I am in attunement with all that surround us, and I am at peace with it. My grandmother taught me about the inherent value of life—a concept I would later come to know as *ahimsa*, a Sanskrit word meaning "nonviolence"—as she refused to kill even an ant. Instead, she fed them so they would leave the house on their own. As a child, observing my grandmother's reverence for all life taught me the spiritual views and values by which I live today.

I have also been deeply influenced by the spiritual teachings experienced throughout my travels in India, where I came to fully appreciate the Living Universal Consciousness. This expansive worldview recognizes the Divine within each one of us. As we feel the blessings of what each of us brings—our divine expression of who we are—we can mirror that in one another. In Mayan tradition we believe that we are all related to one another, not just in an abstract sense but as real family. As I look at nature and its wondrous expressions, I am in awe and delighted about the colorful array. The same is true of our human family—how boring it would be if we were all uniform and without our own unique definitions. My knowledge and experiences have been deeply influenced by the spiritual awareness I learned as a young girl. Later I discovered that even contemporary men of science have expressed an understanding of the subtle spiritual nature of reality: "Everyone who is seriously involved in the pursuit of science becomes convinced that a spirit is manifest in the laws of the universe—a spirit vastly superior to that of men."[2]

I believe that the challenges of living with diversity grow from a cultural socialization that promotes separateness as opposed to oneness. I believe that this perception of separateness is the biggest challenge, as it creates the false view that my manifestation, my religion, my country is better than yours. In this way it serves to divide people. In Guatemala there was a sense that people, ideas, religions, and other things that were of European origin were inherently better. This can create for many the belief that Native ways, people, and beliefs are to be avoided or forgotten, which is very sad. Of course, this was fueled by many religions promoting the old European concept that Native indigenous people were savages to be dominated, Christianized, or killed. To this day, this perception continues to fuel a division between the indigenous people and those of mixed Native and European ancestry.

For me, the blessing of diversity is to experience ourselves as interconnected, integrated in all that lives. We are called to experience the gift that when we stand for each other, greatness can bloom before our eyes. When we accept that every member of the human family has an ultimate reason and a purpose for being on the planet at this time, only then can we joyously experience existence. When I can be my unique self by embracing who I am at my highest, I can offer the same divine right to the rest of the world. I believe that "we are each of us angels with only one wing, and we can only fly by embracing one another."[3]

How can we reconcile the challenges and blessings of diversity? Our first challenge is in recognizing when we slip into judging, distancing ourselves from walking a mile in other people's shoes, and slipping into a place of separation from that oneness. Separation eventually leads to despair. The blessing is our opportunity to embrace "what is" without wanting to change it into something else. I intentionally choose to experience myself and see everyone else as a jewel in Indra's Net. As the author Stephen Mitchell wrote in his *The Enlightened Mind*: "The Net of Indra is a profound and subtle metaphor for the structure of reality. Imagine a vast net; at each crossing point there is a jewel; each jewel is perfectly clear and reflects all the other jewels in the net, the way two mirrors placed opposite each other will reflect an image ad infinitum. The jewel in this metaphor stands for an individual being, or an individual consciousness, or a cell or an atom. Every jewel is intimately connected with all other jewels in the universe, and a change in one jewel means a change, however slight, in every other jewel."[4]

In this world, where there is so much emphasis on money, power, prestige, and fame, when the TV news is largely tragic and undermining our happiness, it can be easy for some to forget our true divine nature. When we get caught up in the world of pain and loss, it is sometimes easy to forget the wonder and joy of our cosmic heritage ... that many of the very elements that make up our bodies were fused within stars in the distant past ... that we are all one, and one with all there is. Keeping this knowledge alive in our hearts through ritual and ceremony can help us step outside of our small selves and experience the world and its people as sacred.

My values and spiritual traditions take me to far and distant lands to meet with authentic indigenous leaders, where I may sit at their feet and in ceremony remember who I really am, and bring forth the innate wisdom whispered by my ancestral spiritual guides. My spiritual values were shaped by the traditions and practices with which I was raised—yet my cultural and spiritual identity continues to evolve throughout my life by my learning, sharing, and celebrating the diverse traditions of others. Perhaps the greatest blessing of diversity is that it is a great teacher—for in appreciating our differences, we come to realize in some fundamental way at our very core, within our heart of hearts, that we are all brothers and sisters on the road of life. In this way we consecrate the path we tread as we make our way in the world. Each one of us has a higher purpose as a sacred manifestation of the divine. When we pursue this purpose, we contribute to manifesting a world in balance, where women and men can fully express their divine origin as being complementary opposites in a world where there is no "other."

Susan Quinn, born and raised in the Jewish faith, has also practiced Buddhism since the early 1990s. She leads a meditation group in Poinciana, Florida, and teaches several types of meditation. The author of *The Deepest Spiritual Life: The Art of Combining Personal Practice with Religious Community*, Quinn also publishes a monthly newsletter. She has owned and operated training and consulting businesses since the 1980s. Her specialties are managing conflict, helping organizations and individuals deal with change, and facilitating team building and problem-solving workshops.

Faith in the Transitions of Not Knowing

SUSAN QUINN

A short while ago—it seems so much longer—I made one of the most difficult decisions of my life: I ended my relationship with my Zen teacher. She and I had worked together for fifteen years, and I was in the final stages of becoming a *sensei* (teacher) when I realized that it was necessary for me to move on. Although I was certain that I had made the right decision, it was nevertheless a painful one, and I am still going through the grieving process. Even so, my spiritual practice has served me well through this time of transition; it has helped me understand how I arrived at this decision, how to work with the raw emotions that have arisen, and otherwise heal in so many ways.

My spiritual practice has empowered me to reflect deeply on where I am, who I am, and where I am going. Zen practice has been my most profound teacher and my healing balm during this period. It has provided me with many tools—experiential as well as philosophical—to both learn from and heal from my experience. Although my relationship with my teacher has ended, I am more committed than ever to my personal practice. I'd like to share how it is guiding me through this time.

Sitting through My Sorrow

In Zen Buddhism we call meditation *zazen,* or "sitting practice." Zazen is central to Zen, and it has grounded my life in peace and, often, clarity. Medical research validates my belief that when I meditate, I change my brain! Early on I experienced calmness and less stress, as I incorporated meditation into my daily life; over time I have continued to experience more openness and joy in my life. In the past when times were tough, I had convinced myself that meditating was the last thing I wanted to do. After all, with my mind going crazy, why bother! Over time and with a deeper understanding, however, I realized that *not* meditating was simply not an option. Choosing not to meditate would be like not getting out of bed in the morning. So after leaving my teacher, I continued to meditate. Sometimes my mind flew everywhere, remembering the past, worrying about the future, with sadness welling up along with disappointment about all that had occurred. But in between those thoughts were moments of peace, solace, even joy; although my practice reminds me that the "good emotions" can't be held onto either, I recognized that as the days and weeks went by, I was comforted by more periods of spaciousness and lightness.

Recognizing and Embracing Loss

I knew that by ending the relationship with my teacher, I would be filled with anxiety, sadness, anger, confusion, disillusionment, and a myriad of other emotions. But knowing the results of my decision was completely different from allowing myself to experience them. At one level I knew that I had to allow myself to experience whatever arose in order to move through my grief, but who really wants to embrace misery? Instead, one of the first things I recalled was the basic premise of Zen, the Four Noble Truths. These truths reminded me that life is filled with suffering, disappointment, and loss; that we suffer, not because of these experiences, whether they are annoying or excruciatingly painful, but because we hold onto our desire to keep things safe, predictable, and consistent; that we don't have to live in these constant cycles of loss and clinging; and that there is a path to moving through them to freedom. I gently and regularly reminded myself that everything is impermanent, and how I responded to the outcomes of change was up to me. With all that said, though, I was still suffering! By continually reminding myself that my grief was also impermanent, however, I could breathe into my fragile and vulnerable condition and discover that even moment to moment there was also peace and well-being.

Nevertheless, I'm human, and the paradox of life is that even when we have tools to deal with difficult times, we still feel our deepest emotions. As grief, tears, sadness, anger, and confusion arose in me, I allowed myself to fully experience these emotions. As the days went by, I noticed the ever-changing quality of these emotions, how they came and went, intensified and dissolved. Zen has taught me that all the thoughts and feelings I was experiencing were ungraspable, empty of any fixedness, and would pass. I was especially surprised to notice my feelings shift regarding my teacher. Although I felt we both had contributed to the tensions in our relationship, and my desire was to credit her with "most of the blame," when I let go of blame and simply owned my contribution to the breakdown in our relationship, compassion for both of us suddenly had the space to emerge. I knew that she too was experiencing grief and loss, and I recognized that the sadness I was going through was the loss that everyone in the world experiences not only from time to time, but actually in every moment.

Practice Is Not Enough

Although my Zen practice was a key to my transition, I knew that it was not the only step I could take in this healing process. I'm one of those people who tends toward introversion; although I love being with others, I replenish my energy by taking time to myself. In the past, during stressful times I would tend to withdraw; no one wants to be around an unhappy, hurting person! I've realized that much of my spiritual growth has been a result of being in relationship with others. My husband, bless his patient heart, is my teacher and dear friend, and over time I have come to treasure my friendships with others as well. Rather than pulling into my cocoon, I chose to reach out to my closest friends and ask them to help me through my grief. They were extraordinary. They bore witness to my decision and my experience, offering comfort, a ready ear, even laughter. Along with my practice they have been a balm to my aching loss and have reminded me often that I am loved and treasured. My practice serves me well in teaching me that we are not separate, but in relationship with everyone and everything. And in the midst of suffering is also growth and well-being.

And Then There Is the Future

During this time of transition I also experienced the unavoidable question: What next? I asked myself every imaginable question, so that I could bear witness to all my choices and opportunities; I put all possibilities on the table. Did I want to continue my Zen practice? Did I want to continue leading my meditation group? Did I want to find a new teacher? Was I motivated to complete my teacher training? A part of me wanted to know the answers to all these questions immediately. Being in the place of not knowing is such an uncomfortable place to be! I knew, though, that this not-knowing place was the perfect place to be. I have trained all these years to learn how to rest in uncertainty, to open to possibilities, to be curious. This time of my life offered me the perfect opportunity to just not know. I also realized, however, that some of those questions might already be answered, because of who I am and how I live.

In the everydayness of life, I am a wife, consultant and trainer, meditation teacher, friend, daughter, sister, writer, and speaker. Intermingled with every single role that I play, I am a Zen practitioner. There is no way for me to separate that from who I am; so I still practice. I love providing a space for meditating and leading my meditation group; so I still welcome them into my home. To be in that leadership role responsibly, I feel that participants and I would benefit from me having a teacher in my life, a person to consult with, with whom to explore ideas. At this writing, I am investigating finding a new teacher. Finally, because there are a number of hurdles to overcome and steps to take if I decide to pursue and complete my training, I am letting go of my need to make that decision right now. Instead, I am free to move through whatever life presents in the days and weeks ahead.

Where I Am Right Now

So here I am: writing this piece for you; feeling a gentle breeze drifting from the fan overhead; sensing the heat of the Florida afternoon; wondering what is next. I am healing: my breathing is easier, my heart is lighter; my fingers tap on the keyboard. I notice my thoughts shifting: lighting on the past, touching to the future. My Zen practice reminds me that with all of that, there is just this unique and precious moment, here with you.

Karen R. Boyett, MA, is the executive director of the Interfaith Council of Southern Nevada. She teaches religious studies at Regis University as well as anthropology and sociology at the College of Southern Nevada. She also serves on the board of directors for the North American Interfaith Network and on the editorial board for the *Interfaith Observer*.

Practicing Empowerment

KAREN R. BOYETT, MA

My body ached from lying in the hospital bed. Scattered thoughts and bursts of emotion surfaced in between the queasiness and disorientation from the morphine. How did I get to this point? How am I going to get past this? How can I take care of all my responsibilities—my children, my livelihood, myself? My chest felt heavy. Every breath strained to be expressed. Tears of confusion and desperation steamed down my face. I wanted to escape, run away, or at least bury my head in the pillow so deep that everything would magically resolve itself.

Even though I am only thirty-three years old, chronic illness and physical maladies are not new to me. I have always been a "delicate flower." From my early teens I struggled with environmental sensitivities and body malfunctions; from headaches, sinus infections, irritable bowel syndrome, easy bruising, back and neck problems, food sensitivities, and fatigue. I remember a friend in junior high making a comment about the frequency of my headaches and achy back, telling me that I was acting like an old lady. In searching for an excuse for my physical state, I began to joke that my older brother (who is athletically talented and is a buff firefighter) had taken all my mother's immune system while in utero, leaving me with but a few remnants. References to my lack of physical hardiness have even found their way into my relationships with men. One boyfriend often commented that my delicateness freaked him out. Another boyfriend affectionately called me Florecita (little flower).

I was twenty-seven years old when I had my first child and had my second just before I turned thirty. I became more fragile with each pregnancy and with the real-life consequences of the 24/7 care babies and toddlers require. From early on, I was in essence a single mom; my then-husband was either physically not present and/or emotionally unavailable. For years now I have been the sole provider for my children and have worked two full-time jobs to make ends meet. This made for the perfect storm—a downward spiral that landed me in the hospital and out of work for five weeks.

I was raised in what I call an American Jewish liberal home. I attended Hebrew school on Sunday mornings and after school on Tuesdays and became Bat Mitzvah, the Jewish rite of passage, at age thirteen. But we didn't observe the Sabbath, and we ate bacon and shellfish … a lot. My mother is Jewish from two parents who are Jewish. My father is not Jewish. He was raised in Louisiana and reared in the Church of Christ until he was eighteen or so and decided that path was not his. We observed major Jewish holidays at home, where my father participated, but he was absent at anything that required synagogue attendance. We celebrated Hanukkah and at varying degrees we celebrated Christmas as an American cultural event. I got an Easter basket but never was Jesus mentioned.

> "Rendering: I come to pray, but sit in silence. I am listening for You to talk to me. You whisper, 'Come, let go your heavy burdens. Raise up your weary arms, all the light and yearning they hold. Into my hands, rest your hunger and hurt. Believe all you seek is not beyond hope. Trust it is not outside your being.'"
> **—Miranda Claudius**

I have always identified as a Jew, although the way I have related to Judaism and the ways I have expressed my Jewishness have been anything but traditional, orthodox, or even mainstream. I have always been spiritually inquisitive—a soul searcher, soul rebel, and spiritual adventurer. I have tended to look outside the box and have never been shy to explore and be led by my heart, no matter what seemingly wandering paths it has sent me down. While an undergraduate student, I began to delve into yoga, Hinduism, and Buddhism. These Eastern traditions, with their emphasis on the body-mind-spirit connection, deeply resonated with me. They provided practical tools for me to work with my mind and to deeply connect to my body, both of which had been areas of intense need. The more I learned about these Eastern traditions, the more curious I became about my Jewish roots and Judaism in general.

As I have grown and matured, that spiritual inquisitiveness has led me to hone my skills of observation. The contemplative practices of yoga and Buddhist-style meditation have helped me develop a deeper awareness of myself and the world around me. I have learned that the universe guides me and gives me messages. When I don't heed them, they keep coming, only with more force and frequency. The intensity builds until I respond, process, do the work that needs to be done, and incorporate the lesson seamlessly into myself. My stint in the hospital and the subsequent weeks of being bedridden were a message for an issue I had yet to resolve or even adequately manage. Now I clearly see all the earlier messages that had come my way, the days I could barely function from fatigue, the migraines that knocked me down for days, the bouts of the runs that kept me close to a restroom. I did the best I could to deal with these "messages" within the established structure of my life. I realized, though, during this last episode of illness, that it is time to make drastic changes in my life. I need to honor my body and what it's telling me in a whole new way, a way that redefines what living successfully means, a way that isn't dictated by social conventions and cultural norms, a way that is a unique expression of me and what I want for myself and my daughters.

What does it mean to be an empowered woman of spirit and faith? Or perhaps a better question is, What does it mean *to me* to be an empowered woman of spirit and faith? What I have found is that my answer changes and grows. It reflects where I am in my life, the point in the cycles of my life in the present time. My expressions of spiritual empowerment at age thirty-three look different than when I was twenty-five or sixteen. Even with varying forms of expression, I have found two central themes that keep arising and inserting themselves into my life, two themes that take on different shapes and keep showing up in obvious and not-so-obvious places. These themes keep surfacing and somewhere along the way I have picked up on the directives: "Karen, honor your body and own your expertise." Well, that sounds so simple. Of course I need to honor my body. Of course I need to own my expertise. What most of us know, though, usually through finding out the hard way, is that simple doesn't mean easy. It is one thing to know with the brain; it is an entirely different thing to know with your whole being.

I am reminded of one of my teachers, Khenpo Choga Rinpoche, a Tibetan Buddhist meditation master, who during a teaching pointed to his head and said, "This is shallow-thinking." He then pointed to his heart and said, "This is deep-thinking." I know that I get myself tripped up by mistaking my shallow-thinking for deep-thinking. When I recognize that I am doing this, my perspective changes. Shallow-thinking paints a picture where being empowered is static, fixed. I am either empowered or not empowered. There is nothing in between. It is dualistic, black and white. It discounts as irrelevant all the other colors and shades of life. Shallow-thinking perceives empowerment in a straight line with a definite direction, a set trajectory, and an end point. Shallow-thinking confines its perceivers to a harsh, rigid view of empowerment.

Deep-thinking, on the other hand, frees me to see that empowerment is dynamic and expansive. It expresses itself in ebbs and flows. It is the antithesis of the linear and instead recognizes the value of process and seeming sidetracks. Deep-thinking sees that inherent in empowerment is gentleness and compassion toward oneself. Deep-thinking knows that being an empowered woman of spirit and faith is an ongoing practice outside of the realm of a definite end point. Empowerment is a practice, not a destination.

In a workshop she gave about women's voices in the media, Jamia, a dear friend of mine, emphasized the necessity for women to own their expertise. As soon as she said the words "own your expertise," deep-thinking kicked in. My modus operandi for as long as I can remember has been to discount my skills and gifts. I am understanding, caring, empathic, compassionate, and collaborative. I value people and their experiences. I connect with people easily, and people know I am safe and nonjudgmental. I am genuine and value authenticity. I excel at understanding the big picture and distilling it down for practical application, especially in the realm of interfaith work. For so long I have easily minimized what I bring to the table because it comes naturally to me; I don't know any other way. I had not recognized that what comes easily to me does not necessarily come easily to others. I have gotten stuck in the assumption that all people are like me, so there is nothing special in my talents. This skewed thinking has led me to devalue my natural talents as not holding a lot of weight, and thus I frequently disown my expertise. I have been preventing myself from acknowledging my own wisdom and celebrating it.

I have learned (the hard way) that not owning my expertise has a physiological effect on me. It is downright exhausting. It mentally and physically drains me. Every time I disown my gifts, natural talents, and the skills I have honed, I deplete my own creativity and impose limits on myself that are stifling. I now see the interconnectedness of the two themes that keep surfacing in my life. Owning my expertise allows me to honor my body. This process frees up energy that I can use for healing and for creating a lifestyle for me and my family that honors the needs of my body. Instead of expending energy on self-doubt and fear, I can practice tapping into my own wisdom. I can be open to possibility and have the clarity to understand and make the changes I need to. Acknowledging and valuing my expertise relieves a burden on my body and creates space for well-being.

One ordinary day, in my early twenties, I had an experience of empowered knowingness that has stayed with me like a trusted companion. In the process of cleaning the bathroom in my apartment, I was sitting on the cool linoleum floor organizing the contents of the cabinet below the sink. Upon finishing that task I stood up. Immediately I could see my reflection in the bathroom mirror. There, gazing at me, was an

> It will take all of us to hospice, this old culture as the new one is forming. We can't see it yet. It is providing us with little tangible comfort in the moment, except for faith. My faith holds off the fear that this culture feeds me every day in large doses.
>
> —PARTICIPANT AT A WSF GATHERING

> The most major professional insight is that women are having this same conversation all over the country right now, in different contexts and communities. There is something bubbling up across many different fields and that's thrilling. I have been looking for what it is like to be a woman leader and how to develop professionally, how to pursue excellence in a feminine way. I am someone of deep spiritual commitment yet want to fully embrace the opportunities ahead of me in a skillful way surrounded by male-dominated structures.
>
> —PARTICIPANT AT A WSF GATHERING

image of myself. It was me but a version of myself I had not yet known. I was radiant and bathed in an illuminating golden wash of color. The image serenely smiled and exuded an exquisite balance of tranquility and vitality. In those fleeting moments, wisdom and empowerment were personified in my image. I knew then that this way of being is my birthright and that I will achieve this in my life.

Being an empowered woman of spirit and faith is a lifelong practice. This vision of myself needs to remain ever present in my mind and to serve as a reminder for what I know I want for myself. It needs to serve as motivation to be mindful and to not slip into shallow-thinking; instead, I must make deep-thinking habitual. For me, my practice is reconnecting to my body through yoga, both *asana* (posture) and *pranayama* (breathwork). My practice is cultivating mindfulness and compassion through meditation techniques like the Tibetan Buddhist practice of *tonglen*. My practice is listening and respecting myself through my body, my talents, and my life experiences. It is the process of revering my innate knowingness and manifesting it in my life, even when it is challenging or goes against the status quo. My practice of empowerment is staying with deep-thinking, resting in it and welcoming my changing experience of it with time. Today empowerment looks and feels like this. I welcome my experience of empowerment now and as I continue on my journey.

Living Our Leadership

Questions

1. How might we animate ourselves to claim our voices/roles as spiritual leaders?
2. How do you embody a spiritual expression as a woman in a position of leadership?
3. What are some of the practices that keep you grounded, centered?
4. Who are your role models, and whom or what do you draw on for inspiration?
5. What is the special contribution of women to leadership? What is the feminine approach to leadership?

Circle Practices: Women Coming Together

When women gather in a circle with a sacred center, a space is created that calls forth collective wisdom and inspires personal passion. The world needs both right now. As women of spirit and faith bringing our skills and leadership in so many different ways, we also need the nurturing, validation, and synergy that a circle can provide its individual woman.

CIRCLES

The moon is most happy
When it is full

And the sun always looks
Like a perfectly minted gold coin

That was just Polished
And placed in flight
By God's playful Kiss.

And so many varieties of fruit
Hang plump and round

From branches that seem like a Sculptor's hands.

I see the beautiful curve of a pregnant belly
Shaped by a soul within,

And the earth itself,
And the planets and the spheres.

I have gotten the hint:
There is something about circles
The Beloved likes.

Hafiz,
Within the Circle of a Perfect One

There is an Infinite Community
Of Light.

—HAFIZ, SUFI MASTER[5]

Getting Started with a Local Circle

Enjoy creating your first local circle.

1. Decide when and where. Plan to spend at least two hours together in a place where you can have privacy and quiet. This may be around your kitchen table or in your living room—or it may be outdoors in a park, at the beach, or in your own back-yard. You can hold your circle any time of the day or evening, depending on when women are most likely to be available.

2. Invite three to six women to join you. This invitation can be sent by e-mail, snail mail, or by phone. Use language that feels comfortable for you and your community of women friends. You can call your circle anything you want—Women's Wisdom Circle, Circle Sharing, Spirit Circle, Dream Circle, Support Circle—or if you think this word *circle* will be confusing for your friends, you can just invite them for a special "girl's night out." Call each of them the day before to remind them. Give specific directions to the location.

> "Spend some time each day in silence and reflection, listening deeply for divine guidance about your next steps and divine assignments."
>
> **—Participant at a WSF gathering**

3. Arrange your space so that seating is roughly in a circle, with the middle of the circle forming a sacred center. In that sacred space, on a small table or even on the floor, create a simple altar with a beautiful scarf, a candle, some flowers, and a few objects that have meaning to you. Items from nature can help symbolize our connection to Earth.

4. When everyone has arrived and had some time to mingle, invite the women to gather in the circle. Welcome them with some words about why you have invited them and help them understand the circle process:

    • Let them know that this is going to be a different kind of conversation, a structured opportunity for each woman to speak from her heart and to listen deeply to others.

    • Share some simple circle guidelines. There are examples of different guidelines throughout this book, or you can mix and match to create your own.

- You might introduce a talking piece to help focus attention on one speaker at a time—a seashell, stick, stone, or any small object. The woman holding the talking piece is the only one who can speak. She sets it in the center of the circle when she is done, and another woman can pick it up. This helps break our usual patterns of chattering with one another in multiple conversations.

"Create do-nothing, buy-nothing, hang-out-together days, perhaps with putting up signs of invitation in a public park."
—Participant at a WSF gathering

- Many circles have a question or topic to focus circle sharing. Keep it upbeat and positive at first, inviting dreams, visions, and hopes. The conversation will be drawn deeper naturally.
- You might also read a poem, prayer, or other inspirational words to begin the circle as you light the center candle.
- After your welcome and introduction, invite each woman (using the talking piece) to check in with her name and maybe one sentence or one word in response to the question, How are you feeling right now?
- Some women may be quiet or uncertain. There may be times of silence. This is not a bad thing, though it does sometimes make people feel uncomfortable at first. It's helpful to acknowledge this by speaking about it after the first silent time.
- Some women may be very talkative and begin to dominate the conversation in the circle. Call for a moment of silence and then invite new voices or remind them that all voices are important.
- As you come to the end of your time together, save a few minutes for one last round so each woman's voice is heard again. Invite the women to reflect, in a single sentence, on how this circle felt to her.
- This is also a good time to schedule another circle. You might want to meet on a regular basis—weekly, monthly, or quarterly. What is the desire of the group?
- Always close the circle by blowing out the candle and saying some words of closure, such as "This circle is now complete."

Blessing: Words for Reflection

Fill a bowl or basket with small pieces of paper, each containing one word from a list of words that have meaning to your gathering of women. Words that describe human qualities work well: love, peace, curiosity, gratitude, silence, commitment, surrender, explore, courage, and so on. You can also create a list around a certain theme—like the names of countries where women are struggling, or the names of specific women needing prayer and help at this time, or a list of intentions for your organization. Each woman chooses one word to silently reflect upon, pray about, and listen deeply for during the gathering and for the coming weeks.

PEACE PRAYER
Lead me to peace,
Lead me from death to life,
from falsehood to truth.
Lead me from despair to hope,
from fear to trust.
Lead me from hate to love,
from war to peace.
Let peace fill my heart,
my world, my universe.
Amen.[6]

How Women Are Leading
Gather the Women

Gather the Women (GTW) was founded in 2001 to, according to the group's website, "create a global community of women committed to practicing compassionate and collaborative use of their power, offering a container for exchange and partnership through local and regional gatherings, conferences and events." The organization's Covenant of Leadership states that "our greatest value will be creating a place where all women can gather with the assurance their gifts will be honored." Please visit the GTW website to read the full mission statement and Covenant of Leadership values.

Gather the Women brings women together for strength, for support, for encouragement, for fun, and for friendship. Women leave GTW gatherings feeling fulfilled, renewed, and inspired. The group has annual gatherings every spring and fall around the same theme, and many of women have regular circles throughout the year. Women are encouraged to meet in circle and use circle principles as taught by Christina Baldwin and Ann Linnea, founders of the educational company PeerSpirit. As Baldwin has said, human beings have been meeting around a cooking fire for millennia. It's natural. With a few guidelines it is a safe and more heartfelt way to gather together.

Gather the Women has thousands of members through LightPages, our Internet portal, and a proactive community of regional coordinators who hold circle gatherings in their communities across the United States and in Canada, and we have a growing community in Europe. The regional coordinators meet once a month on the phone. We have a working circle of conveners (aka the board of directors) who also meet once a month in a teleconference. GTW's founding mothers are called ambassadors. We love staying connected with them and learning what they are doing in their lives.

BARBARA BELKNAP

Circle Connections: The New Story

The majority of us on Mother Earth have grown up and lived with the "old story" that defined God as male and women less than men in knowing the Divine. The "old story" separated us, ranking diversity with white over people of color, men over women, straight over gay, people over nature. People and the environment continue to be exploited with this perceived worldview of having less value, a commodity to be used by those with the power over others. Hierarchies maintain this means of power *over*. Living the ways of the "old story" are destroying the planet.

The New Story brings forth the indigenous ancient stories and a fresh understanding from science that we are One, interconnected and united with God, Creator. The New Story unites us with all creation and, once known in our hearts, opens the floodgates to a greater understanding that we are all loved and magnificent. It is from Source that we gain access to the greatest power ever experienced in becoming cocreators of a new society based on right relationships with all creation. All life will be treated as sacred. It is from this collective intelligence that we acknowledge our place in the history/"herstory" of the Universe and Mother Earth, just a blip in the fourteen billion years of enlightenment. Circle principles are an integral part of this New Story. They guide us in our relationships and unite us. They show us how to access and use power *with* as cocreators of the New Story. The New Story is revealed through art, poetry, dance, music, ancient and modern science, storytelling, as well as how we interrelate to one another. How will the New Story change your life? *Namaste!*

—ANN SMITH

Leadership Tools
How to Meditate

Most of us can relate to the desire to slow down, to gain some peace and serenity in the very busy, scheduled lives that we lead. However, finding or making the time to do so is quite the challenge. There are many approaches to meditation. Here are a few ideas to get you started. We encourage you to find a method that works for you.

One-minute meditation. This can be done anywhere and at any time. Find a place where you can sit quietly. Set a stop watch for one minute (most cell phones have this feature). You might want to close your eyes to eliminate visual distractions. Place your hands on your lap or on your knees. Take a deep cleansing breath. Start your timer. Listen. Whatever you hear—whether external noise or internal conversation—take note and let it go. Keep listening. Take another deep breath when the timer goes off. That's it. Many people find that they are more relaxed when they get back to regular mode. Others report that they feel more at peace. Some say they find their minds are sharper after one-minute meditation, and they see possibilities that they didn't see before. It's like a time-out for your busy mind.

Walking meditation. This is a practice in slowing down and practicing patience. Find a place where you can walk slowly without causing undue attention. You can walk in a circle, in a straight line, or both.

Begin by noticing what it feels like when you stand still, how your weight is distributed, how you are breathing. Take one step as you inhale and one step as you exhale. It may take a minute or so to get into this very slow rhythm. You may feel off-balance for a while. Just stay with it. Notice how you will want to move faster. Keep moving at the slower pace. It is a time to simply be in the present moment, walking slowly. When you are finished, stand still for a moment to reflect on the experience. Feel how much you have been slowed down. Become aware of your pace during your day.

> "Nothing before in my life has met that need to serve in me like holding space does....
> [It] has given me the means to fulfill a lifelong yearning to be of service.... It is a privilege."
> —Lynda Terry

Meditating with music. Many people find that listening to music is a way to slow down and access the quiet place inside them. There are many excellent CDs available with various types of chanting, including Taize, monks from various orders and traditions, and psalms. Whatever you choose, take some time to sit quietly, listen to the music, and allow yourself to be fully present. Take another minute or so when the music stops and reflect on the feelings that were evoked in you.

Yoga meditation. Raja yoga meditation is simple and practical, with no physical postures, mantras, or chanting. Simply relax the body and begin to accept the light of peace, letting go of any tension. Think of yourself as an eternal being, a soul, a starlike being of light, and let peace begin to surround you, the soul and the body. When you feel peaceful, send a thought beyond the stars to the dimension of golden light, where the Supreme Soul, the Ocean of Peace and Love, dwells. Visualize your starlike being moving close to the Supreme Light, also a starlike being, and accept the light of love emerging from that One. Absorb and enjoy that love. The love and peace you experience will radiate outward to the world. *Om shanti.*

Buddhist meditation. This is also known as taking and giving (Tonglen) meditation. Follow these steps:

1. Taking: Begin by visualizing any personal difficulty or the sufferings of others as black smoke. Imagine the puff of smoke before you as you inhale it into your heart center. The smoke condenses

into a black pearl. Notice any resistance, sensation, or thought and let them go.

2. Giving: Pause and watch the black pearl transform into a radiant diamond. Gently radiate white light from your body and envelop you or others.

3. Rejoicing: As you exhale, notice the joy of sharing compassion.

Repeat the steps.

Sacred Space for Birthing Transformative Action

There is a special synergy that can be created in a group where everyone is willing to come together at the heart as well as the mind. In my experience of countless meetings—whether within the NGO community at the United Nations, among visionary evolutionary leaders, or in the tiny meeting room of my local church—I have noticed that a few very simple procedures help to dramatically shift the quality of the experience, and hence the result.

The real key is in the opening, which sets the tone for all that follows. At the United Nations we always begin with a moment of silence. The invitation alone signals to everyone that the meeting will not be business as usual, a contest of wills and opinions. In the silence the heart prevails. Unless it's a very large group, it's good to go around the table letting everyone introduce herself and himself or say a few words of greeting so that each voice is heard, if only

"As we become more transparent and safe with each other, our alchemical outpicturing will take on more substance and form, and it'll become more widely visible. We need to be able to share with each other the formlessness and our individual feelings of that formlessness before the actual form will show up in general consciousness. Like when Columbus arrived with his three ships, the Natives couldn't see them—and the shaman had to step in and describe the ships through their dreams. Well, not everyone can see these feminine ship-forms! We are the new ships actually. We are the forms in person."

—Bonnie Kelley

briefly. Then we are all truly present. In this style of meeting, no single contribution is dismissed. Each person is honored and gently brought back around if necessary. Voting is only to find out how people are feeling, not for decision making, because if everyone is not comfortable with a decision, there is something amiss. I remember one painful meeting where the group simply could not agree. So we stopped and went into the silence again. We emerged clear, aligned, and on track, as though a little miracle had taken place.

Closing is time for acknowledgments in gratitude. If the exhilarating sense of group mind has been created, every person present at the meeting has helped in some way. I like to close with "May Peace Prevail on Earth."

—Reverend Deborah Moldow

Digging Deeper

God Our Father; God Our Mother

In Search of the Divine Feminine

JOAN CHITTISTER, OSB

There is a subject intimately connected to every religion that we are seldom willing to consider. And, if we do, we almost never talk about it out loud. The unknown or unspoken subject that lingers around the edge of thought in this new and cosmic age is the subject of the feminine dimension of God: Is there any such thing? And if there is, are we allowed to consider it? If not, why not? Yet the truth is that what we think of the Divine Feminine will determine what we think about everything else in life. It grips us on both levels of humanity—the personal and the spiritual—and the effects of it are all around us. Women everywhere are denied positions in public arenas, excluded from religion's "Holy of holies," undervalued, underrepresented, underpaid, and largely underdeveloped in social arenas.

Joan Chittister, OSB, is a Benedictine Sister of Erie, Pennsylvania, is a best-selling author and well-known international lecturer on topics of justice, peace, human rights, women's issues, and contemporary spirituality in the church and in society. She is cochair of the Global Peace Initiative of Women, a partner organization of the United Nations, facilitating a worldwide network of women peace builders, especially in the Middle East. She is founder and executive director of Benetvision, a resource and research center for contemporary spirituality. The following is drawn from Chittister's keynote speech at the Alchemy gathering.

The first level of impact is clearly theological. Now this is soul-searing and sober spiritual stuff! Is it heresy, we worry, even to put those two words together? Can we possibly, with good conscience, even say it: the Divine *Feminine*? the *Divine* Feminine? If we ever do dare to say it, will we possibly get out of the church alive before a paddy wagon full of priests, ministers, popes, and potentates snatches us up and takes us away? The second level of the question is a profoundly personal one. It has to do with a breathtaking outbreak of spiritual imagination in women—with entirely new images of spiritual development among women—and the effect of these on roles, relationships, religions, and the definition of human rights, all dearly to be wished perhaps but certain to be contested.

The subject is a tangled, thorny, exhilarating, and highly suspect excursion into the very center of the spiritual life and interfaith understanding. It is precisely this subject that explains both our personal spiritual development and our place as moral, spiritual, political, and professional leaders in a world sorely in need of new forms of leadership everywhere. Why is the concept of the Divine Feminine important? The implications of this question shake the spiritual ground under our feet. In the attempt to lay out the dimensions of the subject, however, I found myself haunted by a story—at first seemingly irrelevant to this topic but down deep, revelatory of the impact and import of this issue, not only to our spiritual lives but to our daily lives as well.

In the story a tribal Elder is explaining to a child the nature of life: "Remember, child," the Elder teaches, "there are two wolves fighting for dominance within each of us. One wolf is good and the other wolf is evil." "But, Elder," the youngster asks, "which wolf will win?" The Elder answers, "It depends, dear child, on which wolf you feed." The story is clear: Who we become as persons depends on what we decide to develop in ourselves, in us and around us. Neurologists tell us that it is experience that forges our brain patterns. What we think depends on what happens to us. We are not born as we are, we *become* it. What we believe derives from what we experience. The relationship of this story to the importance of the Divine Feminine in our own lives is obvious. First, if we fail to nourish the fullness of life in us, male and female, as the tribal Elder implies—both the feminine and the masculine side—in both women and men, the lack of that inclusiveness will warp our personalities and stunt the growth of our souls. Second, it is useless to say that we truly embrace the feminine dimension of life but refuse to be part of the public process that makes respect for the feminine an equally important part of the social fabric.

Newspapers ask, Can a woman really be president? Magazine articles ask, What makes a real man? Researchers ask, Are women and men different or the same? Theologians ask, Can a woman really image God? We ask, How does God really deal with women? Face-to-face or only through male or clerical intermediaries? For example, take our public language. Eskimos have forty words for *snow*. They see forty different kinds of snow. It's important to them to make the distinctions between them because snow is the very context of their lives. We have the same snow, yet we see only one kind, name one kind, because it's not as important to us. However, we have forty words for *dog*—we call them shepherds, poodles, chihuahuas. We have forty words for *car*—Kia, hatchback, SUV, limousine, convertible. But we have only two words for the human race—male and female—one of which we collapse into the other.

We are still teaching our children that when the gender of a group is clear, we may use the appropriate male or female pronoun: "Everyone attending the Women's Athletic Club presented her card," for instance. But when the gender of the group in question is unclear or mixed, it must be male: "Anyone may have his money back" or "Someone left his pen here." In this linguistic system, women become invisible. Clearly, language shapes the mind: if it's not in the language, it's not in the mind. What that says about the importance of women to society, however, is clear: they are simply not seen. What we see creates perception, signals the very importance of a thing.

The book of Genesis reads, as does every scripture of every religion on Earth, about male-female dual creation out of the same substance: "Let us make humans in our own image, in our own image let us make them; male and female let us make them" (Genesis 1:26–27)—that is, God is male and female, not male. The scriptures reflect the reality of it, and the meaning is clear: the way we see God determines the way we see ourselves. The language we use shapes public perceptions about God. If we see God only as maleness, maleness becomes more Godlike than femaleness. Maleness becomes the nature of God and the norm of humankind, rather than simply one of it manifestations. If we limit ourselves to the Divine Masculine, we will never see the Divine Feminine.

The great figures of early Christianity centuries ago—Origen, Irenaeus, Anselm, Bernard of Clairveaux, and Aelred—believed that the womb of God is the Divine Feminine and that without that awareness of the motherhood of God, as well as the fatherhood of creation, we will never know the fullness of God in our own lives. None of us, neither women nor men. In the end the real depth of the spiritual life, the real development of the psychological, emotional life, depends on whether we each nourish the feminine image of God in us and around us as fully as we do the image of the fatherhood of God. When churches refuse the language of the feminine dimension of God, when they delete female pronouns and collapse the male and the female into "all men" and "dear brothers," and "God, our mother" into "God, the father," they deprive us of the whole spirit of God.

But as obvious as the problem may seem, it is every bit as much denied as it is affirmed by traditions that refuse the spiritual insights and the religious leadership of women, by traditions that subordinate women to the male masters (their local gods) who have beaten, burned, killed women around the globe, male masters whose religions justify it, who counsel women into servitude but never into leadership. The full stature of women is every bit as much suppressed by a church's or a religion's absence of emphasis on their moral wholeness—absence from moral and theological decision making—as it is enshrined by their empty insistence on the spiritual value of women. Although theological development omits women, the theological situation is clear: Everything written about us is without us! So we limp through life one-sided, empty-hearted, underdeveloped. We become spiritual amnesiacs, spiritual orphans, spiritual cyclops with a myopic view of God and other religions too. It blinds us—even women ourselves—to our moral agency, our responsibility, our leadership gifts.

Where does this notion of the Divine Feminine come from? Is the question of the Divine Feminine simply a current fad? A silly notion of even sillier feminists? Or could it possibly have deep and ineradicable roots in the tradition itself? However much we mock the idea, the truth is ironically that every major spiritual tradition on Earth carries within it, at its very center, in its ancient core, an awareness of the Divine Feminine. In Hinduism, Shakti—the great mother, the feminine principle—is seen as the sum total of all the life-giving energy of the universe. She is the source of all. In Buddhism, Tara is seen as the perfection of wisdom, and in Buddhism wisdom is life's highest metaphysical principle! Tara is considered the light and the prime source of Buddhahood and of all Buddhas to follow.

In the Hebrew scriptures the ground of the entire Abrahamic family (Jewish, Christian, and Muslim), the God to whom Moses says, "Who shall I say sent me?" answers not "I am he who am," not "I am she who am," but "I am who am." I am Being! I am the essence of all life, I am the spirit that breathes in everyone: the source that magnetizes every soul. I am the one in whose image all human beings, male and female, Genesis says clearly, are made. "I am" is, in other words, ungendered, unsexed, pure spirit, pure energy, pure life. That assurance we have, note well, on God's own word: "I am who am." Let there be no mistake: woman or man, man or woman— the full image of God is in you, masculine and feminine, feminine and masculine godness. Hebrew scripture is clear, as are the Christian and Islamic scriptures as well. God is neither male nor female—God is of the essence of both, and both are of the essence of God.

Actually, lest we be fooled by our own patriarchal inclinations to make God in our own small, puny, partial male images, the Hebrew scriptures are full of the female attributes of God. In Isaiah (42:14), the Godhead "cries out as a woman in labor." To the psalmist, God is a nursing woman on whose breast the psalmist leans, "content as a child that has been weaned" (Psalm 131:2). In Hosea (11:3–4), God claims to be a cuddling mother who takes Israel in her arms. In Genesis (3:21), God is a seamstress who makes clothes out of skins for both Adam and Eve. And in Proverbs, God-she, wisdom, Sophia "raises her voice in the streets," "is there with God 'in the beginning'" (8:22–31), "is the homemaker who welcomes the world to her table" (9:5), shouting as she does, "Enter here! Eat my food, drink my wine."

After centuries of suppressing the female imagery and the feminine attributes given in scripture to establish the patriarchy of lords and kings and priests and popes and powerbrokers as the last and only word of every failing institution in humankind—no wonder we are confused about who God is. But God is not! Scripture is clear: God does not have—and clearly never has had—an identity problem. Our images of God must be inclusive because God is not mother, no, but God is not father either. God is neither male nor female. God is pure spirit, pure being, pure life—both of them. Male and female, in us all.

What signs do we have of the authentic role of the feminine in the spiritual life? Who are the women that God has raised up in the Jewish, Christian, and Islamic scriptures to show us the spiritual power, the leadership roles, and the qualities of women alive and working in the economy of salvation? And what do they say to us today? Moses's mother had an intuition that no woman could see the face of the oppressed and oppress it. So, with great faith and keen insight, she set her condemned Jewish infant where the daughter of the Egyptian king herself would find this doomed child. Together two women—one Jewess, one Arab—joined hands across their differences to subvert the enemy system that male power and an irrational kind of reason had devised. Because of feminine intuition and passion for life, an entire people was saved. It is, too, the midwives Shifrah and Puah who refuse to destroy Jewish newborns, thus saving the children of Israel.

Queen Esther was a woman God lifted up to model the power of feminine strength. Esther is scripture's "well-placed woman." Esther, the Jewess, has after all—on account of her beauty, of course—been taken by the Assyrian king from the Jewish ghetto to the palace harem. She is the one safe Jew in the kingdom. She is respected and established. But Esther is a "lady." She knows her place in a world where self-development is a male prerogative and male protection is a woman's only defense. But Esther, under the impulse of the Divine Feminine, is willing to sacrifice it all—her position, her security, her very life—for the sake of her people. "Though no one may go to the King without being called," under threat of death "I will go to the King to plead for the people," Esther says, "whether he calls me or not. And if I perish, I perish." On her account, the people survived and thrived. Surely this world needs the leadership of Divine Feminine feeling for victims of unbridled power. When men are trained simply to take orders without question, when the best men rock no boats, call no consciences, critique no systems—civil or ecclesiastical—for fear of falling off the corporate or ecclesiastical ladder, someone must be willing to die for the truths of equality and difference.

Sarah, the woman of God, was open to the possibility that what the world called "rational" was not the only possible approach to a problem. "Sarah will conceive in her old age," the angel told Abraham, "and bear a son." The scripture says: "Sarah laughed." But I don't think Sarah laughed. I think she hooted. Nice boys, these angels, but not too smart. She was, after all, way past menopause. Way past child-bearing age. Way past the very thought of pregnancy. And she told the angel so. But when the impossible happened she was open to it. She didn't reject it; she didn't set out to wrench the world to her own design. She accepted her role in this new world and she led the way for others. "Receptivity is the quality," the American Pulitzer Prize–winning poet Mark Van Doren has said, that "takes ideas in and treats them royally, on the grounds that someday one of them may be king." Thanks to the receptivity of Sarah to a new idea of life and her new role in it, a whole people was raised up.

Clearly, women have been an essential part of God's economy of salvation from its foundation in religions in both the West and East. What does all of this have to do with women of spirit and faith here and now? Why should we even consider the subject of the Divine Feminine at all? In the light of scripture's own images of God, in every religion everywhere, what kind of a life-denying, God-diminishing question is it to ask whether there is such a thing as a feminine dimension to God? On what grounds can we possibly deny the feminine face of God

> "This is my beloved daughter in whom I am well pleased."
> **Sister Joan Chittister, OSB**

among us an equal place at every table: corporate boards, decision-making synods, ecclesiastical councils, Qur'anic academies, and shariah judgeships? How can women be denied the chance to be listened to, the right perhaps even to be heard, the fullness of moral agency and a public role to be reckoned with?

The social implications of ignoring or denying a topic such as this are enormous, life-changing, and spiritually stunting. By casting God in human form, in one human form only, we limit our knowledge of God. We ignore the feminine dimension of God in the world and God in women as well. We leave life to the warriors, rather than to wisdom figures. We make masculinity the divine norm, ignoring and devaluing the feminine part of ourselves, in both women and men. We enthrone maleness, masculinity, the macho. God the father, God the avenging judge, God the warrior, God the lawgiver, and God the perfectionist overwhelm the fullness of the image of God. We create a distant and unemotional God that comes with the image of an exclusively masculine God—all rational and all-powerful—that affects our lives at every stage and every moment. The model we have been given of the all-male God exercises power over everything, so we get confused trying to explain God's failure to use his power to save us from dangers.

Without a conscious awareness of the rest of the essence of God, of the Divine Feminine in God, we lose sight of God our mother, who forms us and influences us and encourages us to do good—not to be perfect but to do our best. We fail to remember God the mother who encourages us to repent and repair our mistakes, misjudgments, and immaturities, God the mother who enables us to survive them. To understand God as Divine Feminine is to realize that all creation is cocreation. That creation is at least as much about what we do with creation to complete it, to lead it to new life once we have it, as it is about the notion that it was given to us in a fixed form. God, for instance, did not create nuclear bombs—humans did—and we can uncreate them anytime we want to, provided someone exercises leadership of the Divine Feminine to show us the way. The common response to attempts to reduce nuclear weapons is always seen as a loss of total power—the one attribute that is God's alone. Instead, we pray for peace but do little or nothing to press politicians to practice it!

We must realize that God is the mother who carries us rather than lords it over us, who leads us to face the fact that the fate of Earth is largely in our hands. The God who is both feminine and masculine energy, the God who in ourselves we all image—more of this or less of that—both feminine and masculine in each of us, not only raises standards for us to meet but helps us over the bar. This God—this Divine Mother God—feels compassion for us, as scripture says so clearly: "I have heard the cry of my people," (Exodus 3:7). This Mother God feels anger and pain when we suffer: "I am sending you to deliver them" (Exodus 3:10). This Mother God in us feels care and concern when we struggle: "Be not afraid, Abram, I am your shield" (Genesis 15:1). It is this God and we who go on now creating the world together, feeling together its pain, working together to re-create it, leading other men and women to do the same.

This God is not only the Divine Masculine, medieval lord and master, father, warrior, and judge. This God is also the Divine Feminine—the one who feels, the one who cares as well as prescribes, the one who is nursing mother as well as protective father. The one who is also Divine and Feminine. This is the God who is completely other—and completely like us at the same time—in affection and care, in feeling and hope. This is the God who brings the world together—Hindu, Buddhist, Jewish, Christian, and Muslim—listening, learning, loving the other. If God is all being, all there is, masculine and feminine, then Plato's God of total power, total distance, total indifference, and total emotional detachment is deficient. A God like that lacks love, lacks the will to be cocreative in a cocreative world. A God like that lacks the compassion and the empathy it takes to love the imperfect perfectly well. That male God is the one we have fashioned at our peril. By ignoring the value of the feminine, we have made for ourselves a patriarchal God for a world in which feeling is the necessary glue that holds that world together. We have made for ourselves a God to keep everybody else under control.

It is in the name of the God made male that women have been suppressed and ignored and reviled, called lesser, called inferior, called irrational in every male-controlled religion. Why doesn't God fix such an obvious injustice? Because God didn't make the situation; humans did. It is humans who warp the theology, humans who ignore the scriptures, humans who create a world designed to make the powerful more powerful and to divinize themselves at the expense of every other religion on Earth. It is humans who fail to lead us to a fuller image of God. Humans, to be true to their own image of God, must now undo that imbalance—for the sake of the entire world, for the humanity of women, and for the authenticity of religion. No, God does not "fix" the world for us. But awareness of the fullness of God is the reality that requires us to fix it. God Divine Mother and God Divine Father is exactly what demands that being in all its glory—black and white, gay and straight, female and male—be respected and revered and embraced. Until all are, the fullness of the life that is God is only half alive in us, no matter how profusely we proclaim our rationality, no matter how confidently we argue our righteousness, no matter how sincerely we exalt our religiosity.

As it stands, we have enthroned the image of God the father. We have abandoned the image of God the mother, and as a result women, one way or the other, have become the invisible majority of the human race. By virtue of being female and in the name of God and religion, women the world over are kept out of social systems, out of schools and social status, out of work and financial security, out of property and politics, out of literacy and life support, out of food and water—even out of the pronouns of the language they dare to speak. Not because they are poor, but solely because they are women. Indeed, once we make God male, only males are really visible, only males are really the norm, the crown of creation, especially in our churches! Even there in our churches we call God Rock of Ages, Door of Heaven, Key of David, Dove of Peace, Tree of Life, Father of the Universe—but never, ever Mother. What can that possibly be but blatant sexism as well as bad philosophy, deficient theology, and an edited version of the scriptures? How can that not distort our very notion of leadership? After all, the scriptures demonstrate the essential role and the central place of the feminine, not a glorification of the female in the design of God.

Process philosophers say that feeling is a characteristic of the Divine Feminine. But the male world says that it is feeling that enfeebles a woman. High Vatican officials, for instance, issued documents a few years ago warning the church about the presence of women on marriage tribunals: "Their tender hearts render them unable to make right judgments." Feelings corrode the brain, in other words. Feelings weaken the will, they say. Feelings obscure the truth, they say. While the male world leads us to weapons of mass destruction, the will to ruthless power, and lies about male superiority, they tell us that feelings diminish our effectiveness! Tell that to the woman who washed the feet of Jesus with her tears and dried them with her hair. Tell that to the Marys who, frightened, nevertheless followed Jesus all the way to the cross. Tell that to the women who went weeping to the tomb. Who even remembers and about all the "reasonable" men who were not there where all the world has since wanted to be?

Tell the women philanthropists who, Luke says, "supported him out of their own substance," who recognized Jesus for the rest of us and made his work possible. No women—no Jesus! Tell women that feeling is their downfall and their bane. Tell women that feeling is the disease that renders them unfit to lead, to hold authority, to make decisions.

You see, it is not what sexism says about women that is sinful. It is what sexism says about God that is heresy, that corrupts the spirit. Doesn't sexism really imply that God is all powerful—except when it comes to women; at which point the God who could draw water from a rock and raise the dead to life is totally powerless to work as fully through a woman as through a man? Is this the same God who also said, "Let us make humans in our own image: female and male let us make them"?

What will women bring to churches in crisis and a planet in peril? What will women bring to the spirit of the times? Woman will bring womanhood to where only male lordship has been permitted to lead—distant, indifferent, and dictatorial. It is womanliness that is the invisible gift, the unseen presence, the continuing reminder of the Divine Feminine in and over all of humankind. Woman must bring the feminine to leadership—the missing dimension of the God-life in us all—enabling it in men and fulfilling it in women; the missing link of a theology everywhere, in every tradition not only our own, that understands the nature of God but has yet to make it real so that we can all become what we are meant to become. So that we demonstrate, rather than simply profess, our respect for women, and women's insights, and women's values, and women's experiences. So that the women of our time everywhere may make the fullness of the love of God real for us all. Then we may all come to know ourselves, to be in the womb of our mother God. And right the images of God in every religion everywhere.

No doubt about it, women leaders like Miriam, prophetesses like Huldah, judges like Deborah, liberators like Judith, keepers of the very line of David like Naomi and Ruth, the women at Jesus's tomb—all of them break through the patriarchal world of Hebrew scripture with earth-shaking regularity and clear recollection of the other face of God's presence and power. In a world in which a third live in abject poverty, two-thirds of which are women and girls—the poorest, hungriest, most venerable, most threatened, least cared for, least listened to population in the world—patience is not enough. We need the courage now to lead us to a consciousness of the Divine Feminine in ways that make life changes for the world, for women in every religion everywhere. And, that will, at the same time, enrich the emotional, spiritual development of men.

The Talmud reads, "If we had been holier people, we would have been angrier oftener." May God give us all the grace to feel a life-giving burst of holy anger!

Although I was raised as a practicing Christian, it wasn't until adult-hood that I thought about the implications for Christian women in a religion where God is exclusively He. In my study of female church leaders' perceptions of the gender of God, one of the questions I asked was, "In your mind, is God a man and how does that make you feel?" A majority of the responses read like a description of popular representations of God as a man. As direct questions about gender surfaced, most were quick to note that any gendered perception was only a semantic interpretation, not literal. The standard explanation of this divide between the figurative and literal understanding of God centered on how the Bible was written for a specific culture and thus this area of Christian theology could be reunderstood in our modern, more gender-equal society.

A majority of women had both a gendered god-concept and neg-ative experiences in how that affected them as Christians. After lis-tening to their experiences, I still use male language as a way of connecting to my Creator in a humanlike relationship, yet while God is not male or female, I've found a greater appreciation for the diversity of ways to conceptualize God. In the end we are all created in God's image and thus there is room for everyone to be right.

—EMILY RHINEBERGER

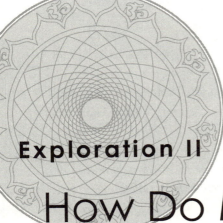

Exploration II

How Do My Spiritual Values Inform Me about Living with the Challenges and Blessings of Diversity?

Creator, maker of all things

This is your Granddaughter,

Sees Birds Medicine Council Woman.

In gratitude to Mother Earth for all she provides for us.

Also, to Grandmother Moon, who shines down upon us to remind us as women to be thankful of our cycle.

Love and prayers for those who are searching for peace within themselves and for the homeless of the world. The children. The elderly and the disabled.

Thank you for all allowing me another day.

I, Shar, was born in Lytton, British Columbia, Canada, on July 19, 1941. My parents were both residential school survivors, as I am. This resulted in the stripping of my culture, language, and self-esteem. I started my spiritual journey in 1998 by attending ceremonies and by learning more about my lost culture. For many years I've been learning and evolving in my spirituality and gaining confidence and knowledge from my Elders and members of the aboriginal community. Today, I am still learning and I am contributing to my people through art and guided healing.

—All my relations, GRANDMOTHER SHAR

The second exploration leads us deeper into our own values and how we express them in the world, moving into the interpersonal aspects of life. How do we as women of spirit and faith approach our differences with grace and tact? What gets in the way of listening to others? How do we collaborate with people from diverse backgrounds? These are some of the questions we asked ourselves as we began our journey. One of the discoveries was the vast types of diversity we live with every day. Not only are we diverse in faith traditions and spiritual practices, we are also diverse in age, race, ethnicity, education, gender, sexual orientation, economics, education, politics—the list goes on and on. We simply have different worldviews. A Cuban proverb says: "Listening looks easy, but it's not simple. Every head is a world." What are some of the underlying spiritual principles that help us along the way?

In addition to acknowledging the diversity of women of faith and spirit, we also want to note that the civil discourse has deteriorated and seems more polarized and hostile than ever. This points to the necessity of finding ways to have authentic conversations about our differences and creating opportunities to explore the hard questions in safe spaces. Many women do this in circle, using techniques of deep listening and compassion—both of which require a great deal of practice. As coeditors of this book, we experienced some differences of opinions too. How did we resolve these differences? Some of us noticed we were having visceral reactions to really digging into the situation. We would rather work *around* the difference—make nice, so to speak. What we learned is the importance of taking the leap and dealing directly, going *through* rather than around. On the other side of that is more bonding, understanding, and creative energy. It's important not to ignore the elephant in the room!

As you read the stories of the women in this part of the book, we invite you to reflect on your own lives. What type of diversity is difficult for you to deal with? What are the blessings of diversity? What is it like to go outside of your comfort zone to develop new ways of building bridges?

Karma Lekshe Tsomo is an associate professor in the Department of Theology and Religious Studies at the University of San Diego, where she teaches Buddhism, world religions, and comparative religious ethics. She is a past president of Sakyadhita International Association of Buddhist Women and the director of Jamyang Foundation, an innovative education project for women in developing countries. Active in interreligious dialogue, she is the author of *Buddhist Women and Social Justice: Ideals, Challenges, and Achievements* and *Into the Jaws of Yama, Lord of Death: Buddhism, Bioethics, and Death*, among other publications.

Buddhism, Women, and Religious Diversity

KARMA LEKSHE TSOMO

Women's unique strengths and potential have the power to heal the disaster-ridden planet. Our voices, as global citizens, and our efforts are crucial to awaken humanity to the even greater disasters that await unless we respond soon. Women need to recognize and work together to correct the root causes of these disasters, paying special attention to the members of the human family, especially women and children, who are suffering from poverty, oppression, and violence. To so do constructively and effectively, however, women must combine our talents and resources and learn to work together with goodwill for others. We need to see beyond our many differences in worldviews, religious practices, and sometimes even values and pay attention to the needs of others—water, nutrition, clean air, education, and equal opportunities. Women's color-blind, inclusive, and concerted efforts can become a model of cooperation across religious and political boundaries. As nurturers and guides of children and youth, women have much in common and can become exemplars of peace, compassion, awareness, ethics, respectful communications, and other qualities that are crucial for human survival. Working together, optimizing our capabilities and potential, we can set an example for the entire human family of how to work together in harmony, embracing differences of religion and culture.

Women have plenty of experience being members of a minority. We are often a minority voice in discussions and decision making. In fact, women are an underrepresented minority in nearly every field, including government and religious leadership, especially at the higher levels. Only in recent decades, with the feminist movement, have these disparities been acknowledged and serious attention given to understanding the dynamics and consequences of marginalizing women. Serious reflection and research are devoted to documenting and redressing women's absence and underrepresentation in the halls of government, the dais, and the pulpit. Many new books, most by women writers, have appeared to celebrate women's historical and contemporary contributions. Exceptionally distinguished women are gradually becoming recognized for their compassion and wisdom. Many, such as Oprah Winfrey, have become models of tolerance and openness in dialoguing with people of all religious backgrounds and no religious background. Women are taking new roles in religious organizations and becoming highly respected as teachers and mentors for others. If we agree that human beings' chances of survival as a species depend on cooperation, the only remaining question is, How can we become more effective in reaching across the imagined boundaries of religious difference?

We can begin by locating this question within current global realities. As technology advances and means of communication expand, human beings are drawn, at least virtually, ever more closely together. Images of veiled women, praying monks, and exotic religious celebrations are beamed to us over countless media channels, greatly expanding our religious vision or at least our awareness of people's different ways of being religious. Religious diversity is gradually becoming a daily reality for billions of people. In response, we may either regard religious diversity as a global competition for numbers and ideological supremacy, *or* we may see it as an amazing opportunity for expanding human awareness, particularly our own thinking. Instead of assuming that we are right and the other six billion people are wrong, we can visualize a world of religious harmony where human beings openheartedly respect each other's choices and priorities, even when we may disagree.

It has frequently been observed that, despite groundbreaking scientific and technological advances, many of us are still stuck in the nursery school stage of development, kicking sand in the face of anyone we disagree with. Although we can now easily communicate around the globe, exchanging images and ideas with millions of people with the click of a mouse, we remain consumed by the same old patterns of anger, attachment, jealousy, and aggression that have enslaved humanity since, presumably, the beginning of time. Despite higher levels of literacy worldwide, wars and corruption continue to proliferate. Instead of using scientific and technological advances to ensure happy lives for all, we remain chained by ignorance and self-interest. While millions of children go to bed hungry and thirsty, the privileged take luxurious showers and overconsume in abundance. We are literally bleeding the earth dry.

As members of the human community, especially as givers of life, women have a responsibility to help turn this around. By expanding our awareness of religious diversity, each of us can become a force for good in the world. We may work on a private level, learning and teaching our children about the shared values and virtues of the world's religious traditions and also helping understand the differences in worldviews. Or we may take a public role, engaging in dialogue in the community and in the media about our own and others' worldviews. Either way, the cause of greater understanding is served, and consequently the chances of conflict based on misunderstandings decrease. Thus, simply by educating ourselves and others about the views and practices of others, we can make a significant contribution to global understanding and world peace.

All people of good aspire to eliminate human suffering. For Buddhists the key is working to eliminate the causes of suffering: greed, hatred, and ignorance. If women become models of universal values and further human understanding, we can serve the important role of inspiring others to be the best human beings we can be. The planet needs more qualified "teachers" who have hearts of compassion and wisdom to help humanity dig itself out of the hole we are in. Together, beyond the ideologies and attachments that separate us, we can work to develop compassion in our hearts and free all living beings from suffering.

The majority of people are concerned about their own lives, their own families, their own communities, their own organizations, ad infinitum. In reality, though, no one operates in isolation from others. Yet few people have a broader view that encompasses the entire world. To ensure our survival, we need more human beings who are open and able to expand their global vision—not just a view of world dominance by our company's products or our religion's followers, but a wise and compassionate global vision of humanity as healthy, creative, happy, respectful, and flourishing. When all human beings have enough to eat, enough to drink, and hope for the future, we are all enriched. Extending genuine concern for the whole of humanity, we can effect a complete turnaround that replaces self-interest with a sincere concern and commitment to human survival and well-being—extending especially to those who are suffering the most.

At the very least, awakened women can become a model of *not* using bottled water, *not* taking twenty-minute showers, *not* resolving conflicts through violence. Beyond that, women can become models of compassionate awareness, advocating for human services and protecting vulnerable sectors of the human family from wasteful, exploitative practices. Expressing our wisdom and compassion proactively, we can move from awareness to action to advocacy. Using our allegedly higher intelligence, we can imagine new solutions to the problems that beset our sisters and brothers around the globe. Using our multidimensional religious awareness and interreligious connections to advantage, we can help protect the human family against its own miserable, senseless suffering and demise. Why not envision the fullest, happiest future imaginable?

This is where Buddhist women can make a difference. According to a 2007 UNICEF report "Gender Equality: The Big Picture," women do 66 percent of the work in the world and produce half the world's food, but earn only 10 percent of the world's income and own only 1 percent of its lands. If this is true, then women are not only overworked and undercompensated, but also have less of a stake in maintaining the miserable, exploitative status quo. On the contrary, it means that women stand to benefit most from transforming unjust structures.

Human survival depends on the overall health of the human community. People of goodwill cannot simply stand by and watch planet Earth and all its beautiful inhabitants self-destruct. Women must work together, across boundaries of religion and culture, to preserve our precious human and natural resources. We can no longer afford to ignore or devalue women's spiritual potential or confine it within the narrow frame of self-concern. As soon as we recognize that our families, communities, and nations are intertwined with the well-being of all life, we can work together for the whole of humanity. From a Buddhist perspective, clinging to labels is a source of conflict and sorrow. Seeing beyond labels to common human values, such as loving-kindness, enables us to combine our precious human resources into a force that can overcome all negativity.

No Buddhist text says that enlightened being must be male. In fact, the Buddha confirmed women's equal spiritual potential and encouraged women by establishing an order of female enunciates who independently pursued the path to awakening. This path, by whatever name we call it, is key to awakening the world. Combining our efforts in the practice of the six perfections—generosity, ethical conduct, patience, joyful effort, concentration, and wisdom—we can awaken humanity, save the planet, and liberate limitless beings from suffering.

Jamia Wilson—feminist activist, organizer, expat-brat, networker, truth seeker, cartwheeler, and storyteller—is currently vice president of programs at the Women's Media Center in New York, where she trains women and girls so they are media-ready and media-savvy, exposes sexism in the media, and directs the WMC's social media strategy. Formerly Wilson served in several roles related to youth leadership development, grassroots organizing, and communications at Planned Parenthood, People for the American Way, and New York University.

Faith's Challenges

The One We Seek

JAMIA WILSON

> If I were really asked to define myself ... I would start with stripping down to what fundamentally informs my life, which is that I'm a seeker on the path. I think of feminism, and I think of anti-racist struggles as part of it. But where I stand spiritually is, steadfastly, on a path about love.
>
> —BELL HOOKS

Every day women fight for the right to express their values and beliefs—from Kabul to Paris, from Tehran to Salt Lake City. We are demanding to be recognized in our spiritual and religious communities and challenging our traditions to remember the stories about our roles in our religious histories that have been rendered invisible. These narratives provide us fresh opportunities to identify how we as diverse women are working together to develop new perspectives that will empower women spiritual leaders. Despite our differences in beliefs and the conflicts therein, our ability to honor the sacred voices of women of spirit and faith emboldens us. Our own endeavors to ignite novel opportunities for challenging the existing limitations to our expression appear in both national and international religious and spiritual discourses.

In June 2011, Gallup released the results of a nationwide poll that showed that more than nine in ten people in the United States claim a belief in God.[1] These statistics confirm that the majority of the population continues to acknowledge a spiritual connection. Although we differ in our sacred journeys, we are bonded by our shared identity as spiritual seekers. Despite each of our unique approaches to a relationship to "God," "divine energy," or "the universe," we are unified in a search for connectivity with a greater power.

I have learned that my experiences with spiritual traditions that differ from my own complement my personal religious practice and open my mind to a new, richer appreciation for my relationship with the divine. Throughout my life I have developed and strengthened my spiritual consciousness through traditional Baptist prayer and song, when kneeling in front of an emerald Buddha in Thailand, while practicing yoga in the Catskills, and by watching hordes of diverse and devoted pilgrims in white clothes board planes to Mecca. I understood God's nature when I marveled at black Madonnas in Italy, meditated at a Zen Buddhist temple in Brooklyn, and watched an eighty-one-year-old woman take her last breaths with peaceful eyes as a priest read her last rights. Even though I have followed a Protestant tradition for much of my life, I have come to understand Sri Swami Satchidananda's mantra: "Truth is one, paths are many."

As I learned to appreciate our intrinsic oneness, I also became increasingly alienated by fundamentalist and extremist expressions of all faiths. It seems that a fervent fear-driven thread ties all of these reactionary and destructive movements together, igniting an energy that threatens all of us who know that unity and respect for our differences is what is required to heal—and bring us closer to the Divine. The current media climate often inundates us with divisive coverage of interactions between different faith communities, rather than highlighting the intersections and connections that exist between our diverse ideologies, rituals, and traditions. We see stories of strife, condemnation, hate, and violence and hear far less about forgiveness and interfaith partnerships. Without more conversation about the hopeful opportunities to appreciate our oneness, we might never experience the truth about what happens when we let go of our fear of losing power and allowing ourselves to be vulnerable—to be able to listen to each other about the spaces where our spiritual goals and ideas intersect and, in some cases, depend on each other.

As we challenge ourselves to realize the goal of galvanizing women's spiritual collective power, it is crucial that we engage in spreading the word about our common vision. At the same time, we must respect that fragmentations and tensions that emerge from our differences exist, but we can't allow them to overshadow our shared humanity. We discover the solidarity in spirituality-seeking sisterhood. It is imperative that I acknowledge that we are all subject to being tested on our tolerance and respect for ideas that are not our own. Even though I espouse that we celebrate our diversity without judgment, I would be remiss if I didn't reflect on the reality that we are often conditioned to be prejudiced about ideas and traditions that may oppose our own.

During graduate school I served as an assistant residential life director in a large residence hall. Every day I interacted with students and supported them with resources, advising, and conflict-resolution services. One day a group of three freshmen women living in an interfaith living and learning community entered my office, demanding that I grant them a room change. When I inquired about the reason behind their request, they explained that their roommate was a "card-carrying member of the Church of Satan," whose beliefs threatened their personal religious values. Throughout my time in my residential life role, I never experienced an internal struggle like the one that emerged during this conflict. The students who visited my office were Muslims and Christians from various cultural backgrounds who explained that they were frightened by their roommate's all-black attire, loud heavy metal music, and insistence on writing controversial language on her clothing and body parts as well as on the door to their room.

The women articulated that they were repulsed by this roommate's bragging about her brazen sexual liaisons with men she had met from the Church of Satan community. They were repulsed by what they described as her open veneration of what they considered to be extreme indulgence, vengeance, and unabashed hedonism. Next, they brandished a ripped poster listing a diverse group of faiths, saying that their final breaking point arose when this roommate had added "Satanism" to the interfaith signs throughout the hall. Because my job was to serve as an objective party that advocated for a safe, nonjudgmental, and mutually beneficial situation for all of the students involved, I listened quietly and documented their complaints. While expressing concern for their well-being and safety, I reminded them of the importance of inclusion. I explained that there were no additional rooms in the building that they could move to, so we would have to engage in a roommate mediation meeting.

As these young women vividly described the toxic relationship they had with their suitemate and begged me to intervene immediately, I pondered how I would help resolve this situation, where three roommates opposed living with the fourth because of their concerns about her religious values within the designated residential community. Although my personal religious beliefs were biased toward the Muslim and Christian roommates, I understood that justice would only be served if I fostered an inclusive community where all beliefs were celebrated as long as students abided by campus policy and refrained from behavior that threatened the health and safety of other residents.

After I met with the residents, I invited their roommate to my office to hear her side of the story. As soon as she entered, she stared at me and smiled wildly during every moment of silent tension in our conversation. Despite the fact that she seemed unfazed by the conflict in her room on the surface, I sensed her anxiety and hunger for recognition. A flicker of vulnerability in her eyes demonstrated to me that she felt alienated and sought connection. At this moment, when I was both terrified and uncomfortable with her and her faith, I realized I was not as tolerant of diversity as I thought I was.

Although I honestly resented her lack of respect for the divine, I understood that compassion was the only answer. I looked her in the eye and smiled and said, "Tell me what your vision is for a better living experience with us and your roommates in the interfaith community." She replied that her belief in the Church of Satan represented her rejection of conformity and abstinence and her celebration of pleasure and freedom without guilt or limitations. She regarded me in silence for a second, as if she was assessing whether she could trust me before saying, "I just want to be happy, and I want my roommates to be happy too. I would never hurt them or anyone else, and I only want to be able to be open about who I am without being ostracized. People have misconceptions about who we are." She went on to say that she did take responsibility for vandalizing all of the signs on the floor because she felt that it was unfair that Satanism was left off of the roster of religions represented in the community.

During our conversation I realized that I had already judged this woman for her beliefs before she walked through my door. I had condemned her in my mind because I didn't understand how someone could be devoted to Satanic attitudes and beliefs and equate her right to this lifestyle and belief system with my own freedom of religion. I recognized my bias and decided that even though I was shocked and appalled by her behavior and expression of her ideas, it was her right to nonviolently practice her religion as long as she respected the rights of others in the community. When she mentioned that she had joined the Church of Satan because she was looking for a community to connect with when she moved to New York and had met a group of close friends through her musical and theater community, I realized that this young woman too was a seeker, even though our spiritual paths were in many ways diametrically opposed to one another.

After she explained to me that she felt hurt and alienated because her suitemates, the resident assistant, and the rest of the students in the community did not include her in activities and whispered about her in the hallways, I invited all of the roommates back in to talk openly about their concerns in a safe space. After three intense hours of honest and authentic conversation, we developed a written agreement between the women in the suite about shared community standards they could all agree on to feel safe and comfortable in their space. At the end of the dialogue, we all emerged with a greater understanding about each other and the complexities of who we are. I was pleasantly surprised that they remained together for the rest of the semester, once all of their fears about each other's beliefs were expressed openly and addressed.

I share this story because it was one of my greatest lessons. Even though fear initially enraptured me and led me to judge another woman's ideologies based on my preestablished beliefs and assumptions, I learned to ask questions before drawing conclusions that limit growth and progress rather than engendering understanding. As we grow toward manifesting a movement, with compassionate and heart-driven work, we must devote ourselves to recognizing the possibilities that come with both oneness and the tensions between us. A mindful and compassionate approach to social justice fosters open dialogue and celebrates our common humanity. When we reject fear and choose to have faith in each other as seekers partnering on a path toward truth, we will spark a spiritual uprising that unearths new opportunities for mind-altering paradigm shifts and transformational changes in our hearts, in our relationships, in our communities, and in our world.

Legendary rock icon Jimi Hendrix said, "When the power of love overcomes the love of power, the world will know peace." Hendrix understood that hegemonic and oppressive expressions of power stand in the way of positive social change. He recognized that our social and cultural obsession with domination-driven power diminishes our humanity and our potential to transcend from war, violence, and the fear that separates us. His sage words apply to the movement to ignite women's collective transformative power because they remind us of the energetic, spiritual, and cultural paradigm shifts that occur when devoted hearts set their intentions on peace and justice. These words also provide us with a glimpse at the possibility of a sustainable and sacred way to live and lead through a common truth most of the world's traditions revere: love.

Diane Tillman is a licensed educational psychologist and the primary author of the Living Values Education (LVE) book series. Currently a member of the International Advisory Committee of the Association of Living Values Education International, she has coordinated content for this global educational endeavor since 1997. She has written nine educational resource books for educators of young people at risk. Tillman teaches meditation and has been involved with several international initiatives and global conferences over the past thirty years as part of her involvement with the Brahma Kumaris.

Living My Values

DIANE TILLMAN

I wear two main hats in my life. One is as a Brahma Kumari (BK), coordinating a raja yoga meditation center for an international peace organization, the Brahma Kumaris World Spiritual University. I was attracted to the spiritual knowledge of the BKs in the early 1980s while traveling in India. I had taken a sabbatical from my job as a school psychologist to get to know myself again. I was quite surprised when the Australian blond teaching me the raja yoga meditation course in Rajasthan listed the eight virtues I had always wanted to have in my life and didn't know how to get—humility, sweetness, fearlessness, patience, cheerfulness, tolerance, introversion, and purity. Their meditation offered a method to explore and experience those virtues and opened a connection to peace, pure love, and a level of happiness that I knew intuitively was possible but had not experienced.

I was intrigued with the Brahma Kumaris organization as it was administered by women. With nine thousand centers in more than a hundred countries today, the three women in charge are in their eighties and nineties. Having become BKs in their teens, their peace, love, and power are palpable. When the organization was formed in 1937, women were second-class citizens. It was felt that women would benefit spiritually by learning to take power, and that men would benefit spiritually by putting others in front and becoming egoless. The goal: spiritual balance. My cynicism melted away as I observed the sweetness, humility, happiness, and wisdom of both the men and women participating in the meditation course.

I returned to my job as a school psychologist when my sabbatical ended. I decided to open my home to people who wanted to know how to experience more peace through the meditation, much to the dismay of some of my family and friends. "You're a vegetarian?" "You're not drinking wine anymore?" "What's happened to you?" Within a year, though, the skepticism and disdain of some had changed into appreciation for my completely new level of peace—and relief that meals at my home were just as delicious!

It was initially hard for me to understand the BK teaching that the world today is at a critical yet beautiful juncture. Before I was involved with their meditative practice, I was frequently in despair when reading stories of callousness, cruelty, and injustice in the morning newspaper. Now I can read news about wars, violence, corruption, and abuse of power spiraling out of control and instead of going into despair, I use that information to strengthen my determination to work for a better world. The only positive factor in all the negativity is that the situation is finally dire enough to fuel increased awareness of the need for fundamental change. I have adopted the belief that each person can contribute to a culture of peace and well-being for all. Every moment that we enjoy being in a state of peace, send light, listen compassionately, and lovingly accept the self and others is a moment that supports real change and enriches all of humanity and the planet. Radiating peace helps the world immensely, for when we do, we strengthen ourselves to live as beings of peace—caring, courageous, humble, and benevolent. Not a second of giving peace or love is ever wasted.

In time, I ventured forth as a BK during vacations, participating in a peace conference in Costa Rica, science and consciousness seminars in Greece, and giving personal development workshops around the world. I had found a niche in combining psychology and the spirituality taught by the Brahma Kumaris. The core beliefs that I took from the BKs were the knowledge that we are all souls and that as souls we are all originally good; peace is our nature. That perspective changed my life and indeed my attitude toward others. I no longer measured people on the yardstick of wealth, appearance, position, clothes, religion, or culture. Diversity had ceased to exist. We were all just points of light, eternal beings, originally good, one family, and my duty as a yogi was simply to have good wishes and pure feelings for every soul. I had anchored in the values of peace, love, and respect. I was gradually learning how to stay in a state of peace and slowly beginning to change my own measurement of myself from body conscious to soul conscious. All of this deepened fifteen years later when I was asked to don another hat.

The second hat evolved into becoming the primary author of the Living Values Education series of books. These educational resource books offer a practical methodology and a wide variety of experiential values activities to educators to help them provide the opportunity for children and young adults to explore and develop universal values and associated intrapersonal and interpersonal social and emotional skills. Educating hearts and minds for the past fifteen years has been a fascinating journey. This work has carried me to five continents, including refugee camps in Thailand, UNESCO conference rooms in Paris and Lebanon, seminar rooms in Nigeria and Malaysia, and street children centers in Brazil and South Africa. I have loved this sojourn and learned a lot about values, how they are learned, and how profoundly values impact our lives as well as the lives of others around the world.

One of the most joyous moments of my life was riding in a jeep through a rocky riverbed into a refugee camp for one of the minority tribes in Thailand, two years after Living Values Education had been implemented there, and realizing how the people in the camp had changed. The houses were the same, made out of bamboo poles, joints tied with strips of the outer bamboo skin, with roofs of large leaves, but the children and adults were different. The violence and depression were gone; the hitting had changed to holding, the depressed stares had changed into loving and curious looks—and the children were enjoying playing. The Living Values students would spontaneously go up to other children not in the program who were fighting and say, "You don't need to fight; you can solve your problems. Would you like us to help?" Teachers had stopped beating students and instead guided their hands and listened to their feelings. The children who before would just stare at us and watch us for hours, and never play, were playing creatively, spontaneously, happily.

They were creating their own toys and games out of bamboo, stones, and homemade balls. I was overwhelmed with joy and gratitude.

For the first nine years of my work with Living Values Education, we held international train-the-trainer seminars in Oxfordshire, England, at the BK's Global Retreat Center. Held during the long summer days, these were special times in which seventy to ninety educators from all around the world, of many religions and cultures, would gather to share, dialogue, learn, and explore together our own values and values education. One day I asked Dadi Janki, now the administrative head of the BKs, what the difference was between virtues and values. She said, "A virtue is a quality that you have. It becomes a value when you use that virtue all the time." "Wow," I thought, "all the time!" That deep understanding has allowed my life to be simple. Now, when there is a challenging situation, I just ask myself, "What is my value?" Depending on the situation, sometimes the value needed is peace. At other times it may be love, integrity, or respect. These are my four main values. What are yours?

Values dramatically affect the world. Think about a positive person who was important in your life, who made a difference in your life. What quality or value did she or he have that made a difference for you? What would the world be like if everyone "lived" that same value? What two values do you think would completely change the world if everyone held them, lived them? I enjoy asking this question in values education workshops, for the answers from each person are often different, and yet each one is completely true. Yes, if everyone had love and respect, the world would completely change. Yes, if everyone was honest and compassionate, the world would transform completely. Once that is actualized, change will be instantaneous. But first we have to grow to a place where we can hold those values, all the time.

I love the theoretical model of Living Values Education. Pilar Quera, an educator who was asked to contribute to the initial Living Values Educators' Kit, and I spent a month together in Spain in 1997, near the beginning of LVE. We discussed the needs of children. After a week of dialogue we agreed on five qualities that would benefit children in any situation: if students felt loved, respected, valued, understood, and safe, they would grow toward their potential. We contrasted this with young people being pushed toward the emotions of inadequacy, hurt, fear, shame, and feeling unsafe. As the LVE workshops have evolved over the years, one of my delights is to see educators, facilitators, and parents begin to evaluate every action in terms of that model, whether the behavior was positive or negative. We help them fill in the positive and negative factors affecting their classroom, home, school, or organization. Building further skills, we explore acknowledgment, building positive behaviors, active listening, nonviolent discipline, and conflict resolution. Why shouldn't every child grow toward his or her potential? Is that not a human right?

To apply this to my own life, and to the adults in my world, has provided me with opportunities to reflect on what I am really doing. What are my motives and intentions? I remember once I was chairing a board meeting and all of a sudden realized I was using guilt inducement. Oops! It is a moment of self-awareness and learning to move beyond manipulation based in fear to clear motives—and means—based in caring with a strong desire for benefit for all. One of the strengths of women is to deeply desire benefit for all. Women have had much more of a role in the governance of Rwanda since the genocide in 1994; now the Rwandan legislature has a majority of women. Since this switch, there have been major positive changes, including a great increase in access to education. The United National Development Program usually does projects with women, for then the resultant income is spent on food and education for children, rather than squandered by men on other things. Not that there are not wonderful men. There are many incredible, wonderful, compassionate men. If we are to have a better world for all, we need to go beyond our need for personal gain and work for the benefit of all.

To lead with love, to give with love, to correct with love and a true desire to benefit the other person rather than blame—to me this is where grace meets power and true leadership flows. How can we stay light and encourage? How can we keep ourselves unselfish, in a state of gratitude, and maintain the balance of self-respect and humility that allows us to be an example, a true leader? How can we detach from challenges, make mountains into molehills, and use love, integrity, and intelligence to create solutions and realities that benefit all? The understanding that love, kindness, compassion, and mutual respect are far more important than power greatly adds to the beauty of a person. These qualities and values empower people and actually increase productivity at the level of the individual and the society. Communities and organizations that are values-based have greater cooperation, caring, collaboration, commitment from their members, and sustainability. I see this awareness growing. Perhaps not growing as rapidly as many of us would like, but it is growing.

The following statements reflect how my faith and personal understanding teach me how to live with the diversity of this world:

- Take care of yourself.
- Lovingly accept the self, both the flaws and the strengths, for then it is easier to continue steadily and accept others with humility, humor, gentleness, and compassion.
- Never compare the self with others; feeling disheartened or developing arrogance does not serve the self nor others.
- Each one of us has our own puzzle piece; enjoy making yours beautiful.
- Take time to enjoy the self and family and friends.
- Pray and/or meditate with God every day, filling the self with that divine peace, love, and power.
- Enjoy moments, little successes, and know that when things are tough or don't seem successful, it is only an opportunity to learn a virtue more deeply.
- Know that each thought of peace and love is incredibly important, for the self, others, and our planet.
- Know that each one of us is loved by God.

The Reverend Lorenza Andrade Smith is with the Ministry for the Poor and Marginalized in the Rio Grand Conference of the United Methodist Church in San Antonio, Texas. She describes herself as "a five-foot Hispanic/Latina born in the U.S./Mexico border town of Brownsville, Texas." She has been described by others as an ultra-radical, feisty, muckraking rabble-rouser, prone to calling injustice for what it is, and generally creating chaos and mayhem in the most peaceful way.

Where Grace Meets Power

REVEREND LORENZA ANDRADE SMITH

Intriguing is the "meeting" of grace and power. Interesting is that both grace and power are gifts from God, yet they are both used in ways that at times severs well-being. Not accepting God's gift is often as detrimental as abusing God's gift. Sacred is the meeting place, that holy ground, of grace and power that brings forth the well-being of all people. I define the meeting as an eschatological event; the now-but-not-yet. (Eschatology is the branch of theology concerned with the end of the world or of humankind.)

This is much the same way as I define the U.S./Mexico borderlands of my birth place. The border is an eschatological event of the now-but-not-yet, for a multitude of people. For many who sacrifice everything to reach and cross the border from the south, grace certainly meets power at the border. And it is in this meeting that the eschatological event ensues. Our deepest identity lies in relationship with our God, as migrant-immigrant. Our creation is a teleological event, and we are living in the eschatological borderland meeting realm of the now-but-not-yet, always migrating.

When I first met the San Antonio DREAMers, I felt a profound spirituality. These University of Texas at San Antonio students were gathered downtown in front of the San Fernando Cathedral. They were crying out to our nation to pass the DREAM Act. They were on their fourth day of a hunger strike, and I could only hear the word of God as found in scripture in the book of Isaiah: "Is not this the fast that I choose: to loose the bonds of injustice, to undo the thongs of the yoke, to let the oppressed go free, and to break every yoke?" (Isaiah 58:6). I knew then I was being called to be in communion with this community—to do justice and to be in solidarity. As I was seeking to understand my role within this community, another message came from the sacred text of my tradition. It was nearing Thanksgiving and I knew this scripture was a word from God: "Do not worry about anything, but in everything by prayer and supplication with thanksgiving let your requests be made known to God" (Philippians 4:6).

I began, not a hunger strike, but a spiritual fast in prayer on Thanksgiving Day, November 25, 2010. This was an act of solidarity with the DREAMers and an act of prayer for all our legislative process, especially for the men and women involved in the process. To love kindness is nourishing and absolutely foundational to meet the great requirement for all Christians: "Love the Lord your God with all your heart, and with all your soul, and with all your mind. This is the greatest and first commandment. And a second is like it: You shall love your neighbor as yourself" (Matthew 22:37–39). As time passed, I would continue to engage with scripture for sustenance.

This word of God continues to be a maturing process for me.

Do justice.

Love kindness

Walk humbly with your God.

I think I can do these things; I think I want to do these things; I think I'm called to do these things; I think my soul yearns to do these things; I think this is my created image. What I do know is that from the depths of my created image, I cry out, "This is where grace meets power."

It was at the San Antonio city jail that I encountered that holy moment with God. God worked through the events of a civil disobedience act of Monday, November 30, 2010. As I was handcuffed, fingerprinted, photographed, and escorted into the holding tank, there was that burning bush. Even to the last detail, before entering the cell, I heard the words from scripture: "Remove the sandals from your feet, for the place on which you are standing is holy ground" (Exodus 3:5). It was then that the officers removed my shoes from my feet. I entered the cold cell barefoot. I gave thanks to God, was assured of God's promise—"I will be with you" (Exodus 3:12). As I entered the cell, I returned to the word of God: "The Lord is near. Do not worry about anything, but in everything by prayer and supplication with thanksgiving let your requests be made known to God" (Philippians 4:5). With this word I lay my body, barefoot and clothed with a skirt and a clergy blouse, on the cold floor. I was at peace and ready to find rest in God. As the storm brewed around me, having been arrested with fifteen others, I remained still, basking in my holy sabbath. As I awoke, I found socks on my feet and a jacket covering me. These were the sacrificial offerings from those whom God had placed around me. I was in the palm of God's hands— warm, secure, and empowered by the Holy Spirit.

The process of moving from city to county custody began with the shackling of not only my hands but also my ankles. I was driven in a wagon to another facility and processed; I was arrested Monday and I finally was assigned a bed on Wednesday. I denied my bond and I denied food. I was committed to the spiritual fast in support of passing the DREAM Act. I was taken to a medical office to be evaluated to see if I belonged in the infirmary. I was cleared yet threatened that if I continued to go without food, I would be force-fed. I was committed. I continued my time in jail and I continued my spiritual fast. I had made a statement that I would remain in jail and continue to fast until others would join me in fast to advocate for the DREAM Act.

On December 7, 2010, two days after I announced a complete fast from food and drink, members of the community began to commit to a rolling fast. My clergy colleagues posted my bail (which was returned by the bail bond company because of their support of the DREAMers), and I was released. As I left the jail, I was asked what sustained me. I responded that the Spirit of God through scripture was my stronghold, especially the word from Philippians: "For I have learned to be content with whatever I have. I know what it is to have little, and I know what it is to have plenty. In any and all circumstances I have learned the secret of being well-fed and of going hungry, of having plenty and of being in need. I can do all things through him who strengthens me. In any case, it was kind of you to share my distress" (Philippians 4:11–14).

The week following my release, I weaned off the fast. To this day, clergy and laypeople around the country have committed to take my fast in solidarity with the DREAMers. There is someone fasting every day this year in support of the DREAM Act, and we will continue until the DREAM Act is passed. I thanked God then, and I thank God now, for being in the place that I was and in the time that it was, a Kairos moment ... serving time—God's time!

Serving a Life Sentence

I believe Christ, like the narrative in scripture described in the gospel, is certainly abiding with the homeless and the migrant-immigrant. Simply, I want to be a follower of Jesus. I began a new ministry appointment in July 2011. I am living among the homeless, appointed to ministry with the poor and marginalized, advocating for just systemic changes. Though there may be dark valleys and dark alleys, I am assured and comforted with words from the Twenty-Third Psalm: "Even though, I walk through the darkest valley, I fear no evil; for you are with me." Being in God's presence is the longing of our created image. It has been living through the lens of global migration-immigration that has shaped my spirituality with the challenges and blessings of diversity. Immigration is not only a Texas Hispanic-Latina event, nor even just a multiethnic-cultural U.S. immigration issue. Neither is it about global migration, nor is it contained in our biblical narrative and scriptures, as much as all these are part of the immigration-migration event. Migration is greater than all of these combined.

Migration is a God event. God created us to search God out, to be with God and have communion with God. We are created to ever migrate toward God. To be holy as God is holy. We are all immigrants in the eyes of our creator. God did not forsake God's children in the wilderness. In times of darkness God leads the way and remains steadfast. We are in a dark valley and in a dark time in our history. It was not until I walked the seventy-five-mile Migrant Trail Walk in the desert of Arizona, in remembrance of the hundreds of men, women, and children who die every year in the desert trying to find a place of dignity, that I knew that my blistered and cracked heels served to remind me and to represent the cracked and blistered immigration system that distorts our humanity and causes such pain.

Yet in God's mercy, goodness, and steadfast love, I am assured that God will provide healing. God will provide that pillar of fire for us in this dark wilderness of ours as an immigrant people and people in solidarity with immigrant people in the community I serve and around the globe. In my faith tradition the Holy Spirit is represented by fire and wind. Filled with the Holy Spirit, led by the Holy Spirit, driven by the Holy Spirit. God is with us! What a privilege to walk humbly—full of grace, dignity, and hope—with our God.

Jan Booman Saeed is the director of spiritual life at Westminster College. She served as chair of the Salt Lake Interfaith Roundtable for the Salt Lake Organizing Committee (SLOC) for the 2002 Olympic Winter Games and was a founding member of the Utah State Martin Luther King Human Rights Commission. She was instrumental in the publication of and additions to the Olympic version of *World of Faith* by Peggy Fletcher Stack and Kathleen Peterson and edited the section on the Baha'i faith.

Best Friends Forever

JAN BOOMAN SAEED

As I'm listening to my answering machine messages, I find myself laughing out loud as I hear the voice of one of the editors of this book saying sweet words of encouragement: she knows I can put my story down on paper. Little does she know how difficult it is for me to write my own story. I love to write about other people's stories, but mine? It's like pulling teeth. But in this interaction she says something like, "Helloooo, BFF! Best friends forever! How's it going? We need you for the book! You can do it. Just do it!" This friendship, as so many of my interfaith women collaborators over the years, has been nothing less than precious, an inspiration, and a support that no matter how little or infrequently we speak, I feel highly supported, and as she said, best friends forever! And so to support her, I know I must share my story.

My interfaith work and the blessings that I have felt from these experiences started at a very young age. I was probably eight or nine years old. I remember being out in the front yards of our homes in Idaho Falls, Idaho, playing night games: kick the can, Red Rover, red light green light, and others I'm sure that I've forgotten. After playing, we would end up talking about religion and have a great conversation with some of my closest friends, a Lutheran, a Mormon, and me, a Baha'i. My family had joined the Baha'i faith when I was six years old. This was seen by me as an adding to, not really leaving, the Methodist Church. I really didn't think that much about this back then. I just knew my mom would tell me it was important to be friends with people of all religions, a tenet of the Baha'i faith. I would later come to understand this as a basic principle of the faith she and my father had now embraced. As I look back on a family portrait of my extended family, I notice many years later that more than thirty members have also embraced this faith. It had touched the hearts and minds of this group of people that highly valued the importance of education, independent investigation of truth, the equality of men and women, as well as the principle of the harmony of science and religion.

I could never have imagined the opportunities and experiences that have come my way through the transformative nature of this interfaith work, influenced by my own faith and spiritual transformation. As a young, fresh-eyed Swedish immigrant background girl from Idaho, heading out to college in Salt Lake City, Utah, off to the world center of the Mormons for my first college experience, who would have thought I would one day be chair of the 2002 Olympics Interfaith Roundtable? That I would serve on the North American Interfaith Network's board of directors or have the opportunity to serve this generation of young scholars at Westminster College as their director of spiritual life? I never pursued any of these opportunities for leadership as something I was driven toward, but as areas of service where I might offer some assistance, to be of service to humankind.

Speaking of Service, Family First

The summer before college I attended a Baha'i Youth Conference in Champaign-Urbana, Illinois. At this conference, with more than three thousand Baha'i youth from across the country, I met my future husband. He was also going to attend the University of Utah that fall. After serving together on many Baha'i committees and organizing Baha'i campus activities, we decided we were a good match for each other and got married. We have three wonderful children, now adults. I am so thankful to them for enriching my life. One of the important catalysts for my work in issues of diversity sprang from my sincere desire to have my children understand the oneness of humanity as a basic principle of the world we live in, from a

Baha'i perspective. If I wanted them to learn about this, they had to have some hands-on experience. Their lives were filled with many Persians from my husband's side of the family as well as Swedish European mixes from mine and the general community at large.

If my children were to see that there is more than this in the world, I needed to give them opportunities to experience other cultures, races, and religions. This desire to bring diverse groups of people together catapulted me into working with many other women and men to create a weeklong event that we called "Color Me Human: Raising the First Generation Free of Prejudice." It turned out to be an amazing event, with support from the mayor's office, the Utah Humanity Council, and the Institute for the Healing of Racism—to name just a few of the more than fifteen organizations and faith communities that helped with the service activities, educational programs, and celebrations. This work was inspired by one of my favorite quotations from Baha'u'llah, founder of the Baha'i faith: "Know ye not why We created you all from the same dust? That no one should exalt himself over the other. Ponder at all times in your hearts how ye were created. Since We have created you all from one same substance it is incumbent on you to be even as one soul, to walk with the same feet, eat with the same mouth and dwell in the same land, that from your inmost being, by your deeds and actions, the signs of oneness and the essence of detachment may be made manifest. Such is My counsel to you, O concourse of light! Heed ye this counsel that ye may obtain the fruit of holiness from the tree of wondrous glory."[2]

Walk a Spiritual Path with Practical Feet

Growing up, I recall often hearing the phrase "to walk a spiritual path with practical feet." This made so much sense to me that even today I often say it to myself and try to figure out what it means in any given situation. This guidance is simple, but that is what keeps me centered: simplicity and balance. I believe the Baha'i education that I was raised with has influenced my choices in what I do and how I act. Another quotation from the Baha'i writings that has greatly affected my outlook on life is: "Work done in the spirit of service is the highest form of worship."[3] These are two spiritually educative guidances I hold dear in all the work or volunteer service that I do. It resonates with my soul that the work or service that I am doing is like offering a prayer, as if worshipping God. As much as I enjoy praying and times when I can be alone and meditate, I find great comfort in the knowledge that when life is crazy-busy, frustratingly rushed, or when I just feel that I need to be with someone in need, this too is as prayer. This too is nourishing my personal spiritual life.

The Baha'i faith and its teachings about the importance of the equality of men and women have greatly influenced my ability to act with confidence in the most amazing and unexpected situations. I wasn't always able to sit at a conference table with leaders from around the world and comfortably share my opinions. I am no longer that young girl who would rather stand in the corner of a meeting hall with her father, too shy to really want to go visit with the rest of the group. I was happy to have a dad who also preferred to be in the corner, watching. Over the years we both changed and have had numerous opportunities to share our thoughts and connect with others all over the world. In one instance he moved to Vienna, Austria, speaking there with people from all over the world about international safety; I would later be in Barcelona, Spain, speaking of global peace and justice through consultation and interfaith understanding, at the 2004 Parliament of the World's Religions.

Both my mother and my father emphasized the importance of the spiritual teaching of the equality of men and women. It was only because of a lack of education, opportunity, and encouragement that women have not been able to give their gems of inestimable value to society at large. Being encouraged by my loving parents, I took the following words to heart: "The world of humanity has two wings—one is woman and the other man. Not until both wings are equally developed can the bird fly. Should one wing remain weak, flight is impossible. Not until the world of woman becomes equal to the world of man in the acquisition of virtues and perfections can success and prosperity be attained as they ought to be."[4] The visual of a bird trying to fly without the use of both wings is poignant. I have the ability to take my own initiative and help that bird of humanity to fly, or to feel sorry for myself and not develop my skills and talents and let it continue to do circle laps.

As women, we know we have different strengths that are needed and will be cherished in the world as the whole of humanity learns of these benefits. Some of these strengths are collaboration, cooperation, compassion, intuition, and emotional intelligence, even a new way of looking at what defines success. These are all part of the gifts that I hope I am bringing more fully to the table of community building and global service. Through all the opportunities that I am currently having—from helping with an amazing literacy project involving our college and a small community in India, to the regular discussions with interfaith leaders from around the world set up by the UCCD (Utah Center for Citizen Diplomacy), to the interactions with the individuals I meet every day—I hope that my personal spiritual transformation can make a difference in the world in some small way.

As I recall my dear friend, my BFF, encouraging me to share my insights about women, spirituality, and transformative leadership, I close by sharing that my BFF is not only this coeditor and the many other sisters around the world with whom I have collaborated and presented, sharing our ups and our downs. There is also an Unknowable Essence that is my real Best Friend Forever. This prayer encourages me to continue on, when I am feeling less than, sad, or grieved about something, or when I think I don't quite have what it takes, when I need some divine encouragement. I share this prayer with you, so that you too may find comfort in my Friend, who is your Friend as well.

O God! Refresh and gladden my spirit. Purify my heart. Illumine my powers. I lay all my affairs in Thy hand. Thou art my Guide and my Refuge. I will no longer be sorrowful and grieved; I will be a happy and joyful being. O God! I will no longer be full of anxiety, nor will I let trouble harass me. I will not dwell on the unpleasant things of life.

O God! Thou art more friend to me than I am to myself. I dedicate myself to Thee, O Lord.

—ABDU'L-BAHÁ[5]

Shareda Hosein is a graduate of Hartford Seminary in Hartford, Connecticut, with a master's degree in Islamic studies and Christian-Muslim relations and a certificate in Islamic chaplaincy (equivalent to a master's in divinity). She is a lieutenant colonel in the U.S. Army Reserves and serves as a cultural adviser for Operation Iraqi Freedom and Enduring Freedom.

God Said

We Have Created You from a Single (Pair) of a Female and Male

SHAREDA HOSEIN

I was always the "other" in all the settings in my life, because of my gender, my religion, or my ethnicity. My life as a Muslim, female, brown-skinned immigrant has been filled with the challenges and blessings of diversity. My most important insight about diversity of gender was disclosed to me in my thirties, when I attended the Landmark Forum.[6] I became conscious of the reason I chose male-dominated professions. That marked the turning point in my personal journey to consciously own my space, as a female. While my Indian culture posed its requirements on me as a female, I was happy to learn that my parents had vowed to break the old tradition of sending sons abroad for higher education rather than daughters; it was their key reason to come to America. My mother, my first role model, was the dominant force in the decision to emigrate because she didn't want to sacrifice my opportunity for higher education as the oldest and allow my brother, the second-born child, to go ahead of me. She is my biggest cheerleader and takes special pride and joy when I share the stage with my male counterparts.

In 1972 my family emigrated to Boston, Massachusetts, from my small island home in Trinidad, West Indies. It was as if life began at age eleven, when my new friends at elementary school quickly made me aware, through their many questions about my many differences of ethnicity, skin color, language, and religion. They themselves had hyphenated ethnicities; a quarter Irish, one-eighth German, a quarter Italian, a half Polish, and so on. I was rather disappointed and jealous that I had only one: I was 100 percent Indian. I too wanted to fit in and have multiple ethnicities. However, I was aware that when it came to my faith practice, I was content to keep the one I had, Islam, and did not feel the need to change. My father had shared from his heart that the most important thing for him was for all his children to practice the faith of his ancestors. This element of my diversity became the main theme in my life and has been my strength for having compassion, understanding, and acceptance for my fellow human beings.

My first two teachers in understanding diversity in my youth were the Boston Public School system and my mosque, the Islamic Center of New England. In the 1970s the public schools began a period of desegregation and I faced real challenges, struggling to find my place within American society. It would take two decades to feel fully integrated. My mosque, located in Quincy, Massachusetts, and built by a few second-generation Lebanese families, became my family's refuge, with the varied cultures that shared our faith. I learned to appreciate the depth of my faith, and this community gave me a sense of being part of the American fabric of religions and ethnicities. As much as I loved this community, its limitations also pushed me out the door to learn more about what my faith had to say about equality for men and women. I first traveled the secular route and joined the military and later the business world. It took me at least two more decades to find my second route and get to the most important answers to my faith quest of gender equality, which is still an unfinished story.

The Iran hostage crisis in 1979 was the beginning of my military career as I watched the military tactics go from the cold war strategies to focus on the Muslim world. I realized that the two elements of religion and gender would become issues in my new job. I was able to be silent about my religion but couldn't hide my gender. My "going along to get along" personality and the military's zero-tolerance policy of discrimination helped me navigate the environment of gender fairly well. Even though the men didn't want women in their ranks, our presence became a beneficial force and strength to overcome the discrimination that many blacks were experiencing and helped diversify the force and build a professional all-volunteer military. I became an army reservist in the 1980s, reconnected with my religious community, and finished my business administration degree. I held three job titles—officer, volunteer worker, and business woman—for many years as I strived to bring about gender equality and support the women and young girls in my mosque community to stand up and speak out, by taking some sort of leadership role within the community.

It was a lonely challenge for me because most of the women wanted the change but weren't willing to butt heads with the men for their rights. The few that did became marginalized. My other program within this community was my desire to help the youth integrate their American lives with their religious and ethnic lives as a way to heal the schism as the first of a second generation living in America. I encouraged the children to have fun through faith by going on ski trips and then praying in community at the respective prayer times. This was a challenge for many of the youth because they were embarrassed to pray in public, but I believed it helped with the integration process for them. Because I made a difference with the community's children and was on the board of directors for six consecutive years, I earned my place and was accepted as the only female in many male-dominated meetings and events. At social gatherings in homes I would flutter between the living room (with the men talking about worldly matters and the mosque community's future) and the kitchen (with the women talking about food and the children). In reflection, I believe the men saw my value to the community and their children and thus accepted me on my terms.

As I became active in my mosque community and tried to overcome the gender role dilemma, I wasn't fully satisfied to go along to get along. I was now a captain in the U.S. Army and armed with more knowledge. I realized that I had to make lemonade with the lemons given to me rather than go head-on with the men. The turning point for me with winning the gender battle was to turn to God, which showed up in this simple verse in the Qur'an. God said: "O mankind! We created you from a single soul, a (pair) of a female and male, and made you into nations and tribes, so that you may come to know one another (not that you may despise each other). Truly, the most honored of you in God's sight is the greatest of you in piety. God is All-Knowing, All Aware" (Surah Al-Hujurat 49:13). I saw God's words as validation that I am equal and began to own my space as best as I could with all the compassion I could muster to embrace this community, that I so wanted to transform. My two guiding mantras during this period were doing good works for the community "purely for the sake of God" and "leading from behind," a phrase I coined at the time. I struggled to help this community undo the gender bias and was also guided to the profession of chaplaincy, where I felt I could support a broader community in helping many diverse groups of people while representing my faith in God.

My chaplaincy training began with great urgency because September 11, 2001, was my second day at seminary. The thoughts going through my head were: We are at war and I will be called up; there will be many body bags coming back home; and we were attacked by people using my faith as their reasons for this horrific act on the U.S. My new challenge became religious diversity rather than gender. This past decade has been the most stressful of my life so far and at the same time the most enlightening for my faith journey. Although a large percentage of Americans felt threatened by Muslims after 9/11, many said that evil is evil—it doesn't matter about one's color, ethnicity, gender, or faith but how one acts. I feel more at home in an interfaith setting than my own faith setting because I feel that I am doing what God commanded in the verse that guides me: "I made you into nations and tribes so that you may come to know one another." This decade began to fulfill my life's journey in honoring our differences because it is the key element for the harmony of the human race.

Although I did complete my chaplaincy training, I did not have the privilege to be a chaplain in the military. Within my faith I could only lead prayers for women, not for men, hence the military ruled that I couldn't be accessioned into the ranks of the chaplaincy. Since I couldn't become a military chaplain, I pledged that the gender hurdle would become my personal challenge, to advocate for the dream of women becoming U.S. military chaplains. This is the continuation of the dream of a *male* Marine gunnery sergeant in 2003 who thought I might be that person when he endorsed me as a chaplain. What I have learned so far about myself within the realm of diversity is to have patience, perserverance, belief in the power of intentions and prayers. My ultimate prayer is that the diversity of gender becomes a moral right, that women are empowered to reach their full potential with the support of men, and that both genders work in partnership to support and lead God's people in striving for goodness in generations to come.

The Right Reverend Mary Douglas Glasspool was elected eighth bishop suffragan of the Episcopal Diocese of Los Angeles in 2009, the second woman to be elected bishop in diocesan history. Her areas of specialization include ecumenical and interreligious ministries, diocesan schools, LGBT ministries (lesbian, gay, bisexual, transgender), and overseeing one-third of the congregations in the diocese. Before her election, she served nine years as canon to the Bishops of the Episcopal Diocese of Maryland.

Remembrance, Witness, and Action

Fuel for the Journey

THE RIGHT REVEREND MARY DOUGLAS GLASSPOOL

Early in May 2009, a colleague of mine approached me and asked if he could nominate me for bishop suffragan of the Diocese of Los Angeles. At first I thought he was joking. It had been six years since the Episcopal Church had ordained and consecrated the Right Reverend V. Gene Robinson as, among many other gifts and skills, the first openly partnered gay man. This was an event that many in the Episcopal Church celebrated, but it had also resulted in international tension, debate, and even violence for the Anglican Communion, especially in those African countries in which homosexuality is considered sinful or worse.[7] I asked my colleague for some time to think and pray about it, and began gathering information, talking with some close friends, including my partner of twenty-two years, and doing the work of discernment. At the time the Episcopal Church was preparing for its seventy-sixth triennial general convention in July in Anaheim, California, and would almost certainly be addressing the status of LGBT people in the church.[8] Since the election in Los Angeles was scheduled for early December, whatever happened at general convention would probably inform the election one way or another.

The Power of Remembrance

As the head of the deputation from the Diocese of Maryland, I was also making preparations for general convention. While doing so, I dug out an old file from the first general convention I had ever attended: the sixty-sixth convention in Denver, Colorado, in the fall of 1979. Out from the file fell a single, folded, withered sheet of lined paper on which I recognized my own handwriting of thirty years earlier. I read through what I finally remembered as the three-minute testimony I had given at the open hearing on the "Report of the Standing Commission on Human Affairs and Health," a report that had addressed the issue of homosexuality. The last two sentences were: "I trust that God's love at this convention will transcend the issues and address the people—all of us—in our wholeness. I trust and pray that that same love will prevent any of us from condemning others—particularly in this case, homosexuals, in our human, and full, and loving wholeness."

I found myself on the verge of tears as I thought, *We've been dealing with this for thirty years and I could practically give this same little speech in Anaheim this summer.* It was at that moment that I knew I would say *yes* to the colleague who wanted to nominate me in Los Angeles—not because I am a lesbian but because I had the gifts and skills and experience that the Diocese of Los Angeles said it was looking for. I would not let the fact that I am a lesbian preclude me from offering these gifts. The power of remembrance had removed an internal barrier.

The Power of Witness

The concept of *witness* and *witnessing* plays an integral role in the history of Christianity. From its early Jewish roots as a legal term for one who had firsthand knowledge of an event or fact, to the later Christian Testament meaning of one who attests truths about God or Jesus, the act of witnessing had everything to do with the growth of the religion. One of the Ten Commandments forbids us from bearing false witness against our neighbor, and Jesus, at the time of his ascension into heaven, commissions his followers with these words: "You will be my witnesses in Jerusalem, in all Judea and Samaria, and to the ends of the earth" (Acts 1:8b). So bearing witness to that which I know to be true has been a core value in my life.

In early May 2011, I received an invitation to the White House for a reception in celebration of LGBT Pride Month to be hosted by President Barack Obama and his wife, Michelle. I could bring one guest and I needed to RSVP as soon as possible. The first three people I consulted about whether I should go (it was not, after all, in my job description as bishop suffragan for Los Angeles!) said, "You must go! We'll all be so proud of you!" One fellow bishop, whom I deeply respect, even said that my presence at this reception would be a way of bearing witness to the Church. Wednesday, June 29, 2011, was as sunny and clear a day in Washington as one could have wished. My life partner and I drove into the city and parked near the White House. We had also been invited to an LGBT Pride Month Policy Briefing at the Eisenhower Executive Office Building, about which I was quite curious. We arrived at 9:30 a.m. for the briefing to be cleared through the rigorous security system and be ready when it started promptly at 10:00 a.m.

For two and one-half hours we heard from high-level officials, many of whom were openly gay or lesbian, about such issues as "Don't Ask, Don't Tell" and its implementation in the U.S. military, LGBT and Health and Human Services Initiatives, and an HIV/AIDS Update. For me the presentation that hit closest to home was the one made by David Pressman, director for war crimes and atrocities, White House National Security Council. Contrary to his rather frightening title, Mr. Pressman was warm and gentle in demeanor. He was bringing us up to date on International LGBT Administration Efforts, and I was rather curious about what that might be.

One story that he told immediately caught my attention because of the name David Kato. Kato was a gay rights activist in Uganda who had been brutally murdered on January 26, 2011, in what was certainly an act our own country would have called a hate crime. He was an Anglican, and while Mr. Pressman did not mention that fact explicitly, his words went straight to my heart. At Kato's funeral service, attended by hundreds of gay activists as well as family and friends, the presiding pastor launched into an antigay tirade that shocked and angered most of those in attendance. The microphone was grabbed away from the preacher, a scuffle ensued, and the police were called in to escort the pastor away. Finally, someone got up to address the gathering and read to them President Obama's press statement released the day after Kato's murder.

President Obama described David Kato as a powerful advocate for fairness and freedom and made the statement that LGBT rights are not special rights; they are human rights. The president pledged to continue the work of David Kato throughout the world.[9] The mourners were comforted and the service continued. After Mr. Pressman finished this story, I rose to thank him for the witness our president's words had made at David Kato's funeral. I expressed my own wish that the Christian witness would be a more positive one, but assured all gathered that most of us in the Episcopal Church were continuing to work toward the goals of full inclusion and equal rights for all. The power of witness had comforted those who mourned David Kato and confronted a hate-filled diatribe with words of truth and hope.

The Power of Action

Remembrance is about the past. Witnessing has to do with the present. *Action* is movement into the future. Action is the way we live into a new reality, and when we act out of the authenticity of who we are as people, as leaders, as human beings, we help create that new reality. President Obama gave a brief set of remarks at the reception celebrating LGBT Pride Month, and at times I experienced hearing the good news of the gospel being preached! Here, in the White House, I was hearing words from our president that I had longed to hear from church pulpits.[10] But it was a helpful reminder that truths about God transcend politics and the church. God is bigger than all of that, and the good news can come from the White House as well as a faith group.

Among the many aspects of President Obama's remarks that were striking were these: "But I think it's important for us to note the progress that's been made just in the last two and a half years. I just want everybody to think about this. It was here, in the East Room, at our first Pride reception, on the fortieth anniversary of the Stonewall riots, a few months after I took office, that I made a pledge, I made a commitment. I said that I would never counsel patience; it wasn't right for me to tell you to be patient any more than it was right for folks to tell African Americans to be patient in terms of their freedoms. I said it might take some time to get everything we wanted done. But I also expected to be judged not by the promises I made, but the promises I kept."[11] This was the way in which President Obama articulated movement into the future, getting it done, creating a more perfect union.

In the ministry I am privileged to share with so many wonderful people in the Episcopal Diocese of Los Angeles, the power of remembrance, the power of witness, and the power of action have been fuel for the journey. When I remember the past and can integrate the memory, barriers can fall and I become more authentically the person God is calling me to become. When I bear witness to the truths about God and Jesus, hate can be overcome, and truth and hope prevail. When I move into the future as the fully authentic person God created me to be, I can be part of creating a new reality that is closer to what we in the Christian tradition call the *reign of God*. No one does this kind of work alone. We do it together. And that is where *grace* meets *power*.

MOTHERING GOD
> Mothering God, you gave me birth
> In the bright morning of this world
> Creator, source of every breath,
> You are my rain, my wind, my sun.
>
> Mothering Christ, you took my form,
> Offering me your food of light,
> Grain of life, and grape of love,
> Your very body for my peace.
>
> Mothering Spirit, nurturing one,
> In arms of patience hold me close,
> So that in faith I root and grow
> Until I flower, until I know.
>   —Jean Janzen[12]

For most of my life I have been an activist, a left-winger, and a member of a socialist party in Britain. This is what has defined me and has determined many of the friends, activities, and major decisions in my life. That life has not been without difficulties and deep contradictions, but socialism was a story line that endured, a home I could keep returning to, both figuratively and literally. I grew up on protests and picket lines, places where people took control of their lives and discovered a whole new way of living, deciding, and being. I looked to these forms to change me also, and so it was quite a shock when my own transformation came via a very different means.

Growing up in a socialist family, I had disdained the idea of religion and spirituality from a very early age. Spiritual women were silly and self-absorbed, I thought; not the kind of people you could build a movement with, not interested in changing anything but themselves. But acute emotional pain has a habit of opening up the mind, and finding myself in such a place, I reached out for help and discovered a whole new world. The people I encountered on this journey have taught me that spirituality and practicality are not mutually exclusive traits. Today my definition of socialism and spiritualism are beginning to blur into one another. At their best, they both represent the power and goodness that exist when human beings consciously decide to act together in love.

Despite this, the process of emerging into my spiritual self has not been without growing pains. I do not tell my activist friends that I am developing this side of me, and I *definitely* do not mention that I occasionally darken the door of something that might be considered a sort of church. Among my spiritual community I feel less inclined to keep silent and am open about my politics. Still, I have kept the two separate, almost as if I am carrying a dirty little secret in each camp. Attending my spiritual community one morning, I was delighted to hear that members would be marching in the Gay Pride parade, and I decided to go too. The only problem was that I knew my comrades would be marching in the "economic justice" contingent. I had to make the decision: whom was I going to walk with? Somehow the decision was not a difficult one at the time: I walked with Unity, even donning one of their T-shirts, emblazoned with "God Loves All Her Children."

Recounting the moment to my sister the next day, I told her of the conflict I continued to feel around the issue, and as I agonized over the intricacies of my dilemma, she giggled, fixed me with her beautiful blue eyes, and said, "Laura, you 'came out' at the gay parade!" And I suppose I did. What a strange, multicolored, wonderful life it is.

—LAURA PASKELL-BROWN

Living Our Leadership

Questions

1. How do we create safe spaces to ask questions, explore issues, attend to our own souls?
2. What are the obstacles for genuine listening to and learning from each other?
3. How do we embrace and encourage diversity without it seeming contrived?
4. How do our cultural and religious backgrounds influence our choices?
5. How can we make one another feel truly seen, heard, and valued?

Circle Practices: Guidelines

Here are samples of various circle guidelines:

Women of Spirit and Faith Guidelines (www.womenofspiritandfaith.org)
When we are in circle conversations, we agree to
- Speak from our heart and from our own experience.
- Listen with respect, compassion, and curiosity.
- Hold stories or personal material in confidentiality.
- Be willing to discover and explore, noticing patterns, themes, new questions.

Millionth Circle Guidelines (www.millionthcircle.org)
- Create a circle.
- Consider it a sacred space.
- One person speaks at a time.
- Speak and listen from the heart.
- Encourage and welcome diverse points of view.
- Listen with discernment instead of judgment.
- Share leadership and resources.
- Decide together how decisions will be made.
- Work toward consensus when possible.
- Offer experience instead of advice.
- When in doubt or need, pause and silently ask for guidance.
- Decide together what is to be held in confidence.

- Speak from your own experience and beliefs rather than speaking for others.
- Open and close the circle by hearing each voice (using check-ins and check-outs).

PeerSpirit (www.peerspirit.com)
These are our components of the circle:
- Intention
- A welcome start point
- Center and check-in/greeting
- Agreements
- Three principles and three practices (see below for details on these components)
- A guardian of process
- Check-out and farewell

The circle is an all-leader group. Here are our three principles:
1. Leadership rotates among all circle members.
2. Responsibility is shared for the quality of the experience.
3. Reliance is on wholeness rather than on any personal agenda.

Here are our three practices:
1. To speak with intention, noting what has relevance to the conversation in the moment.
2. To listen with attention, being respectful of the learning process for all group members.
3. To tend the well-being of the circle, remaining aware of the impact of our contributions.

Blessings

You might open with some words for reflection. One idea is to fill a bowl or basket with small pieces of paper, each containing one word from a list of words that have meaning to your gathering. Words that describe human qualities work well: love, peace, curiosity, gratitude, silence, commitment, surrender, explore, courage, and so on. You could also create a list around a certain theme—like the names of countries where women are struggling, or the names of specific women needing prayer and help at this time, or a list of intentions for your organization. Each woman chooses one word to silently reflect upon, pray about, and listen deeply for during the gathering and for the coming weeks.

CREATING GOD

> Creating God,
> for those who are wise
> to the ways of your earth:
> thank you.
>
> For those who listen
> to the language
> of tree, rock, river, earth,
> ocean, stars, creatures, sky:
> praise.
>
> Teach us the vocabulary
> to convey our care,
> the words to tell the earth
> we hear her crying for peace,
> the syllables of solace
> for all we have lost,
> the gestures of healing
> for all we have harmed.

—JAN L. RICHARDSON[13]

Secret Listeners

This works well for a retreat setting when a smaller group of women will be together for several days. Put slips of paper with the names of every woman in the group into a basket. At the opening session, each woman draws a name. This woman will be her secret listening partner. For the duration of the gathering, she will secretly listen especially deeply to this woman. At the closing session, time is set aside for each woman to reveal her secret listening partner and give a one-minute reflection about what she has heard and learned. (The editors thank Nontombi Naomi Tutu for this wonderful idea.)

How Women Are Leading

These are the stories of two women, one in California and one in New York, who were inspired to action after 9/11. One created the Spiritual and Religious Alliance for Hope (SARAH); the other created Women Transcending Boundaries (WTB).

The Spiritual and Religious Alliance for Hope (SARAH); www.sarah4hope.org

SARAH was founded in Orange County, California, as a women's interfaith organization in response to the events of September 11, 2001. Women of diverse faith traditions gathered to share their highest and deepest values and to explore new solutions to old problems. We immediately saw that action as well as dialogue is essential. SARAH is a community-building organization founded on shared leadership with an advisory council of eleven women and "SARAH Sisters" worldwide. We are committed to creating a loving, safe, and harmonious world through our personal actions and community service.

SARAH meets monthly and has a weekly newsletter and a dynamic website (www.sarah4hope.org). We often visit places of worship to understand each other's faith traditions and learn the commonalities. We provide educational opportunities for the greater community by facilitating panel discussions and dialogue opportunities for groups, congregations, and local colleges. SARAH has been published in the University of California Irvine's *Difficult Dialogues Report* as well as Harvard University's *Pluralism Project*. SARAH'S Peace Tapestry artwork, created by children and adults at community events, has been sent to peace organizations throughout the world as well as to U.S. government officials. Each year we award a Vision of Peace to someone who embodies our vision of someone who accepts his or her personal responsibility to creating a more safe and harmonious world.

Since 2009 we've mobilized into action more than three thousand people from Christian, Jewish, Muslim, Buddhist, Earth-based, and other traditions, as well as non–faith-based groups in an annual interfaith weekend of community service. We believe one of the most enduring paths to peace is working shoulder to shoulder with shared goals and common values. The women's interfaith initiative is a collaborative and supportive dynamic. We collaborate with con-

centric circles of interfaith groups, both men and women, upon
whose shoulders we stand while we blow in their sails.

—SANDE HART

Women Transcending Boundaries (WTB);
www.wtb.org

WTB was formed in the wake of September 11, 2001, by a group of
women concerned about the harassment of Muslim women in the
community. Ten years later WTB is an established local grassroots
organization of diverse interfaith women dedicated to community
service and education. Through programs, events, and social interactions, we seek to nurture mutual respect and understanding by
sharing information about our diverse beliefs, customs, and practices and working together to address our common concerns in this
post-9/11 world. We educate, serve, and share our personal and collective experiences with the wider community.

Nationally and internationally we have aided victims of the
Southeast Asia tsunami and Hurricane Katrina; raised funds for a
secular school for underprivileged children in rural Pakistan
(Ibtida); partnered with Women for Women International to
finance women's business ventures in war-torn countries; raised
awareness about and funds for African grandmothers caring for
AIDS-orphaned grandchildren; and supported a newly forming
girls' school in The Gambia, West Africa. Locally we have supported women overcoming abuse or poverty, adults needing literacy skills, underprivileged school children, inner-city youth
advancing to higher education, and relatives acting as surrogate
parents. We have helped new refugees create a community garden
and a cottage industry project and supported the local grassroots
group Mothers Against Gun Violence in its mission to reduce violent crime in our city.

Acts of Kindness Weekend, which we launched in 2010, has
become an annual event. A-OK! Weekend seeks to transform the
date of September 11 from a day of mourning into a day for people
from all walks of life to come together and work on projects to
improve our community, get to know one other, and enhance our

mutual values of community well-being and cohesiveness. When we work together, we foster respect and understanding by challenging stereotypes of the "other."

—BETSY WIGGINS

Leadership Tools

The art of listening. If there is one skill we could all use in every interaction, it's the capacity to listen. Remember a time when someone was deeply listening to you. You knew they were there with you, not thinking about what they were going to do next, or say next, or where they were going to go next. They were simply there, present with you, listening attentively to what you had to say. What was that like for you? Most people say that it is such a validating experience to be heard in that way. They also say that it doesn't happen very often in our culture. Listening has become a lost art.

Speaking is seen as the more powerful role in our culture. It certainly gets the most attention. However, listening is equally as powerful but is less well understood. Without listening, there is no power for speaking. The quality of our listening can make a profound difference in any conversation. As Jerry Seinfeld said on the *Oprah Winfrey Show*, "It's all about listening." Defining the art of listening is not easy. These four points are a beginning:

1. It's the art of becoming a listening presence.
2. It's a way of being that opens us up so we can listen to people from diverse, cultures, religions, belief systems, and points of view—those not like us.
3. It's about being a presence for understanding rather than for judging.
4. It's about being open, curious, and attentive to others in such a way that at the end of the conversation, they have fully expressed themselves and feel more alive.

There are some practical ways we can learn to be better listeners. Try out the following list of behaviors and notice the difference it makes.

Top Ten Powerful Listening Practices

1. *Stop talking.* One person speaks at a time. One of the most irritating listening habits is that of interrupting. We have two ears and one mouth—a reason to listen twice as much as we speak.

2. *Pause before speaking.* Allow the person who is speaking time to complete their thought. Another variation on this is to ask, "Is there anything else?" There almost always is. Become comfortable with silence. Stay present with the other person.

3. *Listen to yourself.* Be in touch with your inner voice. Ask yourself, What wants to be said next? Learn to wait for your inner wisdom.

4. *Listen for understanding.* You do not have to agree with what you hear, or even believe it, to listen to understand the other person.

5. *Ask for clarification.* If you do not understand what someone is saying, just ask. Use open-ended questions. Be wary of starting your question with "Don't you think that...?" That's what *you* think.

6. *Let the speaker know that you have heard her or him.* Use body language such as nodding and various facial expressions. If you are not sure what is appropriate in another culture, ask the person how she or he knows someone is listening and do that.

7. *Be patient and present.* Listening well takes time and your presence. We speak at about 150 to 200 words per minute, and we process at about 300 to 500 words per minute, so there's a lag time.

8. *Listen with an open mind.* Be curious and appreciative of what you are listening to. Listen for new ideas. Let go of judging and evaluating. Get to know your own hot buttons, so when they come up you can identify them and let them pass, rather than be hooked into a debate about them.

9. *Pay attention to the environment.* Stop what you are doing to listen. Turn off background noise when possible, move to a quieter corner of the room, and clear your desk. Stop looking at your cell phone!

> "Like a pearl and the grain of sand ... turning inward grates often in the moment. There is a calling, however, that simply exists, and listening is the only way it will abate. Turning or tuning within silence manifests worth. There is no place else to go."
> **—Clare Peterson**

10. *Listen with empathy and compassion.* Let go of your agenda for the moment. Put yourself in the other person's shoes. Each one of us has a story to tell. As the listener, your job is to find out what it is.

It only takes one minute a day to become a better listener.

- *Practice silence.* Spend at least one minute a day intentionally silent.

- *Practice reflection.* Ask yourself, What is emerging now? What needs to be done now? Then wait for your inner wisdom.
- *Practice mindfulness.* Spend at least one minute a day aware of what you are doing each second.

KAY LINDAHL

Shared Praxis Circle Process

Shared praxis is an interactive and dynamic way of listening and learning. It assumes that every participant has insights worth sharing. Each step builds on prior discoveries; what is learned in the previous step is used to expand understanding in the present and the following steps. There is interaction between and among participants that builds toward interaction of the whole group and weaves together all participants' insights. This specialized circle process can be used in any setting— from a small group of five to a large conference. In a conference setting a facilitator leads the whole group through the praxis, with participants seated in circles of five to eight. This allows the group members to easily see one another and opens expanded give-and-take along with the possibility of developing increased trust. Give these steps a try:

1. The first step in the shared praxis circle process engages all the participants individually as they respond to two questions posed by a facilitator or moderator. Each individual reflects on the questions by jotting down some thoughts on paper. This step primes the pump by generating personal reflection in both introverts and extroverts.
2. The second movement is a one-on-one exchange between two participants in response to these questions: What have you learned? What are you thinking now that you have reflected on the earlier two questions individually? The focus is not on reading what the other participant has written but on listening and speaking to one another, although what each participant has written could be shared. Sharing what an individual has learned in the personal reflection and listening to another person's responses further energizes and expands the dialogue.
3. Next, the circle/table gathers together and is asked, "You have reflected individually and with another person. What have you learned? What are you thinking now?" Remarks are listened to

and recorded on newsprint without comment; they are simply received, not judged or evaluated.

4. In a conference setting a keynote speaker or panelists then present their material. This can be especially effective if panel members have also participated in the first three steps; they may have further developed their own thoughts and will be more aware of issues and feelings in the whole group. This will facilitate richer conversation by and among the panel members as well as more connection with the audience. If you are in a smaller group setting, you may want to have a conversation about the remarks on the newsprint at this time, or you can omit this step.

5. In the conference setting, once the panelists conclude, again several questions are asked: "Now that you have reflected individually, with one other person, with your table, and heard the panelists' expertise, what have you learned? What are you thinking now?" This is followed by discussion between the audience and the panel members. In the smaller group you can simply ask the questions, "What have you learned? What are you thinking now?"

6. Finally, everyone is asked, "What are you going to do with what you have learned? What action will you take in the next twenty-four hours as well as in the long term?" Depending on your situation, the answers to these questions could be written as personal reflections or discussed at the tables/circles. The process can be varied and include other forms of expression than written and verbal (like simple art, for example); however, the central objective remains engaging every participant in the process so that her participation expands her sense of her own expertise.

JOY MILLS, MA, MDIV

Leading from a Whirlwind

Faith and Courage in a Swiftly Changing World

VALARIE KAUR

For me the whirlwind appears in those moments when we decide to challenge the status quo, something that I think almost every woman knows a little something about. I feel as though we come into the world handed a script, and this script assigns us roles based on our race, our class, our age, our orientation, and our religion. Sometimes we are assigned speaking parts. Other times we are assigned nonspeaking parts. There are times that the script demands that we stay in the kitchen or in the pews, that we don't make waves, that we laugh at certain jokes, that we say certain prayers with certain pronouns, and that we recite certain claims. In these moments our

Valarie Kaur is an award-winning filmmaker, writer, advocate, and public speaker. Her critically acclaimed documentary film *Divided We Fall* (2008) on the rise of hate crimes after the tragic events of September 11, 2001, has inspired national grassroots dialogue. She has clerked on the Senate Judiciary Committee and traveled to Guantanamo to report on the military commissions. She teaches visual advocacy as founding director of the Yale Visual Law Project. She is also director of Groundswell, a broad-based initiative to spark and empower the multifaith movement for justice at Auburn Theological Seminary. The following is drawn from Kaur's keynote speech delivered at the Alchemy conference.

124

hands begin to tremble, and the script that we have been handed doesn't necessarily ring true. In these moments we have the choice to either bury our head in the script for safety and security—indeed some women must make that choice—or to follow a certain stirring in our hearts, turn ourselves toward where our moral compass points, face the whirlwind that has appeared, and leap into it, taking action that challenges the world as is, for a vision of the world that ought to be.

In my life I have faced three whirlwinds. My sense is that another whirlwind may be brewing among us now. The first time I leapt into it, it was for truth. The second time I leapt into it, it was for justice. And the third time I leapt into it, it was for love. Each time I leapt, it felt like flying. I felt invincible. It feels really good to be courageous. But each time I leapt, I fell down in a dark hole, broken, bruised, sometimes bleeding. But every time I fell, I discovered something, some gem that made the leap worthwhile, some discovery that set me free. My story begins with sound.

> *Tati vao na lagai, Par brahm sharanai*
> *Chaugird hamare Ram kar, Dukh lage na bhai*
> *Satguru poora bhetya, Jin bant banai ji*
> *Ram nam okhadh diya, Eka liv lai*
> *Rakh liya tis rakhan har, Sab byadh mitai*
> *Kaho Nanak kirpa bhai, Prabh bhayo sahai*

These are the words my grandfather used to sing to me as I fell asleep at night. These are the words he sang to me as he drove me to school in the mornings. These are the words I would hear him sing as he marched his garden at sunset. This prayer was his favorite prayer. It was a Sikh prayer and, to me, it was the secret to his fearlessness. My grandfather was the most fearless person I know. He survived war, riots, religious massacre, and yet he embodied the ideal of the saint-soldier, the heart of the Sikh faith, the idea that you are deeply connected to the One True Divine, even as you walk in the world by soldiering and serving those around you.

It was these prayers that I would recite when I woke up from my nightmares. When I was a little girl, I grew up in the Central Valley in California, near Fresno. My family had settled there almost a hundred years ago, so I had deep, deep roots in America. I never found a contradiction being Sikh and being American until I went to school. The kids at school tried very hard to convert me to Christianity. I would have nightmares of judgment day and hellfire. When I woke up, it was my grandfather's prayer of fearlessness that lulled me back to sleep. These experiences created a deep curiosity about religious violence, what it means to live in a world of radical difference, and how we might find peace. Years later, I brought these questions with me to Stanford University, where I studied religion and international relations. That's when the whirlwind first appeared.

The First Whirlwind

On September 11, 2001, I was crumpled on my parents' bedroom floor, watching the Twin Towers fall over and over again set between images of Osama bin Laden with a beard and a turban. It wasn't long before I realized that the image of America's new enemy looked like my grandfather, like my brothers, like my cousin, like my family. I was handed the social script that divided everyone into two camps: those who are with us, and those who are against us. Anyone who was Muslim or Muslim-looking fell on the wrong side of the line. We were rendered automatically suspect, perpetually foreign, and potentially terrorist. This social script didn't ring true to my experience, and as we began to hear news of hate violence sweeping the country, my discomfort turned into sorrow.

On September 15, Balbir Singh Sodhi was murdered in front of his gas station in Arizona by a man who called himself a patriot. He was the first of at least twenty-four people killed in the yearlong aftermath of 9/11. It felt as if an uncle had been murdered. I ran into my bedroom and locked the door, and I hid for days because I didn't know what to do with this script. That's when the words of my grandfather washed over me. His prayer of fearlessness made me face the whirlwind outside my bedroom window and decide to leap into it. I grabbed my camera and a list of questions, got in my car, and began a journey across the country to capture stories that we weren't hearing on the evening news. These are some of my experiences on the road in that aftermath:

I'm at Ground Zero, and the rubble is still smoldering. I'm with a young Sikh-turbaned man who has a thick Brooklyn accent, who was running from the burning towers that morning with thousands of other people. A group of men across the street looked at him, pointed at him, and said, "Hey, you f-ing terrorist, take that turban off." Amrik found himself running for his life a second time, within fifteen minutes.

I'm in Queens, and there is a small room with a mattress on the floor and a man moaning and groaning in pain. He looks like my grandfather. "Waheguru, Waheguru," he says over and over again: God's name. They had beaten him with baseball bats the afternoon of September 11 because he wore a turban. He died a few months after my interview.

I'm in Santa Barbara with a Sikh woman who wears her hair in a bun, who said that she had been stopped at a stoplight a few weeks after 9/11, when a motorcyclist pulled up next to her. He opened her car door, put a knife to her throat, and said, "This is what you get for what you people have done to us. Now I'm going to cut your throat." Bleeding and broken, she drove on until she found the arms of her friend who took her to the hospital. During my interview there was a noise in the back of her store and she jumped. She said, "I've my lost my safety. I've lost my security. I came from Kenya to find it here in America, and I've lost it."

I'm in San Jose and there is a small Muslim boy who's eight years old. His name is Samir, and he is telling me about how the kids at school throw their lunch pails in his face so that he can't breathe. "They call me Bin Laden's son," he says. "But I'm not a bad guy. I'm not a bad guy." I said, "Okay, Samir, what would you do if you saw the bad guys?" and he said, "Well, I would attack them with my karate." "Okay. How would you know they were the bad guys?" He says, "They have turbans on their heads."

There were dozens of stories like this, hundreds of stories like this. I thought this road trip would last months, but it lasted years. I discovered that directly after September 11 and in the past decade we have seen resurgences of anti-Muslim violence break onto the surface of the national landscape. It happened after 9/11. It happened at the onset of the Iraq War. It happened after the Madrid and London bombings. It happened after the arrest of the Fort Hood shooter, after the arrest of the Christmas Day bomber. It happened during the campaign and election of Barack Obama. It happened in the fall of 2010, during the controversy around Park 51, the so-called mosque at Ground Zero. It happened again, in spring 2011, when U.S. Representative Peter King held his congressional hearings investigating so-called radicalization in the Muslim American community.

A few days before those hearings, in Elk Grove, California, two elderly Sikh men with turbans took their afternoon walk—the same way that my grandfather always used to take his afternoon walk—when a pickup truck pulled up next to them, fired shots, and gunned them down. The police and community suspect it was a hate crime. One of the men died instantly. The other, Gurmej Atwal, fought for his life in critical care for weeks but ultimately lost his struggle. I don't know if many people know these stories. I don't know if many people are connecting what we hear in the news and the hallways of power and on the airwaves with the kind of violence that we're seeing on our city streets in our own communities.

Perhaps what's even more devastating than the outbreaks of violence are the subtle, daily acts of prejudice that thousands of people of color encounter every single day. The men and boys who are searched two times, three times, four times at the airport; the men and women punished by their employers for wearing turbans and veils; the families who stay at home out of fear of retaliation after the latest news flash. What most breaks my heart are the kids who have grown up in the shadow of 9/11 who say, "You know, the teachers at school, they stop kids who call other kids the N word, but they don't stop kids when they call me 'terrorist,' even though 'terrorist' is my N word." We have an entire generation growing up in the shadow of 9/11.

When I leapt into this whirlwind, although I felt courageous at first, my journey soon grew darker and darker. I think the moment when I hit rock bottom was when I was coming home from college. I was writing my honors thesis about stereotype threat—the idea that stereotypes are embedded inside of the social landscape and we can't help but absorb them, even if we don't endorse them. As I was walking home from school, I was thinking, *Okay, I need to go out and tell all the other people about the stereotypes and racism within them. Of course, I am free of such racism.* But imagine what happened: a black kid was approaching me and I crossed to the other side of the street, pulled my bag close, and noticed my stomach tightening. For the first time in my life, I asked myself, *Why is my body responding this way before my mind has said a word?* I thought back to when I was a kid and I watched all those TV episodes of cop shows, where the bad guy is always this young African American male.

> "I need to be grounded in my own voice to be able to stand for others."
> —Valarie Kaur

I was thinking, *My God, I'm educated*, but those images were so powerful, so in the air, that my body couldn't help but absorb them.

In Nebraska a few years ago an elderly woman approached me and said, "Valarie, I just saw your film, and I want to apologize because I saw two Sikhs at the airport with turbans after 9/11, and I was scared, and I want to apologize for being scared." I was just about to accept her apology when I realized, *Wait a second—I too have done this*. We *all* have done this. Our guilt can cancel out because it's not the first moment over which we have responsibility. It's the second moment. In this second moment we can decide whether we go unthinkingly with the way that our bodies have been programmed to see others—to see gay people out to destroy our faith, the illegal immigrants who are taking our country away from us, the terrorists who live among us. Or, in that second moment, we can choose to draw upon other voices, other faces, other stories, to undo what has been done to us.

The truth that I discovered lay at the doorstep of the widow of Balbir Singh Sodh, the first man who was killed after 9/11. I visited her in India. She was wearing all white, the color of mourning. There were dark circles under her eyes. I just asked one question: "What would you like to tell the people of America?" And this widow, this woman from whom I was expecting anger, a holy righteous anger, said to me, "Tell them thank you. When I went to Phoenix for my husband's funeral, they came out in the thousands—Christians, Muslim, Jew—and they wept with me. They cared for me. They showed me their compassion and love."

When she said that, I realized that there are very few people in the world whose faces are so hardened by hate that they can't be transformed by our stories and that in Phoenix they had told Balbir Singh Sodhi's story well. The local community worked with the local news to talk about how he had come to America to escape religious persecution, how he would never see the faces of his grandchildren, how his widow's heart was now broken. This story broke people open, made them care, made them show up. Her words pushed me to finish my film, which I've shared in over one hundred and fifty cities across the country. I thought that the value of the film would be: "Okay, everyone. See the stories of the Sikh American community. See these people. Stand up for them." What I discovered was quite different. In Chicago an African American man stood up and said, "My braids are my turban." In New York a gay man stood up and said, "Just as we have to fight for the right for gays to come out of the closet, we have to fight for the right for Sikhs to wear their turbans." In the South an evangelical young man, a man with whom I thought I had nothing in common, said to me, "You know, you and I are not so different. I too have been seen as an outsider."

What I discovered were these remarkable gestures of solidarity, this recognition of ourselves in another's story, this recognition that we all have a shared desire to be seen the way that we see ourselves, and that we all remember a moment in our own lives when we have been outsiders at some point. Our task, really, is to throw out the scripts that divide the world into "us and them," to throw out the binaries and instead embrace the incredible multiplicity and pluralism. Our equality is not in our sameness. Rather, we need to hold up a picture of ourselves as a mosaic, as people who are willing to be different from each other, because those differences matter. We should not merely tolerate those differences but respect, embrace, and celebrate them. In this first whirlwind I learned that stories have the power to change how we see the world.

The Second Whirlwind

The second time the whirlwind appeared, I leapt into it for justice. It was 2003 and I was at Stanford. The war drums were beating, and the Iraq War was just about to begin. The script that I had been handed as a young person, especially as a person of color who had been asked to be patriotic, divided the world into victims and oppressors. It said that we achieve justice through slaying oppressors. The United States had been the victim on 9/11, so the only way that we were going to win and conquer terrorism was through war. But the script didn't read true to me, as it hasn't read true to many generations that have come before me. I had a choice as a young American: keep my mouth shut and do what I was told, to support my country; or face the whirlwind outside of my dorm room and leap into it. I leapt, and I joined a multigenerational movement of people who were standing up for peace through intelligent, creative demonstrations. It felt like flying. It felt like we could almost stop the war. We were making the news; we brought city streets to a halt the day the war began. Some of you may remember the incredible stirring of activism in 2003 in the San Francisco Bay area alone. But when we leap, we fall, right?

I was in New York City in 2004 for the Democratic National Convention. I was there as a legal observer with my camera to document a protest, to protect against police brutality. The NYPD came in with tremendous force, knocked people down, bloodied people up, saw me with a camera—a young woman of color with a badge—and arrested me. We were taken to what has now been called Guantanamo on the Hudson, a place of razor wire, diesel on the floor, big cages. When I stopped being able to sense feeling in my hands, I asked the lieutenant to loosen my cuffs. He said, "We're not here to make you comfortable," and he twisted my arm. It felt like he had sliced my hands off.

In that moment of pain the words that came to me were words from Sikh scripture: my grandfather's words of fearlessness. The prayer helped me cross that gulf of pain. I remember being so scared and so alone, crumpled on the floor of the cell, facing the bars with my dead hand crumpled on my chest, thinking, *Oh, my God. I am a citizen; I can speak English; I am well-educated. And I can be treated as if I am not a human being. What happens to people* without *these protections? What happens behind the locked doors of the prisons down our street?* The thought was horrifying to me, and down in that darkness I knew that I had to do something. A door cracked open and I could see the open water of the Hudson River on the other side, and in that moment I decided to apply to law school. Somehow that was my way of responding—I committed to learn how to wield the law as sword and shield once I was free again.

So I went to law school. I drew close to the language of power. I resisted it. I struggled with it. Along the way my professor told me that there was a spot on a military plane to Guantanamo—the real Guantanamo. He wanted me to go to report on the military commissions held on the base. I

> "On the challenges of—and possibilities for—bringing feminine spiritual leadership into the workplace, one woman said, 'It may be as simple as being aware of this special quality of the Feminine that we carry within us.' Another woman spoke of how her male co-workers will come to her office to confide fears, share sorrows, ask advice. She said, 'I think they reveal their softer, feminine side with me because I'm patient, accepting, and hold a space where it feels safe to do so.'"
>
> **—Participant at a WSF gathering**

thought, *Okay, I guess this is what it means to leap into the whirlwind for justice.* On the night before my trip I opened my suitcase and packed it. Then I unpacked it and I packed it again. It didn't seem appropriate to wear bright clothes, so I stuffed my suitcase with grays. How does one dress for a symbol of evil? When the plane descended over Guantanamo Bay, Cuba, and I walked out onto the platform, I looked around and it was one of the most beautiful places I have ever seen. There were sparkling blue waters. There were green rolling hills. There were bright blue skies. My grayness suddenly felt out of place. We crossed on the ferry and there was water splashing in our faces. When we got to the other side, we entered a little town that looked, felt, and tasted like the Main Street of Disneyland. Talk about dissonance. There was a McDonald's. There was a paintball center and football fields and tennis courts. There was even an Irish pub.

I felt a deep dissonance between this manufactured resort and the prisons on the other side of the hill, where dark bodies had languished for years without crime, without charge, without conviction; where we heard allegations of torture, allegations of being force-fed, allegations of murder. That dissonance was something I couldn't understand, so I looked at these soldiers and guards as if they were the oppressors. I needed to figure out how they could live with themselves. I began to talk with them and ask them questions.

You know what they said, almost unanimously? They said, "Those terrorists in those cells? They get more freedom than we do. They get to say and do what they want. We don't get to say and do what we want. We are the prisoners." I escaped to the ocean and gazed upon the sunlit waves, just as I had looked at that water out of my cell in the Guantanamo on the Hudson. It was the same water. I remember thinking, *How can it be that these oppressors—the police officer who hurt me, the guards and soldiers at Guantanamo—can't see those of us on the other side of those bars?*

It slowly began to dawn on me that the soldiers I was speaking to were eighteen, nineteen, twenty, twenty-two. They were young. The man whose hearing I went to had been fifteen when he was captured in Afghanistan and imprisoned in Guantanamo for nearly a decade. He was young. I was sent here as a student to observe the military commissions. I too was young. That we were all young people—the guards, the soldiers, the detainees, the nurses who force-fed them, and the observers sent to report on their trials. We were all young people who had inherited a system not of our own making. We were, in fact, captives of a system that required us to dehumanize others. The responsibility did not belong entirely to these soldiers, just as it did not belong to the police officer who had hurt me.

I had leapt into the whirlwind for justice because I wanted to challenge the script that divided the world into victim and oppressor, that said that the only way to win was to destroy the oppressor. But that script actually perpetuates cycles of violence. Perhaps true liberation requires not to slay the opponent but to hear the opponent's story, to change the system so that the oppressor is released just as those of us behind bars are released. Those soldiers, those guards, that police officer who had hurt me, and those of us on the other side—*we're all trapped.* A new time has come for us to find a way to transform the systems that cause us to dehumanize one another. That's what I learned when I leapt into the whirlwind for justice.

The Third Whirlwind

This last whirlwind is the most personal one, the one I leapt into for love. This one appeared to me in Toronto, outside a museum. I met a young man—warm and funny and intelligent and deeply supportive with an appetite for the world, and for stories, just like me. I had a choice. I had the social script in my pocket, and it said: You are a young, Sikh American woman; you are in a community and a family that will ask you to marry a young Sikh American man. But I had this young gentleman standing inside of a whirlwind in front of me, and I was crazy for him.

You know where this is going. I rejected the script. I faced the whirlwind, and I leapt into the arms of love. Of course when you leap—especially if it's leaping into the arms of love—it feels like flying; it feels like fireworks. It was glorious. When I went home to tell my parents—deeply supportive, deeply loving—they said, "What will your cousins say? What will your uncles say? What about the rest of the family?" Many of us who marry or fall in love with someone outside of our faith or with someone of the "wrong" gender, face this same resistance. I want to challenge us to think how this experience has been different for women of color. Before 9/11, I would have faced resistance for choosing to fall in love with a man from a Hindu family. But after 9/11, that resistance turned into a sense of betrayal, and that betrayal turned into violence.

Imagine: since 9/11, many people in the Sikh community have felt under siege. Boys and men are called "Bin Laden" on the street every day. Some of them don't know what to do with their aggression. In a patriarchal culture some men take it out on the bodies of their women, their wives or girlfriends or sisters, in the form of domestic violence or sexual incest. When some of them pressure women to carry on the faith the way they dictate it, marrying or falling in love with someone outside is the deepest betrayal, a loss, to the whole community. Many of us who are part of minority communities may know what that feels like. After 9/11 the resistance to my relationship turned into death threats, and the death threats turned into a moment in the park where I was called to meet a relative to talk about what had happened. When I approached him, he threw off an umbrella, and suddenly I was facing the barrel of a gun. I asked, "Are you going to kill me?" But the gun swung around. It was on him, it was on me, it was on him again. In that moment I made a choice: I walked away. As I did so, I turned around and said, "You have no power over me anymore." I turned back around and I kept walking. I was thinking, *Oh, my God. I just told a man with a loaded gun that he has no power over me and turned my back on him.*

> "Invite a cluster of women representing diverse spiritual, religious, and interfaith groups to cocreate a one-day event in your community celebrating women's spiritual leadership."
>
> **—Participant at a WSF gathering**

I could hear the gun sound. I could hear it going into my back. I could hear myself hit the ground. I could hear my silence as I waited for someone to find me. That park was empty. I wondered how long it would take for me to die, if I would die there or in the hospital. But the gun never sounded. Even if it had, I had still walked away. I had walked away from centuries of oppression, where men have power over their women. I went home and fell at the feet of my grandfather—my great, magnificent, wise grandfather. "Papa Ji, what do I do?" He looked down at me and put his hand on my head. "Don't call the police. I don't approve of this match. Let the family handle this. He loves you. That's why he did that." I couldn't find the words to speak.

That moment, my mother—my mother who had an arranged marriage at eighteen, my mother for whom I have been the mouthpiece for almost all of our lives—my beautiful mother stood between my grandfather and me and said, "No more. For too long have women in this family been treated second to men. Not my daughter." She handed me the phone, and I was sitting there gripping it, and I was thinking, *I can't dial the number. They will see this man as Bin Laden in the flesh. They will pull the trigger.* I was thinking about black women in the inner city who can't call the white cops on their men. I was thinking about Latina women who can't call the cops for fear of their men or their families or their children being deported. I was thinking about Native women who feel so isolated on reservations without protection. What does "national security" mean for women? What does it mean for women who can't find protection inside of our own homes, our own lives? If my mother hadn't stood up to provide that protection for me, I don't think I would be here. My mother took the phone and dialed the number, then she told me to go, to live my life. I left with my partner and we did—we built our lives together. But I lost something. I lost the village.

Two years ago my grandfather was dying and I stood by his bedside. He was as fearless as ever—my beautiful grandfather. Parkinson's disease was swallowing his whole body. His digestive system had stopped working. He couldn't lift his hands. He could barely move his head or his eyes. But I stood there and I held his hand and said, "Papa Ji, I'm here." He looked at me and smiled, and he looked at my fiancé next to me and smiled. He gave us his blessing and asked for my forgiveness. My grandfather, who taught me to be such a fearless warrior that I turned around and fought him, gave me my greatest discovery. It happened at his funeral. It was the hardest thing that I had to do, to speak at his funeral. I decided that I wanted to recite the prayer that he had taught me. I realized that I'd never found out what it meant. So I Googled it.

> The hot winds cannot touch me.
> I am sheltered by the divine.
> On all four sides I am shielded by the divine.
> Sorrow cannot consume me.
> I have met the true and perfect one who created all of this.
> I am healed in God's name. I am merged with the One.
> The Keeper has kept me and taken away what ails me.
> Nanak says, grace has fallen upon me and the divine has
>   come to my side.

"The hot winds cannot touch me." In this last whirlwind, when I leapt for love, I discovered the final lesson my grandfather had to give me about what it meant to be fearless. I discovered that when you leap into the whirlwind, you will fall. It will cost you. But *the hot winds cannot touch you* if you have truth or justice or love in your heart.

The Whirlwind Brewing among Us

Lately I've been holding another script in my hands, a social script that I find in many feminist circles among women of faith. This script hasn't been ringing true. There are three parts of it that perhaps were true before or true for some people but don't feel true to me now from where I am standing as a young Sikh American woman.

First, this script describes a god that I don't recognize. It describes only two parts of the divine: God as mother and God as father. God as mother is usually characterized as near, compassionate, loving, sacrificial, and invisible. God as father is characterized as distant, uncompassionate, indifferent, without feeling, and with a will to ruthlessness. This is a dichotomy that sets up God as father as bad, perhaps as evil, and God as mother as wholly good. But since my grandfather has died, I have felt him as part of the divine spirit. I have felt him very near. There is part of the masculine that can be deeply empathetic. We must ask ourselves: Can the masculine be more than a caricature? Can the Divine Feminine? There are many faces to what we're calling the Divine Feminine. The most fierce form of the Hindu goddess Durga is Kali—Kali wants blood as blessing; she is about ruthless power, even as she is mother. Kali does not fit the caricature of the Divine Feminine that I often hear about. Can we challenge what we mean by "masculine" and what we mean by "feminine"? Can we challenge from whose scriptures dominant depictions of masculine and feminine come? Can we engage the multiplicity of the One Divine Truth? I understand the need to reclaim the Divine Feminine in our traditions, but how are we doing it? Are we doing it in a way that holds up a script that divides the world once again into "us and them"?

Second, this script describes people in a way that I don't recognize. Just as the script describes God as male as distant and bad, and God as female as near and good, so too it describes men and women in broad strokes. Men are the ones in power, the ones who deprive us of power, and the ones responsible for all conflict in the world. Women are the ones disempowered, the ones who are absent and silent, and the ones who have the potential to save the world if only we would lead. This approach calls for women to have that holy anger to dethrone men and maleness. In my world, though, God did not make "pink and blue souls." God made us in black, white, red, and every hue in between. Not just as men and women, but as straight, gay, lesbian, bisexual, transgender, and queer people. For my generation these categories that we inherited from the culture wars—religious versus secular, black versus white, Democrat versus Republican, man versus woman—don't really match up with our experience, in which there are multiple genders, multiple orientations, and multiple sexual identities. Too often the word *women* in feminist studies implies the experience of white, straight, middle-class, Christian women—and even that group is full of tremendous diversity—with only passing regard for the perspective and experience of women of different races, religions, ages, classes, and orientations. Can we begin to use the word *woman* in ways that do not set us up over and against men and do not treat us all as the same?

It strikes me that there's almost a spiral of women's development, one that's around leaving the world of men, diving into that fabulous lusciousness of a women's circle, then returning to the other world to show up in a different way and with a stronger and deeper and truer voice and presence, to work and play toward creating a world of women *and* men, men *and* women. I've watched myself go round and round (hopefully deeper and deeper) into this spiral over the past decades. I've witnessed much of the old boundaries and divisions blurring, women speaking with more authentic yang voices and energetic presences (not the old animus-ridden stuff) within women's groups, and men having the courage to speak with softer, more body-centric voices.

That being said, where my real energy is these days is in that reintegration. How can we create structures that allow for both male and female, whatever gendered bodies they show up in? How can we create communities that honor both ways of knowing—being and doing?

—MELISSA GAYLE WEST

Finally, I believe that a script that sets up dichotomous thinking—God as father or mother, people as just men or just women—perpetuates cycles of violence. We can't help but set up that dangerous dichotomy of victim and oppressor. No wonder feminists of faith often call upon holy anger. Yes, we need to be real about our anger to process our healing, but this call to anger inside an us-versus-them framework is a call to dethrone men. It's not necessarily violent action, but it's violent thinking. In this kind of violent thinking, the victims—that is, women—are set up to become the new oppressor. I would rather name, value, and lift up the many different kinds of women who are already exercising many different kinds of leadership. I would rather use their experience to explore pragmatic ways to expand that circle of leadership to include every single one of us—people of all genders and identities. Women are already making this happen. Women from indigenous traditions, other non-Abrahamic traditions, and even Abrahamic traditions, are reinventing the ways that we lead.

In naming what I feel is not right about this script, I am sensing the presence of an altogether new whirlwind. I wonder if you do too. You don't have to, but if you do, can we link arms and enter it together? Can we challenge the script that implicitly preaches God as mother against God as father, and men against women? Can we explore a script that reflects the vast and mysterious diversity of the divine and of humanity? Can we replace that call to holy anger with a compassionate way to change the world that transforms rather than slays our opponents, liberating those on all sides of injustice?

I believe it is possible to enter this whirlwind right here, right now. We will fall. We will break. But I think, down in that darkness, we will find something that is a first step toward freedom. I believe that if we have truth and justice and love in our hearts, we can sit inside that whirlwind and have the hard conversations about what faith, courage, and diversity mean for us in a swiftly changing world.

Exploration III

How Do We Stand for the Greatness of Each Other?

Profound Mystery

The leavening of yeast must have seemed to ancient men a profound mystery, and yet something on which they could always depend. Just so does the supernatural enter our natural life, working in the hiddenness, forcing the new life into every corner and making the dough expand.

If the dough were endowed with consciousness, it would not feel very comfortable while the yeast was working. Nor, as a rule, does our human nature feel very comfortable under the transforming action of God, steadily turning one kind of love into another kind of love—desire into charity, clutch into generosity, Eros into Agape.

Creation is change, and change is often painful and mysterious to us. Spiritual creation means a series of changes, which at last produce a Holiness, God's aim for us.

—Evelyn Underhill[1]

This exploration takes us to a deeper level as we begin to look at how we as women support and nurture each other. We are examining our relationships with other women and the challenges and barriers that seem to appear over and over again. What are the fears that get in the way? How do we cope with that which makes us uncomfortable? How do we prepare ourselves to have difficult conversations? What structures can we create that allow people to express their pain and to help others to see their own privilege at work? Each one of us can probably tell several stories of when other women have let us down. They either didn't speak out on your behalf, when you knew they really did support you, or they sabotaged your idea so they would get credit for it, or they told white lies or withheld information, and so on. It may seem easier to pretend the issue doesn't exist; it's much more comfortable to skirt around it than to move through it. We have no doubt all done the same. Men are certainly not immune from this type of behavior either. It takes courage, practice, and deep listening to stay in these conversations all the way through.

Many of us have also had the experience of people in our lives seeing something wonderful in us that we didn't see in ourselves. Remember how it felt when this took you out of your comfort zone—trying new things and extending yourself in new ways. Yet there was that voice that kept whispering in your ear that there might be something to what they were saying. Maybe, just maybe, you are who they said you are; your voice is powerful, wanting to be expressed. When you discover that they were right—what a gift it was that they called you into your own greatness! How do we do that for each other? What do we assume that prevents us from being on either side of this question? How can we support another woman to feel truly seen, valued, and heard? As you read these stories, think about the way women have stood for your greatness. Reflect on times when you have stood for the greatness of another. Imagine what it would be like if we all practiced standing for the greatness of each other, including those who are very different from us or with whom we disagree. What is the shared greatness that could emerge from our unique greatness?

Adelia Sandoval is cultural director for the Juaneno Band of Mission Indians/Acjachemen Nation, the indigenous people of Orange County, California. She is also an ordained minister of Lifesblessings Ministries in Descanso, California. Her ministry is called Song of the Earth, a Native American Healing service in an outdoor sanctuary. Sandoval is a Trustee for the United Religions Initiative, a global interfaith organization and an adviser to SARAH (the Spiritual and Religious Alliance for Hope) and to Orange County Interfaith Coalition for the Environment.

The Wind Is Blowing from the West and Has the Smell of the Sea

ADELIA SANDOVAL

The wind is blowing from the west and has the smell of the sea. I know this is a good sign. It tells me the Bear is with me and Grandmother Ocean is ready to give her inspiration. I have been taught to pay attention to signs like these from my tribal teacher, Ka'chi. She has been my teacher for twenty years now. I have traveled to the stars, have learned to listen to the birds, and have learned many songs and dances that my Ancestors passed down to us through Ka'chi's family. She has been my inspiration. She has encouraged me to be a leader by being a leader herself. She knows what it is to be a strong woman full of grace and greatness. In her words she would say, "I want you to shine."

This journey has not been easy. The road is very narrow. To follow a traditional way of being in this age of shortcuts and fast-paced living is often a challenge. The spiritual teachings of the Acjachemen people are never written down. Oral tradition is still honored and respected. If I am being taught a song, I must listen carefully and sing along with my teacher.

If I am given permission by Ka'chi to tape a song for learning purposes, I must erase it as soon as I know it. The sacred language cannot be written down, so I learn it through song and prayer.

Anything I make and use for ceremony cannot be displayed in public but must be kept wrapped and in a safe place and only used or worn when ceremony takes place.

When ceremony is to happen, there is much preparation. The time and location are significant. The heavenly bodies are a major factor in this process. The moon and the stars still play a serious role in this twenty-first century. The challenge has also been an opportunity when it comes to teaching this knowledge to the Acjachemen people. I have been given the title of cultural director. It is my responsibility to protect our cultural teachings and to teach the protocol that I have been taught by Ka'chi, our tribal spiritual leader and teacher. The joy that I have experienced in caring for and sharing this knowledge has been immense. This has been my opportunity to stand for the greatness of our people.

The songs are our connection to our ancestors and to our Mother Earth. The land we call our tribal homeland is the very land our ancestors lived on for thousands of years. We have been blessed because we have never been taken from our land. Yes, we have had to relinquish title to it because of how history unfolded here in Southern California, but our strength is still vibrant because we can still dance and sing on this priceless earth beneath our feet. When we sing our songs, the very earth vibrates with our voices. The ancestors sparkle in the heavens with pride when our voices rise. One song we sing states clearly: "We are one people, one people we are." This is our very foundation.

Over the years I have discovered that by honoring and respecting the old ways, I am protecting them. If I follow the path carefully, the teachings are not diluted. The People are empowered and the richness of the ancestral wisdom lives on. There are gifts that have come my way by honoring this path. Imagination has been one gift that I have been grateful for. Imagination is the key to my creativity and self-expression. I have dived in the ocean with the pelicans, sat in the branches of a tall pine as I ruffled my hawk wings and looked out over the Saddleback Valley. My cousins the dolphins are always happy when I swim with them. When I have a problem, I travel to the sacred directions and see from the different points of view, and in so doing a solution comes to me in a wonderful way.

Self-expression was difficult for me as a young person. I considered myself shy and quiet. By being encouraged by Ka'chi, I have learned to speak up and say what needs to be said. There is a time to speak. There is a time to listen. There is a dance speaking and listening do together that brings forth magnificence. This is powerful. When I became aware of my own magnificence, I had a revelation so profound and yet humbling. In this discovery I also saw the magnificence of others. This has been the key in my ability to lead. It is like dwelling in a special secret. I know how amazing a young one is when she comes to me to learn a song. I know how powerful a young man is when he steps forward to be initiated into the spiritual community. I am aware of the magnificence present in the being before me. My role as a leader is to assist them in discovering this for themselves.

My self-expression goes beyond my tribal family. There are things I have been taught that can be shared with those who are not part of the tribal nation I belong to. One day I had a vision of an outdoor sanctuary where people could come to renew their relationship with our Mother Earth. I use the word *renew* because I believe we all have a relationship with the earth, but it has been forgotten just as we have forgotten how magnificent we are. I asked the question, What can I do to assist people to remember what has been forgotten? Song of the Earth, my ministry, was created from asking that question. Song of the Earth is a service that is held outdoors in an open sanctuary. There we can feel the wind in our hair and see the trees around us and hear the birds sing. I speak about how we swam in the small ocean of our mother's womb as we formed into a human being. I encourage people to listen and remember the song Mother Earth sang to them as they grew in their own mother's womb. Each of us has a song, a melody, a vibration. By remembering and experiencing this, it is a way to be renewed.

We can ask ourselves simple questions and the answers can be quite amazing. If the little ladybug crawling across the leaf is a gift to be thankful for, then who are you? If the swallow swooping and chittering outside is a delightful messenger, then who am I? I am amazed how readily wisdom comes when the heart is open, the spirit is on fire, and the willingness to serve is sincere. I am grateful for Ka'chi's encouragement and the wisdom she has shared with me over the years. She has been selfless in her guidance.

She has been a stand for my own magnificence, and therefore I have learned how to be this for others. Leadership is generational. Those of us who find ourselves on this path can look back and see a powerful woman in our past beckoning us on. It is up to us to destroy the myths of insignificance and reach forward, empowering the generations to come. I can imagine joyfully the strong young women yet to come.

Thank you, Grandmother Ocean. The wind from the west is now quiet. The Bear is still.

Carol Lee Flinders is coauthor of the *Laurel's Kitchen* cookbooks, and she wrote a syndicated newspaper column on natural foods for twelve years. She is the author of *Enduring Grace: Living Portraits of Seven Women Mystics* and writes regularly on the places where feminism, spirituality, and evolutionary science intersect. She has taught at the University of California–Berkeley and the Graduate Theological Union in Berkeley. Flinders currently teaches at the Sophia Center at Holy Names University in Oakland.

Mother-Lines of Body, Mind, and Spirit

CAROL LEE FLINDERS, PhD

For several weeks leading up to Mother's Day this year a local newspaper ran photographs of entrants in a "Mother-Daughter Look-Alikes" contest. For me and, apparently others, the contest proved a source of rich, uncomplicated enjoyment. Even when bone structure or coloring was notably different, it was fun to squint at a picture and figure out what it was about this particular girl that made her so unmistakably the offspring of that particular woman. From an evolutionary point of view, the contest's appeal makes perfect sense. Nature badly needs the connections between mother and daughter to be strong, and Nature (read "evolution") has made sure it *is* strong, because raising a human infant to maturity is a huge job that involves considerable expertise—knowledge that has passed, traditionally, from mother to daughter to granddaughter through a mix of osmosis and close observation that psychology defines today as "social modeling."

From their first days baby girls are decidedly more inclined than are baby boys to gaze fixedly at their primary caretakers and all but shadow them. Endocrinologists have identified a sequenced infusion of hormones that encourage this behavior. My hunch is that when we catch a glimpse of a daughter who seems almost to replicate her mother, some atavistic corner of the brain lights up, deducing that all is well: the girl child will effectively *be* her mother, and with the conduit firmly in place, the crucial database of maternal know-how will be passed along. We'll all get fed, we'll all stay warm.

It's a conviction the Navajo People have formalized in the four-day ceremony called *kinaalda* that honors a girl's passage into womanhood. Enclosed with a mentor who instructs her, massages or "molds" her, and washes her hair with fragrant yucca shampoo, the initiate runs footraces every morning with her friends and grinds corn by hand for an immense cake that is baked on the last night in a pit dug by her father or grandfather. When she serves it out in the morning, radiant and fatigued, her hair gleams, because it's been sprinkled with sacred corn pollen. She *is* Changing Woman, and she *is* the Sun. My own fascination with mother-lines dates back more than four decades. Mystics, "mini-mystics," inspired activists, and mystics under heavy cover, the women I've studied and written about have typically been drawn to both contemplative interiority and loving action in the world. It is remarkable to discover in how many of their lives the timely intervention of an astute, caring mother or "allo-mother" made a critical difference.

Anthropologist Jane Goodall's story is a perfect case in point. She has often said that she comes "from a long line of strong, compassionate women," and she credits her enormous achievements to that mother-line. Jane was just five when World War II broke out and her father went off to fight. Her mother, Vanne, moved with her two daughters to Birches, her mother's home in Bournemouth, near Dorset, on the southern coast of England. Vanne Goodall's marriage was a casualty of war, and after the divorce she and the girls stayed on at Bournemouth. A couple of aunts lived there off and on, and the odd uncle would visit, but for all practical purposes, the household was matriarchal. Jane and Judy's childhood there was little short of idyllic.

Vanne's mother's family was Welsh, and Vanne herself was said to have "the gift of sight," but she was nonetheless exceedingly practical. Yes, it was too bad there was no money to send Jane to university, but what about secretarial school instead? She could take those skills anywhere—even Africa! And of course she did, and in time, as we know, an incredible opportunity would open up for Jane to pursue her single-minded passion for animals. There was one snag, however. The Tanzanian government refused to let Jane set up camp at Gombe Reserve and study the chimpanzees there without a companion. Anthropologist Kristen Hawkes has written extensively about what she has called "the grandmother effect"—the considerable advantage a child has whose maternal grandmother lives in her home. Hawkes first arrived at her conclusions by observing the Hadza people, who live, as it happens, in Tanzania. But she could certainly have augmented them by observing the two English women who arrived in Tanzania by boat in 1960. Because Vanne offered immediately to be Jane's companion at Gombe, and she could do that because her own mother was more than happy to remain at home with Judy while her daughter as well as *her* granddaughter followed their hearts to Africa.

Vanne would remain there for five transformative months. She set up an informal clinic for people living nearby, dispensing first aid and aspirin to the local fishermen and their families. She wrote a novel, and she became Louis Leakey's close, lifelong friend and coauthor. It was Vanne who made Jane's initial tenure at Gombe possible, and it was Vanne who enabled her to remain there years later, when Jane's son, Grub, was nine and she'd run out of schooling options for him in Africa. Jane's research was at a critical juncture, but she felt she had no choice but to come back to England with Grub. Nonsense, said Vanne, Grub could come live at Bournemouth and go to school there.

The grandmother effect didn't stop with Vanne's direct support of Jane and her work. Because she had grown up in a strong mother-line herself, Jane was able to recognize and record sharp differences among the mothering styles of various chimpanzee moms and to single out one in particular as a kind of super-mom. Flo, mother of Fifi, headed up a long line of chimp mothers characterized by unusual vigilance, playfulness, tenderness, and all around competence. Technically, Jane's own mother-line stopped with her. She had no daughters, unless you count the innumerable girls who were inspired to follow in her footsteps and become primatologists, veterinarians, or anthropologists. I personally insist on counting the primatologist Biruté Galdikas, who was sitting in an anthropology class at UCLA when the instructor said something about a remarkable young English woman who was in Tanzania revolutionizing the study of chimpanzees. "It was as if a chime went off in my mind," Galdikas would recall later. "And if it's possible to remember your future, I did."

There are genealogical mother-lines, in other words, but there are mother-lines of imagination and vocation too. There are mother-lines that arise out of affinity and proximity and reciprocal need, and mother-lines that have to do with artistry and the intellect, and activism, and shared spiritual yearnings. Lovingly and even reverently sustained mother-lines have played crucial roles in human evolution and recorded history. When we look hard at the tapestry of our collective story, the almost invisible motif is there. But surely it is time to move it into the foreground. A growing cohort of serious filmmakers are doing just that. Gratefully, delightedly, I have begun to offer seminars that focus on their work under the rubric "Story-Lines and Mother-Lines, Mystics and Movies." To watch these films with other women, especially when they represent more than one generation, and talk about them afterward, is pure revelation.

I like to begin with the 1995 Dutch film *Antonia's Line*. Set in Holland immediately after World War II, *Antonia's Line* is the story of a woman who returns with her teenaged daughter Danielle to the village of her birth. We see them striding along its muddy lanes, the warmth between them palpable. On the wall of a building they pass are painted the words "Welcome to Our Liberators," and although the immediate reference would be to the Allied troops that drove Germany out of Holland in 1945, one suspects we are to see Antonia and Danielle as the real liberators. The shadow of the Nazi occupation and its celebration of everything brutish and bestial still lies across the village, distilled in one young man in particular, a lost soul who can only do harm. Antonia has inherited her family's farm. She and Danielle settle in there and work prodigiously, and soon it's on a solid footing. Antonia takes in strays and misfits and puts them all to work. Before long she has built up an extended family that is both matrilineal and matrilocal.

The farmer next door is a good man, and after a while he's grown on her. She sees no need to combine their farms, though, and no need to marry; instead, they build a tiny cottage in the bit of forest where their properties adjoin, and there they repair on romantic full-moon nights. Described by its writer-director Marleen Gorris as "a feminist fairy tale,"

Antonia's Line is a glorious "what if?" that spans nearly forty years and four generations of women. Death is no stranger, nor is tragedy. Still, a quiet radiance suffuses the story and its characters. There is room on this farm for everyone—room for every gift to unfold—and for love in all its modalities as well as for abundance and laughter.

Pedro Almodovar's 2006 movie *Volver* invites us to look at three generations of women whose mother-line has been broken in several places, and it lets us watch as they are painstakingly rebuilt. Here, too, we see how differently two sisters can experience the same mother-line.

Sequins is a lovely French film made in 2004, directed by Eleonore Faucher. Its protagonist is Claire, a teenaged girl who is a talented fabric artist, single and pregnant. Some of the questions *Sequins* raises have to do with the role of "allo-mothers." Realizing that her mother is too preoccupied with her own life to even see her daughter clearly, Claire knows she will have to look elsewhere for help. Her hair is an electric red-gold mop that signals her courage and resilience, and when she reaches out to an older woman, one who shares her passion for exquisite embroidery and all things beautiful, we have every reason to hope she will respond.

Waitress is an American movie made in 2007 by the late writer-director and actor Adrienne Shelly. Once again, our protagonist is pregnant. Jenna Hunterson is not a teenager, but she is so much at the mercy of her abusive husband, Earl, that she might as well be. Jenna is resourceful, smart, and funny, but she's no match for Earl, and as the movie approaches the hour-and-a-half mark, it looks as if the best solution she's going to come up with is to run off with her married gynecologist. The last ten minutes of *Waitress* is one of the great contemporary film denouements. Jenna's baby arrives, and suddenly a woman who had been sleepwalking through a fog of despair becomes a many-armed Hindu goddess with a battle-axe. The hard things she couldn't do or say on her own behalf she does and says with ease for Little Lulu.

The list keeps growing: *Daughters of the Dust, Eve's Bayou, Frozen River, Winter Guest, Ponette, Secrets and Lies, House of Sand,* and—a wonderful recent addition—*Mother and Child.* As we take in each of these movies, a powerful context builds. It is as though the movies themselves were in conversation with one another. As we become aware of all the complications involved in the care and maintenance of mother-lines, whether they are biological or constructed, we see in how many ways mother-lines can allow us to "stand for the greatness of one another." Best of all, we develop an eye for the places in our own lives where we have the opportunity to build them and rebuild them and draw sustenance from them.

ALisa Starkweather is founder of many bold and unique initiatives to support women's healthy leadership, including the Red Tent Temple Movement, an international grassroots initiative honoring our womanhood journeys, Daughters of the Earth Gatherings; the Women's Belly and Womb conferences; Priestess Path; She Loves Life, an Internet TV show; and cofounder of Women in Power. A keynote speaker, writer, coach, as well as a certified facilitator of ShadowWork, Starkweather is featured in the documentary *Things We Don't Talk About: Healing Narratives from the Red Tent.*

Birthing Awake the Dream

ALISA STARKWEATHER

With the rock ledge above protruding out like a stone-shaped labia, the cave opens wide to the lush green forest and sky beyond. Inside the den hundreds of people are standing in obvious confusion. Finally one of the brothers turns to the women with great authority. The crowd quiets to listen. "It is your turn now. You must lead the way." A commotion ensues as everyone starts talking. It has been so long. Has this moment finally arrived? The women nervously begin to face each other, for no one's mother's mother's mother had done this, let alone believed their daughters would ever see this day rise again when the world needed foremost women's leadership. "Who remembers?" whisper the women. No one speaks.

"I know!" pipes up one woman. "Let's just do it like the men do and head straight out of the cave." From the women comes a murmur of forced bravado and mutual consent because a plan is certainly better than the growing discomfort of not knowing. "Yes. Do it like the men." In this night vision I am transformed into the ancient old woman who remembers. Out of my dream mouth comes a most articulate and rousing message. Standing atop of a boulder, transfixing their gaze, I cry out, "No. This is not our way." Breathing like a fire dragon imparting gravity to my words, I continue with their rapt attention:

"We do not lead from here like the men, for they are alone when doing so. We feel everything, the devastations and the awe. We feel both our *yes* for life and also our *no* that holds intense resistance to what is before us. We have our *no* because what is ahead is painful, and we are the holders and lovers of life that is both birthing and dying at once. Our *yes* comes from our hearts urging us to live courageously beyond any fear that might hold us back. Unite women! Form a living birth canal womb to womb, breath to breath, dream to dream. This is the time of the great weaving of women. Together in our merging, we hold all of us who are laboring. With every wave of contraction, we become a container for the sacred. Resistance is where a woman feels her *no*. Her *no* is overcome by an even more intense desire to show up in her fullness, no matter what is before her. Beyond feelings of inadequacy or numbness, she is fully capable. She is a blueprint of innate raw power that is the equivalent of the earth's fiery molten core reflected in the true depths of her primal self. To get to her deepest truths, a woman doesn't ascend but rather descends. This is why she has feared herself where both her *yes* and her *no*, her strength and vulnerability create conditions for her whole self to be both leveled and raised up simultaneously as a vessel of the fiercest feminine power imagined."

In choosing to come into her full power, she commits to being awake. Her humility voices, "I am here willing to live, to give, to love through it all." In response, our actions express, "We are with you. We are coming after you. Together we stand for life." I look into their many faces and we collectively remember this is true of our ways. We begin to form two lines facing one another to become the living birth canal. The wind enters the portal as our ancestors' breath. Unseen great-grandmothers return now as guardians of this holy threshold. Tears of recognition pour down our cheeks in our remembering that our destiny resides in the grace of this moment, when we come together for something greater than ourselves. The first woman feels it all, cries aloud and pushes through her sisters to birth her way home out of this small opening into her powerful birthright of womanhood. Daughters of the earth are coming home.

Just as suddenly, I catapult out of my sound winter sleep staring into the dark night, fully awake. The stars burn above in the skylight, bringing me to what we call the "real world." In this waking life, when I am doing what we do as people—grocery shopping, raising children, traveling, going to the dentist, being at social events—it is inevitable that someone will ask me what I do for work. In nearly three decades of bringing forward bold women's initiatives, recovering lost feminine powers through archetypal ceremonies, I am not able to say what it is that I do. It is not that I am ashamed, hiding, or afraid. Or that my fear of belonging outweighs my ability to name what it is. It is not even that I have not learned about the importance of elevator pitches and branding myself into an expert of someone who you might relate to more easily.

The place I live and work is colorful, deep, soulful, creative, unique, emotional, and forever sacred. I never define my work as new age but as ancient. It is a solid base for activism, where radical paradigm shifts take place just as reasonably as tectonic plates move deep in the earth herself. This is not a fluffy feel-good place or a promise to heal all, but rather a door-way for the brave and committed who are ready to meet life on its terms: messy, uncertain, heartbreaking. Transformation is often undoing identities, letting go, and living larger lives. My work is a feeling place more than any words could convey. Much like waking from a dream whose wonders you cannot recount, much is lost in translation, so I do not attempt to explain it.

I am steeped like a teabag in women's everyday lives, for I am often the first one asked to help when the baby is being born, when the parent is dying, the teen is rebelling, the relationship ending, or the old secret finally needs to be told. Let us meet as spiritual midwives on the bridge between our lives to find a greater perspective than ours alone. See what resonates in our shared wisdom, knowing that disturbance and agitation can also lead to break-throughs of our unconsciousness wanting to be welcomed into awareness.

The question before us is how do we stand for the greatness of one another? Let us look at our present values. What does the greatness of another woman mean to you? Do you size her up? Do you look at the way she speaks, where she was educated, how she dresses, where she works, who she knows, how much power she carries, or how much her prestige elevates or deflates you? Do you relate to her or envy her or even pity her? Are you quick to categorize her into a box? Does the complexion of her skin trick you into learned assumptions that have you believing you actually know anything about her life? Is she "other" by judgments that separate you both?

What do you do that diminishes her light or your own? I ask you this honestly because if we are collaborating by strategy and calculation to uplift ourselves, we are likely putting our support behind those who our culture has taught us are leaders while marginalizing many others, never noticing our own ingrained behaviors.

As a gender, women have long been assigned qualities of kindness, patience, politeness, and nurturing in roles of caretaking. How many of us, however, know that we either are not these things regularly, or if we are, we resent having to be? Being a women's transformational leader and Shadow Work facilitator, I've learned that what we repress—what we do not want to own, what we deny about ourselves—holds power. So we look deeper still beyond our defenses, especially if we are ready to work together as change makers. Every day, women hold up one another's greatness and society benefits. We give our life-force away often selflessly and gladly for those we love—our children, our families, our loved ones. We give ourselves to work, to our communities, to what we most believe in. If it is obvious that we do this, why explore this question?

How we hold up our own greatness is the key. There in the marrow of your woman self, do you unequivocally believe in your self-worth, your own beauty and creative expressions? Here in the place where thousands of years of misogyny have taken their toll in subtle and not-so-subtle ways, defining who you are, what do you do with all those measurements like material wealth, weight, definitions of beauty, professions, our children's accomplishments, our sexual identities, our intellect? When you go for your own greatness, where are you going? What part of your own self gets left behind?

What if your greatness is in your ability to tell the raw truth, to wail loudly without shame in your grief, to be in your body so much that the mere pleasure of a fresh red strawberry on your tongue excites you wildly? What if your glorious spirit cannot be measured by normal cultural perimeters? Perhaps you knew this to be true, but you valiantly kept on trying to be what you thought made you "successful" or "good." What if you absolutely knew you were born precious and no one in this world could ever take that away from you, no matter what abuse you have suffered? What if your greatness is equivalent to how awake and alive you feel unfettered by any addictions that numb you from seeing what is taking place in this world? What if every firing dancing neuron in your belly knows instinctively more than what educational institutions could teach you? You are all this and more.

Learning to stand for each other means to stand for all parts of who we are without apology for being either too much or too little. Facilitating hundreds of women over the years, I have noticed an uncanny track record of no one quitting. Instead, the work brings out our natural joy, loyalty, sisterhood, our physical labor to do whatever is needed in service, and inspiration from our collective gifts that foster important endeavors, even grassroots movements, such as the Red Tent Temple Movement. Our health is in our ability to show up as strong women loving and respecting each other, rather than fearing or acting out forms of harmful hierarchy. Our integrity is living our agreements or re-contracting. We learn to be forgiving and compassionate when we fail. In our network we practice not taking things personally, and when we do, we either learn to laugh or use our skills even if it is swinging the bat on the pillow to let the energy move without harm.

As a committed community of women, we value our friendships even more once we go through conflict because then we have the full realization that we can weather emotional storms without blame, shame, drama, or abandonment. Instead, we grow stronger, closer, and even having seen our worst shadows, we forge lifelong bonds of trust and mutual respect. In our circles we share the voice of women's leadership owning our projections. Humor, humility, authenticity, generosity, and true caring ripple out like waves farther than we can see. Given a new paradigm to work from, women are more than ready to heal from the wounds we have perpetrated on one another carelessly and for far too long. The two most important components are compassion and bringing our dreams into form.

My dream, too compelling not to live, manifested in my finding the cave, only this time in the waking world. Every year we participate in a sacred ceremony giving symbolic birth to a woman of power. Here among beautiful sisters, she meets grace head on. Initiated by her own desire to be all she was born to be and blessed by all those who believe in her, a new woman walks on the earth and we each stand for who she is forevermore.

Dawn T. Maracle, MEd, EdD (ABD), is a Mohawk from Tyendinaga Mohawk Territory in Southern Ontario, Canada. She is currently an artist, muse, writer, educator, trainer, editor, consultant, and doctoral student writing about Haudenosaunee relationships with tobacco. She was formerly the national director of professional development for the National Centre for First Nations Governance and the National cochair of the Post-Secondary Education Working Group for the Assembly of First Nations and Indian and Northern Affairs Canada.

Kindness Empowers

A Mohawk Skywoman's Journey of Thanksgiving

DAWN T. MARACLE, MED, EDD (ABD)

"Haudenosaunee" is an Iroquoian word accepted by all of the Six Nations of the Iroquois Confederacy (Mohawk, Oneida, Onondaga, Cayuga, Seneca, and Tuscarora) and can be translated to "The People of the Longhouse," because Iroquoian peoples traditionally lived in longhouses. The female head of each clan of each nation—for example, the Bear Clan Mother of the Mohawk Nation in Tyendinaga (there is a Clan Mother for each clan in each community)—is located at the center of a longhouse. Members of her family "add on" to the longhouse on the ends, thereby making the home larger and larger. Some centuries-old excavated longhouses in the Mohawk Valley have been said to be more than forty to two hundred feet long, depending on the size of the family of that clan.

In Haudenosaunee culture there are deeply held notions about humans and the world embedded in the stories and legends. These notions have survived all attempts to simply categorize them as archaic forms of human thought or mere forms of creative expression. These notions have so persisted that they have become the means through which a very unique identity has been maintained, despite five hundred years of intended destruction and/or assimilation.[2] Traditional stories show us a window into the worldview of the culture from which it came. Gregory Cajete, chair of Native American studies at the University of New Mexico, has also said, "It is the *oral history* that presents how a people see themselves in their journey as a people. The key is learning to speak in a way that reclaims a people's oral history and cultural tradition for the purpose of constructing a transformative vision."[3] These stories attempt to explain the existence, interactions, reactions, and social organization of different people, animals, and plants as well as their interrelationships. Women, as in life, always have a crucial place in these stories, yet in "modern" society and a plethora of history texts (mostly written by men) women's contributions are often left out of the pages, and their contributions to family, community, society, nations, and international relationships are not acknowledged often enough. It is our responsibility to bring these stories back, and this book is just one of those outlets.

The Haudenosaunee Creation Story teaches a worldview that includes being good to and respecting each other, expressing gratitude, kindness, generosity, thanksgiving, community-mindedness, and teamwork. Everyone has a place, decision, and contribution to decisions that affect their lives, and consensus is often a way for decisions to be reached. Ceremonies exist in part to slow down, reflect, and give thanks for all life and relationships on Mother Earth. Iroquoian women are recognized as natural leaders, are respected, and have specific responsibilities (as do men); they decide who becomes the Chief; and they remove the Chief if he does not represent their clan appropriately.

My personal vision includes using our stories and experiences, from our family, cultural, and/or faith lenses, to connect to others and to provide safe places where polycultural and multifaith exchanges can occur.[4] Skywoman's story of her journey from the Sky World to becoming the first human being on Mother Earth sets the stage for leadership, bravery, strength, and independence. The story also illustrates the importance of interconnectivity and survival. "The story comes from the earliest time in our language—a time when our language, symbols, beliefs, the world we saw around us, and life as we understand it—*were completely different from the way we understand them now....* We lived in a complete world. This story expresses [in part] our understanding of how we came to this complete world."[5]

Although this is not the place for me to retell the Creation Story in any significant detail, I would like to share a brief but graceful, elegant, and intelligent journey of Skywoman. She lived in the Sky World and was told as a young girl about the journey on which she would embark. She traveled to another village where she met a Chief whom she was supposed to marry. Shortly after her arrival, the Chief dreamed of being sick, became ill, and ultimately asked for the magnificent Celestial Tree and its roots, located just outside of his longhouse, to be torn up, leaving an abysmal chasm below. It is said that Skywoman either fell through or the Chief pushed her through the hole. She grasped at the edge of the Sky World to save herself, grabbing the roots of tobacco, strawberries, and corn in her hands, and seeds got caught in her skirt. It is said that she fell in darkness for a very long time; she could only feel the wind and hear the sound of the rattle resembling a heartbeat.

She emerged through the darkness between worlds and was reborn into the sky of a new world—this was Earth, only it was completely covered in water at the time. The animals in the water looked up and saved her: the turtle provided her back for Skywoman to land on, and the otter brought up soil from the bottom of the ocean. With thanksgiving, Skywoman took the soil, and with the seeds attached to her skirts and in her hands, she sang and danced around Mother Earth creating the land, stomping into valleys, and stepping over mountains, dropping seeds to enrich the earth and support new life.

There is so much more to this story, including that Skywoman gave birth to a child, but I will stop at this point. She was calm and carried on throughout her life with grace, intelligence, and elegance. She was wise enough to recognize and accept that she was strong and independent but also dependent on the kindness of others for her survival. In allowing this, with the help of the power of the animals, she changed the history of this planet forever. We are all capable of being Skywomen; brave leaders who are independent but also keenly and deliberately aware that we often share our paths with other women leaders. Despite our various cultures, faiths, and life experiences, we depend on others to teach, support, challenge, and sustain us.

Although I was born a woman of power, creativity, adventure, and kindness, I recently have lost my way. I became a mother, something I had wished for most of my life, which is the most wonderful gift. I am forever grateful. However, there were soon many people in my new family community who were very unhealthy for us. Though I tried to rise above the challenges presented, it was difficult for me to traverse along my path and raise a little one in the best ways possible. These were dark days, and though I created as much sunshine as I could for my daughter, I found that being a constant light source for others soon drained my own energy supply. I isolated myself, slowly stopped creating my Arts, and began censoring and silencing myself to avoid conflict. I lost myself.

When Skywoman fell, she observed herself: the feeling, the sounds, and the darkness. She did not get lost in the drama of falling. Instead, she tried to save herself by grasping at the soil in the Sky World. While she still fell, which was her destiny, she carried life in her hands, on her skirt, and in her belly. The seeds I grasped for were love and support, and the seeds of gentleness, kindness, greater calm, and patience clung to my skirt in my dark times. It was around this time that I met my friend Bev, a Cree woman from Alberta. She immediately told me that I was an incredible, beautiful, intelligent woman and an exceptional mother. She encouraged me to partner up with her to help build her future empire—starting with an Aboriginal fitness studio that she was developing as the Chief Empowerment Sister (CES) and CEO. She asked me if I would like to be her Head Empowerment Sister (HES) on her Empowerment Advisory Council.

Bev had competed twice in the North American Indigenous Games in soccer as a teenager, had been a semiprofessional powwow dancer in her youth, is a mother of three, is a personal trainer, and was working toward starting her own Aboriginal Fitness Studio in Ottawa. She recognized that I was isolated. She said, "Dawn, I used to be like you, surrounded by destructive people. Forget about them. They don't matter. You, me, and your daughter, Tekaronhiakanere, matter. Let's start working together." (Tekaronhiakanere is a traditional Bear Clan Mohawk Nation name given to my daughter by a Bear Clan Mother. The name means "she stares at the heavens," and the root word *oronnia* means "sky, blue, cosmos, sky world, or the heavens.")

Bev started dragging me out for workouts, dancing, and to do newspaper, radio, and television interviews for her fitness studio. She always said,

"It is important to surround yourself with incredible 'Sisters.'" She created an empowerment circle in which she would have advisers help her involve more of the entire community, families, and artists, to create a healthier community for everyone. Although I welcomed "getting back out into the world again" both for myself and for our children who played together, Bev kept insisting that I had more to give than I felt that I had the energy for. She kept insisting and pushing me, while remaining supportive.

In early February 2010, Bev became one of the traditional Aboriginal youth dancers in the opening ceremonies of the Vancouver Olympics. While there, she was on top of the world. However, a week after returning home, on February 19, everything changed. Bev and her partner were in a car accident, and both of them were severely injured. They had brain trauma, were in comas for approximately two months, and had collapsed lungs and other severe bodily injuries. At first the whole community rallied around the family. A few of Bev's close friends and I set up a trust fund for her family and ran many fundraisers, which we advertised in news, television, and radio. Bev's mother-in-law gave up her home and job in Montreal and moved to care for the children. A year and a half later, Bev and Joe have finally left the rehabilitative hospital in Ottawa and have found a long-term care facility closer to their home.

Since waking from her coma, Bev says I am one of the few of her newer friends that she remembers, although her memory from earlier in her life is still intact. She has never regained the use of her left arm and is still being rehabilitated with associated brain injuries (ABI). At every visit she tells me that she can't wait until she walks out of that place, and when she can, she is going to be her own boss again. What a Skywoman! Reach for the sky, friend and Sister! Bev continues to be an inspiration to me. I am thankful that she came into my life and that she started bringing me back out of my shell. I am thankful for her spunk, attitude, and bravado, which are rarely matched. I am thankful that the Parkdale United Church and a core group of kind people who really care have continually been a support to Bev and her family.

I started a group called Kindness Empowers to focus on the strength in groups of people putting more kindness out into the world. Bev's sheer dogged determination pushes me forward, even when I see dark clouds on the horizon. My daughter is benefitting from that. I have been happy to support, entertain, and inspire Bev now, knowing she would do the same for me if circumstances were switched. I sat down to think about the idea of how we stand for the greatness of each other. I thought of many different things I could write about but kept coming back to Bev and how she has stood for my greatness. Despite the tragedy that has struck her family, which will take a long time to heal, Bev is someone who stands for my greatness, even when I question it in my own life. Like Skywoman, Bev and I have fallen through an abyss, accepted it, observed it, and surrounded ourselves with powerful Empowerment Sisters. With grace go we, as we move forward and transform our own leadership. The Taoist philosopher Lao Tzu talks about a great leader as one that the people don't even know is there. Bev will never stop being a leader, and because of the empowerment sisters in our lives, we will still accomplish great things while inspiring others to do the same. This is a "pay it forward" deliberate action that we want our children and future generations to be positively affected by.

It is right here, in these pages in this very book, where we start our dialogues. Our stories give us context and enable us to be both tellers and listeners. I am a child in this world, awed by all I see and perplexed that my world isn't full of happiness. In the words of the contemporary music artist Ani Di'Franco, "I am thirty-two flavors and then some," and so is Bev: past, present, and future. Since everyone has stories and experiences, we all engage the labyrinth (this path that is not always straight and where we usually cannot see the end) on equal footing, provided we have a safe place to share. With respect and empathy, we can stand for the greatness of each other. When we raise up others, we raise up ourselves and the children of this world.

Life is standing at the edge of an abyss of forgetfulness waiting for the light of the world to be born. This birth needs the wisdom of the feminine, and women must take their place in this time of great potential.[6]

Skennen. (In peace.)

China Galland, an award-winning author, speaker, university lecturer, and former wilderness guide, is the author of *Longing for Darkness: Tara and the Black Madonna, The Bond Between Women: A Journey of Fierce Compassion,* and *Love Cemetery: Unburying the Secret History of Slaves.* Recipient of the Courage of Conscience Award from the Peace Abbey in Sherborn, Massachusetts, she is also professor in residence at the Center for the Arts, Religion, and Education (CARE) at the Graduate Theological Union in Berkeley, California. She is a member of the national Alliance for Truth and Racial Reconciliation.

In Order to Heal the World, We Have to Stand for Each Other's Greatness, but "First," the Grandmothers Told Her, "You Have to Heal the Wound between Women"

CHINA GALLAND

I've never forgotten the message of the Grandmothers and the vision of how we are to repair the world and the special role women are to play in its saving. It is a vision that was given to my friend Michel Henry, a woman who was part Cree, part Ojibwa, and part Irish, who was born on the Turtle Mountain Reservation in 1939, on the North Dakota–Canadian border.

Although Michel had been raised in cities, by the time she was in her late forties, she was on her way back to the reservation. She'd become obsessed with vivid memories of some of the Native women Elders from her early years, women she knew who had gathered an intimate, encyclopedic knowledge of medicinal plants for healing. Their numbers had dwindled in the intervening years. She started the Grandmothers Project to document their disappearing body of knowledge and teachings. Looking back, she said she knew that it was important to understand how these women functioned in their societies as well as to preserve whatever knowledge and teachings were left. Michel's own teacher was a Potawatomi Elder from Minnesota, a Firekeeper. I met Michel in New Mexico, where she had gone to live with friends after being diagnosed with terminal cancer and given only a short time to live.

Her black- and gray-streaked hair was neatly trimmed at her shoulders. She was fair-skinned like her Irish forebears, with pale freckles sprinkled across her weathered face. Smile lines marked her eyes with deep creases, for smiling was something she did often and with ease. Her eyes were clear, sea-blue, her body lean but not bony. She'd been "cheating death," she told me, "that's what the Tibetans say," and laughed as my eyebrows shot up in surprise. She wasn't shy about her impending death, nor did she pity herself. She accepted her dying like a change in the weather, sunny one day, wind-scoured the next, with an icy air full of knife cuts, it was so cold. Her attitude put me at ease. "Come, enjoy the sun," she said, patting the seat next to her, inviting me to relax. The sky was cloudless, a robin's-egg blue, the stones reflecting back the sun's warmth. She grinned. "I've beaten my prognosis for two years in a row now. I don't take life or people for granted any more. We shouldn't anyway."

As Michel told me about her work with the Grandmothers Project, she said that one of the differences that stood out between Native Elders and whites or Anglos is that Native people tend to honor the negative powers. Native people don't act as though negative forces are not real, as if they don't exist. Many years before, Michel had a vision in which the Grandmothers showed her a tear in the shield around our planet. The message that accompanied the vision she received was that women would know how to repair this tear. Michel's task was to take part in this repair, at once repairing her own cancer and the tear in the planet's shield.

"I cried and cried," she told me. "I knew I couldn't do this repair by myself. Then I was shown the breaking of our link with the divine. It was the most painful experience I've ever known. I saw the breaking of the heart connections between women. The biggest betrayal has been women betraying women. First we have to heal the wound between women. Once the wound between women is healed, then the wound between men and women can heal; once the wound between men and women heals, the family can heal; once the family heals, the community can heal, and once the community heals, the world can be healed. That's what the Grand-mothers say. That's what they told me."

I thought about Michel's message when I recently heard stories of child prostitution. Although I resist mightily the notion of women bearing special responsibility for the fate of the world—that premise in the book of Genesis has been so destructive—the idea of women healing other women seems undeniably important. I've thought of Michel's vision when I've read stories of female genital mutilation in which girls are often held down and cut by the older women. I've thought of the Grandmothers' words when I heard American stories of young girls sent to their father's bed by their mothers to "save the marriage." There are ways in which we as women collude and participate in the very systems that ravage us. Our participation as women in the destruction of other women, our collusion, is much harder to look at. I began to look at mine. First and foremost, I find it in my silence.

> "By bringing my girls up with good values, by teaching them that men and women are equals—and showing that in my own life as a woman—I am nurturing feminine spiritual leadership."
> —**Participant at a WSF gathering**

Recently I went reluctantly to a women's spirituality conference. The invitation to participate came from a woman whose work and dedication I increasingly respected, although I wasn't especially hopeful for the outcome. Nonetheless, after feeling increasingly alienated from the interests of the white middle-class women who make up the bulk of those able to afford these conferences and spiritual retreats, I was won over by the dedication of the women organizing the Spirit and Faith conference. The older I get, the more fearful I discover myself to be. I once harbored the hope that perhaps women, once in positions of leadership, *might* make different choices. In fact, I now believe—as an article of faith—that as women, if we think that we *can* make a difference in what's occurring in the world, we are morally obligated to make different choices than those we've participated in and allowed men to make for us.

I have no illusions of innocence—either my own or that of educated middle-class women. I am also not an essentialist. Having raised sons and a daughter, and now having both granddaughters and grandsons, has only further confirmed my conviction that gender is not the defining issue I once thought it to be. Men and women are cut from the same cloth and do not emanate from separate planets. Despite variations in brain size and other physical distinctions, we are essentially the same as human beings, although we are socialized quite differently depending on culture, countries of origins, regions of a country, class, and so forth. I know many tender, emotional men, and plenty of hard-edged, calculating women. Stereotypes are especially pernicious and brittle—crude attempts to hide from the reality of an encounter with another person and their inevitable differences.

The model of dominance for which men have been criticized is used by women as well as men. Women too can rush to obliterate differences, to run over them and to threaten destruction—whether it's banishment, social rejection, or actual bombing, torture, and war—if the other party won't change as commanded. We too refuse to speak to one another if someone or some country won't behave as we want. No, I won't give you the possibility of having a reason yourself for your difference. No, either accept my perspective, opinion, behavior, or way or I will abandon you. Are these differences really about gender, or are they not the hubris of the inflated egos that haunt our species? Is not our stubbornness another form of fear, an intransigence constructed on the sands of what passes for power and dominance, the passing ideas of what constitutes wealth, class, and position in human societies?

There is a glass ceiling in the women's spirituality movement, a limit unrecognized because it's conceived of as being based in gender rather than our own human greed, hatred, and delusion—"the three poisons," as Buddhists say. The more I've become involved in issues of race and class in American society, the further away I've found myself from the women's spirituality movement. Women have often gone with me to Europe or Asia on pilgrimages, often to see and revere images and statues of black women as long as they are called the "Black Madonnas" or the "Divine Dark Feminine," but few have joined me in East Texas. Fewer still are inclined to see the regal darkness in the face of faraway religious icons as the same face of women on our city streets in America. The divine in the ordinary, in the difficult, in the small, the familiar—these areas grow more fruitful and difficult for me. Everyday life: our carbon-clogged atmosphere, nuclear reactor meltdowns, glacier melts, warming seas, rising temperatures, "modern" warfare. Until I see women making different ethical choices, myself included, women choosing to sit down together and reason out differences, respectfully, to hold out for honoring rather than dismissing differences, "the women's spirituality movement" says less and less to me.

I think of Deacon Hagerty in Karnack, Texas. He was ninety-seven years old when I met him, some thirty years ago. He sat and stood as straight as redwood. His mind was sharp and engaged. His great pride? The fact that all six of his children had advanced degrees—at least master's degrees, if not doctorates—and most were educators. He turned to me one day and said, "Do you know that there are no African Americans running for school board in our district, yet all the students are black? That's not right. It's always been like that and it never seems to change." He continued, "The Good Book tells us that we have to sit down with one another, we have to reason things out with one another. We have to come together. We have to *love* one another. Don't your people read the Bible? What is wrong with your people?" I didn't know how to answer Deacon Hagerty when he asked me those questions years ago. I don't know how to answer them today. Only now I am asking the question of my good sisters in the women's movement: "Don't you read the Good Book, sister?"

> "The wisdom to do what we have to do is already here. The remembrance of this is what is emerging. We are midwifing one another."
> —Participant at a WSF gathering

There are many Good Books around the world, and they seem to say the same thing: we have to love one another, we have to reason things out with each other, we have to sit down together. If we cannot work out our disagreements, we are told to call in another person to help us; if we cannot work out our difficulties still, we are told to call in the community. We have to work through our differences, offer and accept apologies—seven times seven—we are called to be brother and sister to one another. We have to love one another. We are told to work things out, to make the attempts, and if we fail, we are told not to give up but to ask for more help.

To me this is true leadership, the willingness to humble ourselves enough to sit down with someone with different ideas, varied opinions, with the willingness to consider what might be in the way—in oneself. Could that be possible? If we as women began to behave differently as a matter of ethical behavior, I might begin to believe again, as I once did, that women have a critical role in help-

> "Ask the question, Who are you? Tell me about yourself. Tell me your story. Discover how your story and mine connect. Help me recognize myself in you and you in me."
>
> **—Participant at a WSF gathering**

ing heal today's world, that we might save it one more time, as the Goddess Durga, the Hindu warrior queen, did in the ancient story of the Devi-Mahatmya. Durga saved the world not simply by her skill as a warrior, but by the fact that she used her skills as a warrior to pierce the very heart of the King of Demons.

Piercing the heart, opening it to another. The true path.

IN SWEET COMPANY

We sit together and I tell you things,
Silent, unborn, naked things
That only my God has heard me say.
You do not cluck your tongue at me
Or roll your eyes
Or split my heart into a thousand thousand pieces
With words that have little to do with me.
You do not turn away because you cannot bear to see
Your own unclaimed light shining in my eyes.
You stay with me in the dark.
You urge me into being.
You make room in your heart for my voice.
You rejoice in my joy.

And through it all, you stand unbound
By everything but the still, small Voice within you.
I see my future Self in you
Just enough to risk

Moving beyond the familiar,
Just enough to leave
The familiar in the past where it belongs
I breathe you in and I breathe you out
In one luxurious and contented sigh.
In sweet company
I am home at last.

—Margaret Wolff[7]

Living Our Leadership

Questions

1. How do you balance feeding the positive wolf while fighting away the negative wolf?
2. How do we strengthen the soul of our leadership?
3. What does women's equality really look like?
4. What are the barriers and challenges that prevent us from standing for each other's greatness?
5. How do we create genuine friendships and support for each other?

Circle Practices

Create your own unique circle pattern. Every circle is distinctive and fluid, changing and evolving to reflect the needs of the group. There are many different ways to create the sacred space of women's circles. Try these varieties:

Meditation circles. Some women come together weekly or monthly to meditate in silence. Allow some time at the end of the circle to reflect on any guidance, images, or awareness that arose during the meditation—or not.

Prayer circles. Prayers could be spoken or silent. Focus on a specific issue or need, or each woman could bring the prayer that is most present in her own heart.

Interfaith circles. This circle would be formed with the intention of bringing together women from diverse spiritual perspectives. The circle might specifically invite women to share information about their spiritual beliefs and practices—or you might allow the conversation to arise organically from women's needs and weave in observations and reflections about how our spiritual practice supports and challenges us as women.

Mentoring circles. Here women come together to exchange wisdom and mutual support. This might be an intergenerational mix of women so that younger women and Elders have the chance to learn from one another—or it might be a group of women with a shared passion (like writing a book or taking environmental action).

Dream circles. This is an opportunity for women to gently turn their attention to their dreams. Each takes turns sharing a recent dream; the group reflects on the feelings, images, and symbols in the dream.

Art circles. Women gathered around a table create art—paintings, colored pencils on black paper, collage, multimedia images, and so on. Choose a quotation or a question as the theme of the art. Pieces are completed within a defined amount of time (perhaps an hour), and then the group can take time to reflect on each piece.

Phone circles. Many kinds of circles can be done on conference calls with women scattered across great distances. Even silent group meditation can be effective on a conference call. The same basic elements of circle are essential to phone circles. Create a sacred center as each participant lights a candle, and open the call with a blessing; begin with a brief check-in so every voice is heard; and follow circle guidelines. Close the circle before you end the call.

Blessings

Group gratitude. At the end of a gathering, all of the women cluster together for a big group hug. With arms encircling and eyes closed, one woman explains that everyone is welcome to share an expression of gratitude for one other person or for a specific act of kindness, popcorn style—that is, speaking from her hearts as she is moved to do so.

She starts it off with her expression of gratitude. Others are invited to do the same until there is silence and it feels complete.

MERGER POEM

And then all that has divided us will merge
And then compassion will be wedded to power
And then softness will come to a world that is harsh and unkind
And then both men and women will be gentle
And then both women and men will be strong
And then no person will be subject to another's will
And then all will be rich and free and varied
And then the greed of some will give way to the needs of many
And then all will share equally in the earth's abundance
And then all will care for the sick and the weak and the old
And then all will nourish the young
And then all will cherish life's creatures
And then all will live in harmony with each other and the earth.
And then everywhere will be called Eden once again.

—JUDY CHICAGO[8]

How Women Are Leading

The Heart to Lead

The feminine is reaching a new evolutionary edge of expression—leading a paradigm shift for the benefit of all of humanity, indeed the entire planet. This shift is emerging from a groundswell of grassroots authenticity. Women are responding to an innate impulse to gather together in the spirit of loving-kindness, and we are finding the strength, shared wisdom, and groundedness to speak our deepest truths, to come into appreciation of our own dignity and sovereignty, and to become powerful new allies for the greater good.

The documentary film *The Heart to Lead, Women as Allies for the Greater Good* serves as a transformative spark, an intimate invitation for women to come alive to themselves as inspired agents of change. There is something vitally important—and natural—that wants to emerge through women, something not only to be discovered and spoken aloud, but embodied and activated as a collective. This film sets a precise tone and vibration, which is honoring and nourishing. The companion guidebook, *The Guide to Heart-Knowing*, invites women to linger with one another in circle to discover what wants to arise through them. This requires a gathering of strong/soft, courageous/vulnerable, spiritual/worldly, heart-centered/sharp-focused women to arise and take part. And here we are. We invite you to share your gifts and join us on this journey. For more information, visit www.imaginethegood.com.

—BONNIE KELLY

Leadership Tools

Collaborative Art: Mandala as Metaphor

We don't perceive things as a whole. We take in components with our senses and then our minds join them together, like making a many-dimensional quilt. When we look at a flower, we see the colors and shapes, we smell the fragrance, we touch the soft petals, and if we have previous knowledge of this flower, our memory furnishes a word to name it. Memories also influence how we think or feel about the flower—associations with past loves, allergic reactions, or favorite garden spots.

We have both capacities within us—the ability to differentiate and to make whole, to divide and to unite. Our minds tend toward integration; it's how we make sense of our world. Yet our prevailing Western cultural paradigm has promoted separation as the best method for dealing with and understanding life. Only a few decades ago did the paradigm start to shift. We started approaching health care "holistically" and

> "Plato said the soul is a circle."
> —**Joseph Campbell**

saw "systems-thinking" influence business. We also saw the emergence of ecumenical and interfaith movements in religious communities. The mandala is the perfect art form to illustrate the idea that combining diverse parts can create a harmonious whole. The history of the mandala is multicultural and rich but as a simple definition, it is a symmetrical design radiating from a defined center. *Mandala*

Collaborative Mandala from "The Alchemy of Our Spiritual Leadership," April 2011.

is Sanskrit for "circle"; circular designs are found in every culture and often used in a sacred setting. They represent wholeness, integration, and the cosmos and are used for healing, balance, and transformation. Native American medicine wheels and the Rose Window at Notre Dame are some examples. Their symmetry mimics natural forms like flowers and cacti, and their circular shapes remind us of the sun, the moon, and the eye.

When 150 women came together in April 2011 for "The Alchemy of Our Spiritual Leadership: Women Redefining Power," the conference organized by Women of Spirit and Faith, they gathered with the intention to appreciate and honor the unique expressions of each woman's beliefs, to celebrate the beauty and richness of who they were as a whole. As the art facilitator, my goal was to offer a project that would allow each woman as well as groups of women to create art that would reflect the nature of the conference. During the first two days I set out oil pastels and colored pencils on a table in the back of the room. Before the conference I painted a thirty-six-inch square masonite board a beautiful blue. Then I created a mandala pattern on black paper with thick gold marker and cut out some pieces to let the background blue show through. The mandala pattern consisted of seventeen pie-shaped pieces and a small center piece. There were some decorative pieces to fill in the corners as well.

When I presented the art project on the first night, I only showed the separated pieces, did not explain that they were to be fitted together, and did not show the blue background board. The only instruction was to fill the pieces with color, design, or words. In other words, I provided the structure, then allowed the organic flow of artistic expression to arise. By the next afternoon all the pieces had been filled in, and I spirited them away. Once fitted into place, they created a breathtakingly beautiful mandala. Revealed on stage later that night, the women were surprised and delighted to see what they had created together. As many times as I have facilitated this type of art-making, I too am always amazed and delighted to behold our work.

As an artist who specializes in mandalas, I am aware of the numerous spiritual lessons of this art form, and there is one particularly demonstrated in the context of collaborative mandala-making. God/Spirit/Creator has provided us with the structure and materials (our bodies, our minds, the world around us), and we add in our unique thoughts and actions to become cocreators with each other and with the Divine. Quite often, we have no idea what we are creating or how it fits into the larger picture, but the quality of our contribution, our expression, influences the whole. And the Divine *is* the mandala, perpetually radiating from its center into beautiful creation, in whom the Divine is well pleased.

—CHARLOTTE BACKMAN

Where Do We Go from Here?

When I woke up this morning, this song was going through my head—I can't remember the whole song. It's just one of those songs from my teen years, and the only thing I was hearing was, "Where do we go from here, my love?" I found myself wondering why that particular song would wake me up this morning. I've taught myself to listen to things that wake me up, and this woke me up. It wouldn't get out of my head in the shower. Even as I was coming downstairs, I was trying not to hum it in the elevator because there was a very nice couple in the elevator with me and I didn't want to scare them. The "Where do we go from here?" part seems an excellent question as we reflect on what it means to be women of spirit redefining power.

One of the things that spoke to me was a poem. Before sharing the poem, I have to tell you about me and poetry. I grew up hating poetry. When I was in high school in England—and this carried on even when we went back to Southern Africa, because we were still in the British system—each year we were set a Shakespeare, a Dickens, a couple of more modern

---

Nontombi Naomi Tutu is founder and proprietor of Nozizwe Consulting (*Nozizwe* means Mother of Many Lands and describes the philosophy of the organization, which is to bring together the people of many lands). She has served as a coordinator for programs on race and gender and gender-based violence at the African Gender Institute in Cape Town. Formerly the associate director of the Office of International Relations and Programs at Tennessee State University, she is coauthoring a book on race and racism with Rose Bator, titled *I Don't Think of You as Black*. This essay is drawn from Tutu's keynote speech delivered at "The Alchemy of Our Spiritual Leadership: Women Redefining Power."

fiction things, and a poetry collection. We would study all of those books through the year, and at the end we would have an exam that included all these set books. Whenever we did the section on the poetry, I could not understand what the heck these people were writing about. None of the poems I read made any sense to me. I felt like saying, "Just pull out my fingernails instead. I would do better."

I came out of my high school experience knowing that poetry equals torture. Then I met Rose, with whom I work, who is one of my best friends. She has also served as my spiritual adviser in different instances, and the very first thing she gave me was a poem. I looked at her and I thought, *This relationship is not going to work*. But she gave me the poem anyway, and I read it and thought, *Oh my gosh. I understand it, and, more than that, I like it*. From there on I started paying attention to poems, and I've found them to be such a blessing in my life. I was given this poem on my birthday a few years ago. My birthday is in August, and the day after is the day we celebrate Women's Day in South Africa. My birthday has always been Women's Day in my mind. This friend gave me a poem by Patricia Lynn Reilly. It was being given to women as part of the Women's Day celebrations. It speaks to me of who we are, and how we came to be at the Alchemy conference reflecting on power and spirituality:

IMAGINE A WOMAN I

Imagine a woman who believes it is right and good she is a
woman.
A woman who honors her experience and tells her stories.
Who refuses to carry the sins of others within her body and
life.

Imagine a woman who trusts and respects herself.
A woman who listens to her needs and desires.
Who meets them with tenderness and grace.

Imagine a woman who acknowledges the past's influence on
the present.
A woman who has walked through her past.
Who has healed into the present.

Imagine a woman who authors her own life.
A woman who exerts, initiates, and moves on her own
    behalf.
Who refuses to surrender except to her truest self and wisest
    voice.

Imagine a woman who names her own gods.
A woman who imagines the divine in her image and likeness.
Who designs a personal spirituality to inform her daily life.

Imagine a woman in love with her own body.
A woman who believes her body is enough, just as it is.
Who celebrates its rhythms and cycles as an exquisite
    resource.

Imagine a woman who honors the face of the Goddess in
    her changing body.
A woman who celebrates the accumulation of her years and
    her wisdom.
Who refuses to use her life-energy disguising the changes in
    her body and life.

Imagine a woman who values the women in her life.
A woman who sits in circles of women.
Who is reminded of the truth about herself when she forgets.

Imagine yourself as this woman.

                           —PATRICIA LYNN REILLY[9]

"Imagine yourself as this woman." I believe that is why we come together, because we all imagine ourselves as this woman who celebrates herself and her sisters, who recognizes her beauty and her power, who knows that she is not alone, never has been, and never will be.

    I've been thinking about the Divine Feminine, about the way the feminine has been removed in most of the world's religions, that that picture—

that side of the divine has been removed, denigrated, degraded. The picture that came to me was of myself as a young girl in South Africa going to church in Krugersdorp with my grandmother—my father's mother—who was a member of the Mothers' Union and was so proud of her role in the church. On this particular day I was so proud because my grandmother said to me, "You can come and sit in church today." This was a huge deal, because normally in our churches the children go straightaway to Sunday school and then play in the churchyard until called in to be blessed. But on this day my grandmother said I was old enough to sit in the service. It was a day of confirmation, so the bishop was there.

As I walked into church, I was so proud; I looked at my younger sister and my cousins and said, "No. You cannot come in." I was just on top of the world, and then I sat through the service. Our services are long anyway. In South Africa in black churches our services can go on for three to four hours. But because the bishop was there, and the bishop was white and spoke only English, we had to have the sermon translated. He was preaching and the churchwarden was translating into Xhosa. You can imagine how that added to my joy. Trying not to be bored, I started looking around the church—this church in a completely black township—and all the pictures were of white men. There was this white male God reaching out. As I looked at him, he looked just like the white policemen of whom I was terrified for the power they held over our community. I thought, *How can a God who looks like that love me? How can I possibly be made in the image of a God who looks like my oppressors?* I thought, *Maybe they are right. Maybe the architects of apartheid are right that we are not quite God's children because, hey, he looks like them. I don't see myself anywhere.*

That started for me a time of struggle that went through the rest of my life, a feeling of a huge split inside of me. On the one hand, seeing the church as my family—the women, the men, the children of that church, or the church I went to in England or the church I joined when I went to high school and to college—they felt like a second home. On the other hand, the church felt like a place where I didn't quite belong. How do you make sense of a situation that is a place of nurture and love but also a place of "You are less than"? I continue to have this struggle because if I am made in God's image—nowadays I believe I am (or most of the time, except when I'm having hot flashes, and then I see that white male God again), then why are the images that we make of God not reflecting that? If those pictures that I saw are really God, who are we? Could it possibly be true that we are *not* God? If we are *not* God, we're not human, right? Because we're told that we humans were made in God's image, but if that image does not live in me, that means, logically, I'm not really human. If you listen to the voices of oppression and division, that is exactly what they say about whomever it is they have decided is the other: "They're not quite like us, they are not quite human."

If we say we are those who are lifting up the Divine Feminine, our very first challenge is to be those who are willing to say there is no one who is not made in God's image. That means there is no one who is less than. We say that—and we have people today out in churches preaching this, we have rabbis in synagogues preaching, and we have imams preaching—and we have no one, *no one*, who is less than. Yet the structure of our societies continues to say otherwise. Our challenge is, where do we go from here? When we walk out into the world, are we going to be willing to say that and stand for that wherever we find ourselves?

Right after 9/11 there was a dominant conversation going on in the United States that stated we are all united. Then there was the kind of subtext going on, which was the violence against those whom people thought looked Muslim. There was another subtext in my community, the African American community, that said, "Phew. It feels great to not be the one being profiled for a change." That story has hardly been heard, that we have a whole community of people relieved that someone else is being picked on! What does that say about our wholeness as a society? What does it say that this subtext was hardly ever heard? We all hear stories about a young black man coming toward us and our crossing the street, and that the first voice we hear, the one we have been taught—the one we have been trained to recognize as the first voice—will be the voice of the other. "There's the other. How do we escape?" But that's not the natural first voice. It isn't.

If you want to hear the natural first voice, listen to children, because their natural first voice is, "Oh. You're different, and why are you different? You look strange to me. Can you explain your strangeness?" If we allowed children to receive the explanation of the strangeness, I believe that this first voice would never change, but we stop them because they embarrass us. I'm one of those people who like messing around with my hair, and I was for a while clean-shaven. Once I was sitting on a plane. A young couple came in with a toddler, and as he passed me he said, "Why doesn't that woman have any hair?" You can imagine his parents' embarrassment, "Come on, Johnny." My first thought was, *Oh my lord. This child is going to be terrified of bald women for the rest of his life.* So I said, "Wait. No. It's fine. It's fine. I don't have any hair because I'm too lazy to comb it." That made sense to Johnny. I could see the light bulbs going off. "Aha! I'm gonna shave my hair when I get home."

But right there, when we're beginning to change the first voice in Johnny's head about difference, that first voice ("Tell me about yourself") was now saying, "I'm afraid of you." We need to find the courage to say we are going to be the ones who change that first voice back to what it was meant to be—a question. "Who are you? Tell me your story. Let me find out how your story and mine connect. Help me to recognize myself in you and you in me."

I have had some concerns with our picture of the Divine Feminine. Think about what we might be missing when we simply give thanks for our abundance. What is the message about abundance and divinity that we convey? Two weeks ago I was at home in South Africa spending time with women doing amazing work, without abundance, and in many cases without the bare necessities. I thought, *Where are those women in most of our gatherings? I miss hearing from those women. I miss our concern for them. If we are claiming sisterhood and divinity, we must recognize that they too are our*

"Never take away anybody's faith or pride."
—Nontombi Naomi Tutu

sisters. These women are some of the deepest theologians I have ever had the opportunity to talk to. Their vision of God and God in their lives is way beyond the men in dresses. (That's what President Mandela called my father. At one point my father had criticized President Mandela for never wearing a formal suit—always wearing those Mandela shirts. He said, "You know, head of state, every once in a while, you could put on a three-piece suit and let people see you." President Mandela said, "And this from a man in a dress?")

I hear them say, "Our God is a God who didn't say, 'Nothing will ever go wrong,' but that our God is a God who said, 'She is there with us in the midst of all of it.'" That is how they live their divinity. The divinity of God's presence in their lives through oppression, hunger, and lack. For those of us who live in places of abundance, part of our living our divinity has to be, at the very least, the awareness of how our abundance is connected to their scarcity. We must be willing to hear their story of divinity. We must be willing to go beyond an awareness to being advocates, to being voices for those who are ignored, who are starved, who are beaten. That has to be a part of our claimed divinity.

The other concern is the call to a new leadership. We are called to show the world a different way of leadership, of power, a different way of being in relationship with each other, and especially of being in relationship with those whom we know as "other." Yet what does that really look like on the ground, at home? Yes, this new type of leadership calls for our spiritual fullness. It is absolutely necessary but not enough. I can't remember exactly the prayer from the old Anglican Book of Common Prayer, but it was something about "save us from coming to pray only for comfort, rather than energy to go out into the world." That was one of the prayers that stuck with me—that it cannot be about being filled with my sense of Godness simply for the sake of being filled. It has to be about changing the world in some shape or form. It is so easy to become comfortable in the stories that we know, we don't even recognize that we are telling ourselves those stories. It is easy to be comfortable in our goodness, our rightness with God and so miss those times when our comfort is actually at the expense of the need in the world.

One of my favorite stories about this is when I was speaking at Vanderbilt University about the power of women and people of color in the twenty-first century. I was having the most marvelous time—just having a ball—imagining what our world would look like with the empowerment of women and people of color around the world. I was thinking what that would make our governments and our relationships across national boundaries look like, how different our communities would look. I was basking in my view of the Promised Land. Then it came to a time for questions and answers, and a young man stood up at the back of the room. My first thought was, *Oh, Jesus, Mary, and Joseph. Angry white man. Why would I have to deal with an angry white man as the first person after I've been on this high?*

> "We need to be advocates for other women."
>
> **—Nontombi Naomi Tutu**

He *was* an angry white man, but not the angry white man I was expecting. This young man had spent much of his life on the street, and the other times he had been in mental institutions and had been an advocate for the homeless as well as those both inside and outside of mental institutions dealing with issues of mental stress. This man was angry as he asked, "How can you be having this conversation about the power of people of color, in particular, but also of women in this venue where they are not very welcome?" That's what he was angry about, but I had already started the story in my mind of who he was. Fortunately he was able to put the brakes on it before I had gone the whole way into my story. I would have missed his question. His name is Karl, and we ultimately became friends. Karl lived with us when he was next without a home. He is one of my son's favorite people in the world and he has been a blessing to me. When I think about that experience with Karl, it makes me think how easily we decide that we *already know* these stories. Rarely do we give people the chance to tell their own story. The loss can often be our own.

For us women in claiming our power, that is a dangerous and potentially disempowering place to be. Do you remember when we had the whole talk about welfare reform in the United States? If you noticed, the people who were not involved in that discussion were the women who were on welfare. The reason we did not hear from them is that we, as a country, decided we knew their story. We decided they had nothing of value to add to the discussion of how this system was going to be changed. We "knew" that they were lazy and that therefore, really, our function— our concentration—had to be getting them off their butts into the workforce and being productive human beings in the economy.

Here's the dangerous part. Do you remember the other conversation that was going on in the United States at that same time? It was about how middle-class women needed to get out of the workforce and go back home because children were running wild—that they didn't have a parent at home caring for them. That "selfish career women" were endangering the health and welfare of our children. Do you see the danger? One group of women is being told, "Get your ass out of the house," and the other is being told, "Get your ass back in the house." Because we're not sharing the stories, we don't even see the connection. Divided we fall.

We are not making the space to tell one another our stories and to listen to each other's stories. The most difficult work is the work we are called to in our own backyard, in our own communities, in our own families. It is awesome and wonderful to be able to give—to give financial support, to give moral support, to give voice to women around the world. But how many of us are willing to give voice to the woman on our street corner pushing that shopping cart full of everything she owns in the world? How many of us are willing to give voice and listen to the story of that so-called welfare mother? How many of us are willing to give voice and listen to the story of that woman in the Tea Party? I know. That's the scariest place, that place of allowing ourselves to hear and see the humanity of those who dehumanize us.

These are questions I'm struggling with myself. I listen to those voices, and I'm thinking, *You are crazy—plain, simple crazy. Nothing else. Just insane. Insane. Gone. Lost your mind and don't even know where to start looking.* That's where I start. We have to find a way to move beyond that because otherwise we're doing exactly what they are—*othering*—telling ourselves that they don't have a story. They *do*, and I came to hear one. The *New York Times* did a series about Tea Party organizers. One was a woman who is traveling the country organizing Tea Party rallies and all the rest of it. I'm thinking, *Yeah. Okay. Mm-hmm.* Then she said, "I don't know why, but they respect me in this organization, and they need me." If you were to ask her about the interview, this is probably a line that she wouldn't even remember having said, and yet it was the one that struck me. I thought, *Whoa. I recognize that—the need to be respected, the need to be needed. I recognize that.* What is our position to women like that? It has to be that we have the courage to say, "There are other ways to be respected that are not contingent on disrespecting and dehumanizing others, and we want to be those who show you that respect." We have to be willing to step back from what we know and to be those who are willing to speak our truth and hear someone else's story.

There is a Nigerian proverb that says, "In a crisis the wise build bridges; the foolish build dams." We are in a time where there are a hell of a lot of dams going up—walls separating, walls trying to divide, voices building walls of denigration and dehumanization. If we are who we claim to be—women of spirit, women of divinity and power—we have to be the bridge builders. We have to have the courage, not simply to celebrate our wholeness, but to be willing to share that wholeness and even have it broken so that more can enjoy it, can be part of that whole, can be part of the circle, can be part of the powerful.

We are in a place where we have said we are on a quest for the living God, and the truth is, we found her. She is us, and she is that other out there somewhere waiting for us to help her find the living God in herself, in her brothers, her sons, her daughters, her others. Our quest can only be in our stories. It can only be found in the stories that each of us has within, but also in the stories of all of those people in our lives. We can experience people who are living the African proverb of humanness—the one that says a person is a person only through other people. I see you in me. I see me in you. This is a blessing, and the blessing always comes with a challenge. For that too I am grateful.

This poem of blessing and challenges is one of my favorites, by Dawna Markova.

I Will Not Die an Unlived Life

I will not die an unlived life.
I will not live in fear of falling or catching fire.
I choose to inhabit my days, to allow my living to open me,
to make me less afraid, more accessible,
to loosen my heart until it becomes a wing, a torch, a promise.
I choose to risk my significance;
to live so that which came to me as seed goes to the next as blossom
and that which came to me as blossom, goes on as fruit.
—Dawna Markova[10]

May we always, only, pass on blossom and fruit.

How Do We Catalyze Our Collective Transformational Power as Women of Spirit and Faith?

Fire
What makes a fire burn
is space between the logs,
a breathing space.
Too much of a good thing,
too many logs
packed in too tight
can douse the flames
almost as surely
as a pail of water.

So building fires
requires attention
to the spaces in between
as much as to the wood.

When we are able to build
open spaces
in the same way
we have learned
to pile on logs,
then we come to see how
it is fuel, and the absence of fuel
together, that makes fire possible.

We only need to lay a log
lightly from time to time.
A fire
grows
simply because the space is there,
with openings
in which the flame
that knows just how it wants to burn
can find its way.

—Judy Brown[1]

The final exploration takes us out into the community, into the world. One
of the main tools we have used throughout this book is that of asking
questions. Being comfortable with questions is one of the keys to transformative leadership. The thing about living the question is that we never
know what the answer is going to be. We learn to live in the mystery. We
learn to surrender to what wants to happen, rather than trying to control
everything that happens. We live in a very complex world and we often feel
overwhelmed by it. This can lead to inertia, as there is so much to consider
that we just don't want to consider anything. Asking questions helps us see

opportunities to grow rather than another responsibility to take on. Miracles can happen.

Here are some questions to consider now: What are the possibilities that can flow from our shared wisdom? When you leave behind what doesn't work, what skin have you had to shed? If our dreams came true, what would be different? Where do we find places to share our doubts, uncertainties, and growing edges? What kind of work will transform our shared human experience so that the Earth and all people on it can flourish? Many of us don't want to take on more work. We may feel that we are already doing too much. We invite you to think about ways of being together collectively that do not require that. Let's find a new way of experiencing work. When we each respond to what our hearts are called to do in the company of other women who are doing the same, it is no longer work—it is joyful, graceful, and it flows. How do we come together in collaboration with every human being on this planet, regardless of race, sexual preference, and political ideology? How do we develop partnerships with women and men where we support each other, where we find equality of respect and voice? We invite you to read the following stories reflecting on all of these questions as well as our final question to you: What is waiting to be birthed in the community of women of spirit and faith?

Musimbi Kanyoro, PhD, is the president and CEO of the Global Fund for Women, an international grant-making foundation that supports women-led groups working to advance the human rights of women and girls throughout the world. Formerly she served as the director of the Population and Reproductive Health Program of the David and Lucile Packard Foundation and as general secretary of the World YWCA. She is the author of *In Search of a Round Table: Gender, Theology, and Church Leadership* and *Introduction to Feminist Hermeneutics: An African Perspective.*

Living in God's Amazing Grace

The Power of Faith in Leadership

MUSIMBI KANYORO, PhD

My faith is rooted and inspired by the lives of women globally and by Africa, the continent that gives me roots. As an African and a woman of faith, I hold hope high, even when it is hope against hope. Many on the African continent know conflict and war and the deep suffering it causes. Weapons and words of destruction make hope seem so remote and even unattainable. Women, men, and children at graves; hopes raised and hopes dashed. To believe in God, in spite of and despite everything around us, cannot be explained in terms of the "power to do" or "the power to be," but rather as "God's amazing grace!" For God loved us so much that God gives us the power to hope every day for the best yet to come. I come to leadership with this hopeful joyous spirit, always moved to celebrate the gifts of life and possibilities that each day brings my way. I have been in leadership roles for nearly three decades, and I am immensely grateful for those who have trusted me and formed me during these years.

My current and new space of leadership is the Global Fund for Women. Twenty-five years ago, the courageous Anne Firth Murray dreamed about a different way to share money and resources, a different way to connect people and ideas around the globe. She shared her ideas with three other women, and the four put their ideas and money together. The Global Fund for Women was born. Today the Global Fund for Women is the largest public foundation exclusively investing in women's rights groups around the world. Since its inception in 1987, the Global Fund has granted more than $82 million to more than 3,800 women's groups in 180 countries.

I have joined the legacy of women of courage and action who have sustained the Global Fund for Women as donors and grantees, working together in mutual respect. I have succeeded Kavita Ramdas, a woman who has led that organization as president and CEO for fourteen years, growing it from infancy to excellence. I stand on the shoulders of those women and consider this legacy as sacred. I have to lead with honor and respect, knowing that this inheritance is for many women and societies all over the world. For me, working with women over the past thirty years has completely transformed my life and empowered my faith. I have learned that the most sacred texts are not written in holy books, but on the lines of every human face, regardless of religion. The experience has opened my eyes and filled me with courage to knock at countless doors to bring resources, medicines, and love to women who are trying to heal their communities.

Zina is one of the saints who taught me leadership. Ten years ago she was the ordinary bride of a truck driver. Within a month of her marriage, her husband fell ill and died. Two years later, Zina began to get ill frequently, and the result of her blood tests confirmed that she was HIV positive. At that time she did not even know what HIV was. The doctors gave her two months to live. She proved them wrong. She joined a support group, accessed treatment and good nutrition, and today Zina is the face of her community's battle against the dreaded HIV virus. Her strength shows through her determination to support others and to speak out strongly and clearly against the stigma and isolation of people living with AIDS. Zina, a young woman, is my witness that we can continue to hope.

A Future of Promise

Leadership for me as a woman of faith means I am licensed to see the world through the eyes of women. I listen to women and hear their voices demanding better policies, more resources for social themes, more inclusive participation of men and women in decisions that affect our world. My job description is simply "advocate."

A is for assessing the situation of women and girls in a particular place and time and beyond.

D is for detailing the challenges women experience.

V is for vocalizing the concerns of women.

O is for opposing bad, ill-conceived, or maligned policies and programs.

C is for collaborating with others on positive solutions.

A is for advancing the equality of women and men.

T is for talking with or twisting the arms of elected representatives or leaders to implement justice.

E is for engaging the public on the benefits of justice for women.

I try to live out my faith in doing this job, but it is not without challenges. Today there are considerable numbers of women in leadership positions in every aspect of society, including leadership in faith communities. This is often seen as our achieved equality, and we are told to move on now to other things. In reality, we are far away from achieved justice for women. The truth about our world is told through the persistent faces of poverty and the inequality among the world's people and between its women and men. Less than 20 percent of parliamentary positions globally are held by women. Sexual abuse of women is still rampant everywhere, including in faith communities and within families. Poverty among women is still passed on from one generation to another. Trafficking girls and women has become a lucrative trade, now comparable to the drug trade. The HIV and AIDS pandemic has become feminized, especially in Africa and among young women. Rather than benefitting from new employment opportunities opened by globalization, poor working women are frequently relegated to insecure work in an informal economy where they are exploited and abused.

Investing in justice for women is doing the correct thing, and there are many gains for those who dare make this investment. For those of us advocating on behalf of women, we've just begun and we need to hold hands for the long ride. The overriding question is the mechanism of carrying out the job. Our times are asking for different frames from those of baby-boomer feminist leaders. Today in the women's movement younger women leaders spend a great deal of time exploring the question, How can women and men resolve what keeps us in opposing camps so that we can better recognize our common humanity and responsibility to each other and to the environment? The debate is no longer how can we be strong and fearless as women alone or how can we use our power as women, but rather how can we be strong *together* as women of diverse possibilities and as women and men together?

I grew up at a time when opportunities for women-only spaces were valued: girl's clubs, women's clubs, and so on. These spaces are not as valued or available today. Even though our world is changing and these spaces are now questioned, the purpose for which they were created is still valid. Some believe that keeping women-only spaces isolates issues of justice for women in ghetto-like entities, accessible only to women. Others believe that the way to achieve justice for women is to create more opportunities for men and women to "reason together." The implementation of this latter theory is what is commonly referred to as "gender mainstreaming." The gender approach capitalizes on how societies and cultures influence the status of men and women in society and the values that determine justice or injustice to men and women.

For the past two decades there has been extensive gender mainstreaming in governments, ecumenical bodies, churches, and even women's organizations. The intention is always to ask for greater accountability so that people are not disadvantaged by their gender. Although we don't yet have critical examples of success stories of gender mainstreaming, there are ongoing watchdog activities to monitor and evaluate its effectiveness as a strategy for achieving justice for women. Some of the evidence available shows that gender mainstreaming can obscure the reality of women and in most cases has resulted in greater bureaucracy, invisibility of women's leadership, and lack of safe places for women's self-empowerment. Historically, women's spaces have given women the security to explore, deconstruct, and develop strategies to address the gender roles that society, family, religion, and the media impose on them.

The pervasive discrimination and violence against women cannot be reversed by a handful of promising practices and success. If justice for women really matters, it must be accompanied by arrangements and reforms in structures and systems to protect women's human rights and financial commitment to repair the injustice to women. If women are mainstreamed, caution has to be taken to ensure that there are mechanisms of authority, voice, resources, and accountability needed for women to be equal players and that their issues are not pitted against other emerging critical issues. It is important, for example, that funding for women's leadership development does not get sidetracked to building houses destroyed by storms and that gained liberties for women should not slip away quietly in the interest of including men. I suggest that urgent leadership is needed in four areas: transforming power relationships, scaling up what works for women, accountability to women, and affirming the authority of women.

Transforming Power Relationships

Women's empowerment involves transforming power relationships at individual, collective, and institutional levels. For decades women have used their power to organize and mobilize solidarity among themselves. They have used collective power to move issues such as domestic violence, rape, and reproductive choices from the private sphere to the public sphere. Women have used systems and conferences to get their voices heard and documented in such conventions as the Beijing Platform for Action or the Millennium Development Goals. Women have learned to work with difference while giving each other voice such that even if the power imbalance between and among women is still a reality, there is generally a well-developed global solidarity among women, which needs to be protected.

There are many groups of women and men discussing justice for women, but it is important to be sure that the women at those tables still carry the mandate of other women and they have a passion to bring to the table the reality of the less privileged women. Simply accepting to be on panels with men without caring for the women's agenda is a form of injustice. It is also important that the men who speak for women are humble enough to remember when they must sometimes just listen. It is important to watch out that women do not become even more marginalized and excluded because their only spaces are now shared with men. The question of women's participation and even women-only spaces is still valid. Gender mainstreaming should always be tested on how many more opportunities it has opened for women, rather than how many men are now discussing gender justice for women. As a group of HIV-positive women recently stated, "Nothing about us without us."

Scaling Up What Works for Women

It is time to focus on scaling up what works for women. Girl's education, for example, is one area where returns are good for everyone, and scaling up in every country cannot only mean smart investments. Working to build capacities of women through leadership development, skills training, and other formations is another opportunity for scaling up while correcting the wrong done to women. Providing remedial and support services is another area that must be scaled up. When dealing with violence, for example, it may mean more counseling and shelter services and also resources for a fresh start for those women who choose to make new beginnings. In addition, there is a need to enhance such support services for women as daycare centers for their children, continuing education for teen mothers, health-care opportunities for older women, and strong advocacy programs for emerging issues of every time and generation. The church can work in partnership with others in their communities to scale up such programs as reparation for justice for women.

Accountability to Women

Mainstreaming usually aims at ensuring greater accountability from a more diverse sector of population, but gender mainstreaming must put women at the center as subjects. Accountability means ensuring those women's voices are not silenced even if their story is shocking. If women want to demonstrate against rape or lack of reproductive choices, they must not be muted because of policy that often has to be protected in bureaucracies. Accountability to women is about protecting the human rights of all women in all places, all the time. A woman does not stop being a woman when she is a prostitute or a lesbian or when she is living with HIV or AIDS. Accountability includes setting aside budgets to help meet the needs relating to justice for all women.

Affirming the Authority of Women

In governments where women have been mainstreamed, ministers of women's affairs serve as focal points for women's issues, but they have neither cabinet status nor their own budgets. They are expected to influence others through uncoordinated and underresourced gender focal units. The landscape of marginalized women's rights and gender equality structures is replicated in many different contexts. An important way to affirm women's authority is to enhance the status of women who are responsible for units of justice for women. This is a statement of the fact that they represent half of the world, but even more important it is giving them the opportunity to bring issues affecting women to the highest decision-making tables. Finally, making a commitment to women is vital. Women have been at the margins of society for so long that they require tangible commitments. We still have work to do, and women of faith have each other and more to lean on.

Jean Shinoda Bolen, MD, is a psychiatrist, Jungian analyst, and internationally known author who draws from spiritual, feminist, Jungian, medical, and personal wellsprings of experience. She is the author of *Goddesses in Everywoman, Crossing to Avalon, The Millionth Circle, Goddesses in Older Women, Crones Don't Whine, Urgent Message from Mother,* and *Like a Tree*. She is a major advocate of a United Nations Fifth World Conference on Women, a Distinguished Life Fellow of the American Psychiatric Association, and a former clinical professor of psychiatry at the University of California at San Francisco.

Creative Acts of Expression

Catalyzed in Circles

Jean Shinoda Bolen, MD

I know, as so many of us who are fortunate to be in one know, how supportive a sacred circle can be—as an incubator-womb space in which the courage to be authentically ourselves leads to creative acts of expression. This may include what is usually meant by expressive arts—writing, painting, sculpture, dance, theater, and films—or political and personal activism, transforming relationships to others, or changing institutions. Inevitably, perhaps because experiences of the sacred are so deep and deeply personal, creative acts of expression are expressions of awakening that begin with trusting our own feelings and perceptions, of realizing it is up to us to be real and act on the premise that what matters to us really matters. This is soul knowledge that becomes soul work when we take steps to bring what we know into our personal world and into the world at large. At times of crisis what we do, or not do, can tilt a situation in either direction.

In the silence of undirected inner reflection, prayer, or meditation found in a sacred circle, we tap into a center in ourselves that is also at the center of the circle. In Jung's psychology this is the archetype of meaning, the Self. By meeting as a circle of women, we invite the sacred feminine to come into our midst. This form is archetypal. It connects us to suppressed sources of women's spiritual power, much as an aquifer lies below the surface until it is tapped into, bubbles up, and flows. We tap into an awareness that goes back in time to when divinity was worshipped in many forms—as female, as the Great Mother, Gaia. In the last third of the twentieth century, Merlin Stone's *When God Was a Woman* got archeological support from Marija Gimbutas and other archeologists who literally dug up evidence. Scrolls that had been hidden and preserved by the dryness in Egyptian caves near Nag Hammadi were found in this same period.

These became known as the Gnostic Gospels. These early Christian writings were rich in metaphor and included Sophia, the sacred feminine. Gnostic churches were egalitarian rather than hierarchal in form. Leadership was shared: who did what—the sermon, communion, greeting newcomers—could be chosen by lot. Everyone was welcome. Women served in all roles. Once the Church at Rome had the power to condemn heresy, the Gnostic Christians were persecuted, its gospels destroyed. Our only knowledge of them came from the church fathers, who systematically had destroyed all previous copies of these gospels. This time, it was different. Circumstances had changed. Through the influence of feminism and the women's movement, there now were women scholars in all fields including theology.

In the United States, before the women's movement, men (not women) defined who women were, using religion as authority. It was only after women spoke for themselves and about themselves that "women's spirituality" emerged. Only then, did we speak of what we experienced as sacred and what we knew to be spiritual information. This is *gnosis*, intuitively felt soul knowledge; it is what we recognize in the marrow of our bones, what our heart recognizes as true for us—and from this insight, true for other humans and for the planet. Sacred circles support trust in our own perceptions of divinity, which can be felt as transcendent spirit or felt in embodied holy moments. This is empowering, especially for women who have been told that God is male and demands obedience and that women since Eve are the source of evil, when her choice was knowledge of the difference between good and evil. Reimaging God as other than and more than a male authority will shake the foundation of patriarchy, which is historically based on theology and hierarchy to justify having and using power over others. Monotheism has brought us fratricidal wars of religion in Europe during the Middle Ages as well as the current conflicts in the Middle East. Jew, Muslim, Christian—all descend from Abraham and thus are brothers. Women's spirituality is in conflict with monotheistic, Abrahamic beliefs based on words attributed to what prophetic men in ages past said God said.

Five women friends sitting around a round table began the women's suffrage movement in 1848, an effort that took seven decades for women to achieve, when women finally got the right to vote in 1920. Once accomplished, it became a nonissue. Of course women vote! This is what success looks like. This same pattern is seen in the economic and social gains for women by women in the late 1960s and 1970s. In consciousness-raising groups, women learned about being stereotyped and stifled. Speaking truth to power emerged as a ringing intention, done through demonstrations, conferences, marches, legal suits, and personal confrontations. The idea of equal rights spread. Betty Friedan's *The Feminine Mystique* was a starting point. Others wrote articles and essays; many were published in *Ms.* magazine or in anthologies of women's writings. Women challenged the invisible assumptions of women's inferiority and the right of men and male institutions to limit access to education, professions, and occupations. The consequences of sexism and the idea of equality brought about a huge cultural change in the United States and influenced the world. That gains are taken for granted is a measure of success. Young women now assume that they have opportunities and rights that women never have had as a gender before, and still do not in many parts of the world. Just like the right to vote, once the perceptions and voices of a critical number of empowered women are heard, what was radical and opposed becomes the new normal.

When I wrote *The Millionth Circle: How to Change Ourselves and the World* as a guide to women's circles in 1999, the mechanism through which women's circles with a spiritual center could bring about an end to patriarchy was based on theoretical biologist Rupert Sheldrake's work on morphic fields and morphogenesis. The millionth circle, like the allegorical hundredth monkey that inspired my title, was a metaphoric number. It was the final one to tip the scales, the one that added to all the rest formed a critical mass, after which a new idea or attitude or behavior becomes accepted. A recent example would be global warming, an idea that was resisted and even ridiculed, until almost overnight a critical number of people accepted it. I was aware that it happened between the hardcover publication of *Urgent Message from Mother: Gather the Women, Save the World* in 2005 and the paperback edition in 2008.

Also pivotal for me was Malcolm Gladwell's *The Tipping Point*, based on geometrical progression, another way of explaining how evolutionary ideas spread. It is how a virus spreads or a YouTube video goes viral. It's like how a snowball that starts as the size of a baseball gathers snow and momentum and as it rolls downhill can become an avalanche. It is what I sense is happening: there is momentum, circles form easier and easier, and the more there are, the easier it is and the less time it takes for more to form. A circle with a spiritual center provides support for authentic acts of expression, to discern and commit to what I call your "assignment." Mine is about writing and speaking and spreading the word about circles and assignments. The current vehicle for my message is *Like a Tree: How Women, Trees, and Tree People Can Save the Planet*. I call upon mystical activists and sacred feminine feminists, the men and women I call "tree people" who feel deep connections to trees and the sacred world. If you find yourself wanting to give back or make a difference and are drawn to the possibility, you will recognize an assignment as yours by three characteristics, by your answers to three questions that only you can answer:

1. Is it meaningful to you?
2. Will it be fun? If it draws on your skills and experience, if it calls on your creativity, and if you are in the company of people who share your values and commitment—it will be fun.
3. Is it motivated by love? In the first half of adult life, parenting can fit this description, as can developing an innate talent that will require years of perseverance and discipline, or following a calling into a helping profession. Like Joseph Campbell's "follow your bliss," it does not mean that this will be easy, or that you will be successful, or that others will understand. It is, however, living your personal myth, which we do through the choices we make. Heed Goethe: "Whatever you can do or dream you can do, begin it now!"

Once you make a heart commitment to an assignment or a sacred mission, a trustworthy circle provides spiritual and emotional support. In your circle what is meaningful is important. Prayers are requested. Gratitude is expressed. Often a candle is placed in the center. With or without awareness the sacred feminine is represented by it. For this is a symbol of Hestia the Greek Goddess of the hearth and temple, who was present in the fire at the center of a round hearth; her fire was the source of light, warmth, and nourishment. In women's circles such as these, we are catalyst, witnesses, and midwives for each others' growth and path of individuation. Meanwhile, the world is now in crisis—danger and opportunity exist side by side. There are more than 6.7 billion of us on the planet, doubling since 1960, adding about 78 million every year. For all the concern about sustainability and global warming, left out of the solution is the need for reproductive rights for all women and universal education that includes girls.

Conflicts that could escalate into nuclear warfare continue, while political leaders posture and threaten each other. Women and conflict resolution knowledge are notably not brought to the table, at a time when a growing world population and weapons of mass destruction could make this beautiful planet uninhabitable. Demonstrations for democracy and social justice, a resurgence of feminism, and research support that humans are born good, that meditation changes brain patterns, and that at the quantum physics level we are all one suggest the potential for evolutionary change. It depends on what we do. It would be fair to say that whether matters will get better or much worse will be decided in our lifetime.

I take to heart the Dalai Lama's words at the Vancouver Peace Conference in 2009, when he said that it is up to Western women to save the world. I'd expand "Western" to mean every woman anywhere who has been liberated by the women's movement to define herself by the choices she makes. Western women are the beneficiaries of education, responsibilities, authority, opportunities, democracy, medical advances, and reproductive choice that women have never had in history. As members of the female gender, women respond to stress differently than do men, and we have empathic, collaborative, and communication abilities that contribute to decision making and conflict resolution. When women's maternal concerns for their children extend to all children, when women have an equal say with men in making decisions at every level, when women's ability to look after others and budget-limited resources is valued, then peace and a sustainable world will be possible.

Never doubt that small groups of committed women can change the world: we did before, we can do it again!

Lisa Anderson is the director of Women's Multifaith Programs at Auburn Theological Seminary. She holds masters of divinity and masters of philosophy degrees from Union Theological Seminary. Currently she is a Union doctoral candidate in systematic theology. She has taught Black, Feminist, and LGBT theologies, Christian ethics and liturgy, and she has designed and led seminars on the connection between faith and social justice. She is a regular contributor at Feminist.com.

A Poetic Response

"The Catalyst"

LISA ANDERSON

The following poem, "The Catalyst," was composed at the Alchemy gathering. It was written in response to the question, How do we catalyze the collective transformational power of women of spirit and faith? The poem digs beneath the surface of this question to reveal the many layers of often unspoken complexity and challenge that accompany the desire of women and any configuration of justice-loving and -seeking people to build authentic, inclusive, and lasting communities of belief and action. How is our sense of the "oneness" of women—our so-called "we-ness"—defined and embodied? What is the substance of the transformational power we would claim as our own? Does it reside in how we understand faith and spirit as it pertains to women? If so, which women, whose faith, and what spirit may (or may not) inform our sense of ourselves as wielders of a new transformative energy? What concrete action toward the making of a better world will, indeed *must*, a collectivity based on women's faith and spirit-filled knowledge and experience yield?

The decision to reflect poetically on what I refer to as the unsettling undercurrents of the original question was quite intentional. The evocative and symbolic nature of the medium is meant to invite the reader to not simply analyze these undercurrents, but to feel their impact and influence on the shape women's faith and spirit-driven leadership is poised to assume in the twenty-first century. Toward this end, "The Catalyst" is meant to be read aloud and in community—certainly in the company of other women and ideally within a multifaith group whose diversity also spans the bounds of race, class, orientation, and generation. It is meant to provoke honest and deliberate discussion across these usual dividing lines in the service of creating a space where the spiritual capacity of all women can combine with authenticity and integrity to bring healing, hope, and wholeness to a broken world.

THE CATALYST

It was as if I was walking on air, suspended in space
disembodied
disconnected
floating.
That was where the question seemed to be leading me
which was quite odd actually
considering that our being
as women in the world had seemingly
always grounded us so very intimately in it.

And yet
with the unfolding of the question
"how do we catalyze the collective transformational power
of women of spirit and faith?"
I felt the ground giving way beneath my feet.
How could this be? I wondered.
What could this mean?

I had a thought
at once unsettling
and yet not devastatingly so
that perhaps "we women of spirit and faith"
so-called had not come quite as far on our journeys
of truth-telling and coalition building
as we would like to believe.

Perhaps our desire to come together
across the many lines
of difference and disparity that truly define "us"
still wanted a bolder incarnation—
A "this-world-made-just-and-safe-for-women-and-girls-
    now!"
to steady us
against a vague veneration of earth and sky gods
whose perceived withholding might only be a manifestation
of the Divine's own plea for us to
at long last show up
in force and in fullness for our own liberation.

I reckoned the toll millennia of silences and unknowing
had taken on our ability to become so calibrated
against the scant decades
of new vulnerabilities revealed
and longings shared
And I began to understand that our
wellspring of collective power and possibility
was still more emergent than nearly realized.

My feet touched ground with this revelation—
"how to catalyze the collective transformational power
of women of spirit and faith"—
suddenly removed from the ethers of religious mystery
and rendered imaginable
in and through a steadier cultivation
A holy habit of being for us,
spoken of
written about
prayed over
worked for
realized
The catalyst.
                —Lisa Anderson

Dr. Barbara E. Fields is the executive director of the Association for Global New Thought and cofounder of the Gandhi King Season for Nonviolence. She was program director for the 1993 Parliament of the World's Religions centennial celebration in Chicago and cofounder and director of The Synthesis Dialogues I, II & III with His Holiness the Dalai Lama of Tibet. Fields is a contributing author to *The Community of Religions* and *Two Hundred Visionaries*.

The Meta-Civics of Feminine Leadership

DR. BARBARA E. FIELDS

> Dear reader, traditional human power structures and their reign of darkness are about to be rendered obsolete.
>
> —Buckminster Fuller

This essay is based on a topic I have been thinking about for a while, relative to what is actually revolutionary about the feminine leadership model and its strategic implications for active paradigmatic shift. These thoughts directly reflect, on a daily basis, the spiritual leadership opportunities and challenges unfolding in my own life's journey. However, as I wrote and edited this piece, I had a growing concern that my writing style and conceptual reach might not ring enough of the personal tone achieved by other voices in this book. My next thought was, "But, this *is* my personal tone." Every time I try to soften the intellectual or academic edges of my message and its articulation, the attempt has been motivated by a false mandate that the feminine voice is expected to be more subjective and emotionally resonant. I do not necessarily agree to those terms, as I never agreed to the historical and sociological premise of that characterization in the first place. I think it does a disservice to women's freedom to speak with the whole range of our voices, not just with the chords that reinforce the so-called feminine mind-set. What I have written here is what I truly feel, think, and believe … and here is its voice.

Meta-Civics: Citizen Visionaries in Compassionate Service

There is a new worldview emerging rapidly among feminine leaders in every sector of social discourse. It prompts us to abandon even the baseline assumptions and preconceptions we barely knew we had. For some of us, reality looks like two societies existing simultaneously, occupying the same time and space. One is the system as we know it—static at best yet apparently deconstructing itself. The other might be referred to as the "innovation," or the evolutionary response to these prevailing conditions. This emerging society is present, aware, dynamic, and ingenious. It springs from, is informed by the parent, but it is not simply "alternative" and should not be thought of as a subculture or counterculture. The emerging society is in the process of fully individuating; it should be thought of as differentiated as opposed to reactionary because if all we are capable of at this point is following the two-dimensional swing of history's pendulum, we are lost. The emerging culture recognizes the imperative of synergy, formulating itself into a matrix at once nonhierarchical and complex, driving toward solutions no longer constrained by the fading paradigm at all, but leaping from qualitatively new foundations into a future of absolute potential.

This reality of emergence is intimately bound to the feminine principle. We have passed the point of speculation as to "whether" this phenomenon will constitute a new social meme and are fast approaching practical reasons to consciously name, claim, and frame it—not by default, not in reaction to, and not at the effect of anything but our own choices and skillful self-empowerment. This is indeed a global trend, the measure of which can only be taken by authentic self-reflection and the extent to which we collaboratively innovate for the measurable uplift of the whole system. This signals another factor at play: evolutionary models in natural systems demonstrate that communities thrive when enlightened self-interest is sustained—not despite but *through* support of the collective higher good.

A True Revolution of Values

In the year 2011 we are standing in the midst of nothing less than, as Dr. Martin Luther King Jr. names it, a "revolution of values" accelerating toward a new definition of what it means for a conscious, spiritually motivated woman to engage in the business of leadership as an experiment in shaping her own social reality. Because it demands and demonstrates a complex of *highest common denominator* attributes that must be present for its integration, we endow this new model for leadership with a unique terminology: *meta-civics* (citizen visionaries in compassionate service).

In this country and throughout the global community, leading women are seeking alliances of intent and purpose as vehicles by which they can actively engage in effective social and political change. It is no coincidence that many of us are also committed to personal spiritual practices such as prayer and meditation or are waking up to the benefits of such practice for the first time. Worldwide, there are currently more than a million organizations that use emerging consciousness as an organizing tool to create personal and social change. Although each organization has a specific emphasis, their common founding impulse is that consciousness itself affects the conditions of our lives and the planet. While many of these organizations are officially led by women, nearly all are run and made functional by us.

Women living in the "first world" of economically developed nations are saturated by a culture of unprecedented sophistication. Questions of equity aside, this offers to us the curse and the blessing of having a hand in shaping the messages of evolving global culture. Our "rights" to these staggering material, informational, and technological opportunities are being reframed *by women*, becoming instead our "responsibilities" as citizens living in the most privileged nations on earth. Many Western women in positions of leadership seem to have an innate gift for examining the motivations with which we encounter the stuff, services, and experiences to which we have access. Are our motivations selfish or compassionate? Inclusive or exclusive? Self-directed or subjugated to an outside authority? Codependent, independent, interdependent cocreative, or synergistic? Ultimately, how does this abundance and diversity affect us when it comes to the question: By what source are we inspired to live?

Is existence, for us, sacred or purely material? Beyond that—if sacred, does that impulse come from within or without? Then there is the instinct of compassion—what is ours to do about the gaping global heart wound as members of a human family in which so many are still suffering? The bottom line is that we, as spiritually guided women leaders, hold the magic key to transformation. It is up to us to *educate through embodiment* the social evolution of the sacred secular world that harbors our common future.

Synergy of Feminine Leadership, Empowerment, and Collective Self-Consciousness

As spiritually guided women within many nations, we face a matrix of fragile variables: government, religion, war, peace, military, civilian, economics, politics, faith, material resources, moral and ethical values, human life, livelihood, and power. Knowing that these are inextricably entwined, how must we act to ensure that the highest wisdom is gained from voices of moral authority within each domain? This is an age-old question. But now, with the stakes of life and death ever deepening, hierarchies of "dominator model" decision makers either fail to grasp, or choose to ignore, that salvation demands laying down weapons of war, releasing addiction to greed, and embracing the more enlightened tools of meta-civics. How long can we continue to rely on systems and responses that not only don't work, but entrench us further each day in the mires of social, environmental, and ideological distress?

Meta-civics requires that we pursue new goals through a process consistent with any product it strives to engender. An integral model of citizenship will measure its efficacy according to the synergy it achieves between leadership and grassroots empowerment, guided by methods that call us to simmer in a "self-consciousness of the collective." This spiritually motivated, collectively shared, feminine wisdom leadership phenomenon might be our reverently awaited, radically new paradigm giving birth to itself. It does not stand against or react to what came before, but clears the way for a fresh revolution of values that rises from an autonomous source remembering its unified nature. It is prayerful, meditative, contemplative, thoughtful, devoted, disciplined, compassionate, strategic, inclusive, and courageous. Healing the exile of the immanent from the transcendent, are we beginning to embody a feminine global messiah that defines the moral order we deserve by our birthright and earn by our integral sense of universal responsibility? Although this meme is new and the dots are not yet connected, the agencies of meta-civics can at last be welcomed into our neighborhoods and narratives.

Women Form Natural Collaboratories

Meta-civics can be thought of in part as a laboratory for deep change within individuals, among communities, and throughout society. We, its feminine culture, are a diverse collection of leaders, thinkers, and social architects who have spent years, each in our own way, questioning the mind-set of a civilization that knows and can do better. The prevailing male leadership model generally operates from the belief that progress is achieved by recognizing and choosing between competing objects, ideas, and forces. Although some say that this ingrained combination of dualism, dogma, and discrimination has expedited the development of advanced technology and economic power, it has also produced social institutions and cultural attitudes that have distorted the intrinsic human preference for harmony and universal satisfaction. It has become clear that the world's awakened women are ready to give a living voice to at least one uncompromising assumption: that it is both necessary and possible for humanity to achieve a prevailing consciousness that holds the welfare of all living beings as its highest good, that protects the weak while honoring the strong, and that will assure the health of the earth for all future generations. This sensitivity lies at the center of religious experience but is also reflected in the noblest expressions of social, artistic, and scientific insight.

"A person is a person through other persons.... I am human because I belong, I participate, I share. A person with *ubuntu* is open and available to others, affirming of others, does not feel threatened that others are able and good, for he or she has a proper self-assurance that comes from knowing that he or she belongs to a greater whole and is diminished when others are humiliated or diminished, when others are tortured or oppressed, or treated as if they were less than who they are."

—Bishop Desmond Tutu[2]

The unique methodology of meta-civics is, in fact, to constantly encourage our universal principles and practices to keep emerging quite specifically in a field of diversity where we can see, hear, and feel their power authentically. This points to a critical clue: women intuitively know that the need to work with the energy of our differences has never been greater. Therefore, we must create more opportunities to model to ourselves and to others that, in a practical way, it is at the very edge of our differences that the greatest possibilities for human evolution emerge. To achieve genuine breakthrough, in contrast to temporary concession, requires the systematic development of a mind-set that equitably encompasses and transcends, includes and discerns. The feminine psyche is inherently attuned to this—a kind of meta-mind that senses the intelligence that resides more within a group or holistic experience than in an individual ego.

The goal of meta-civics is to assist in the emergence and expansion of this universality of consciousness. It is, quite simply, a way of setting the intention to inspire "moments of awakening"—to the contradictions as well as the consonance in our own mind-sets—and to catalyze the growth of a more spacious awareness that can accommodate opposing ideas and beliefs, reconcile differences, and nurture a creative integration from which new possibilities emerge. Through intentional, focused dialogues and exchanges, women leaders will become more and more able to identify and suggest ways to address some of the contradictions and complexities that continue to restrain humanity's natural impulse to see the world as one and all beings as deeply interconnected. This is meta-civics and, at the same time, it is the empowerment of evolutionary leadership manifest in the feminine principle.

Whether Discord Is Secular or Religious: Is Spirit the Solution?

The collective "soul force" of the world's sacred traditions is a passionate flame to be reckoned with, and these days it burns far beyond formal religious practice to ignite millions of women who consider themselves "spiritual but not religious." This globally shared natural resource can be understood as the contribution by universal spiritual principles to history's archives of irrefutable treasures: love, compassion, justice, equality, happiness, and freedom. Above all—a reverence for life itself, which *all women know* can only be sustained by a civilization of peace. We are in moral "triage" as a planet. At what point will we say that it is immoral to accept the violent or inequitable methods of problem-solving that seem to be the only resource of many governments? When do we recognize that it is not sane to invest one more ounce of energy hoping to repair or, more precisely, *to gain permission from* a corrupt system to repair a corrupt system? It is the subtlest form of sabotage; we struggle to gain entry through the gates that oppress us, thereby sapping our energy and resources from the vital new terrain yet to be cultivated. The ever-increasing numbers of female religious and spiritual leaders, along with their empowered congregations and networks, must find the sacred authority to take moral and ethical governance back into our own arena. The challenge lies in learning to engage and enlist policy-making institutions in a conversation based on the wisdom of moral and ethical values as a context for successful programs and bottom lines.

Meta-civics is a new start. Today there is no ocean to cross to a New World, but technology has opened up a new world of virtual communications and grassroots potential. In our temples, mosques, churches, synagogues, kivas, rain forests, and humanitarian communities, women have already begun to rekindle sanity and peace by designing and applying grassroots-based "omni-local" nonviolent initiatives to take back the immense power we have entrusted to masculine-led hierarchies that have failed us. Imagine how quickly global wounds would heal if decades of violent and self-serving leadership were enjoined by the meta-civics of feminine leadership. The question is this: Is humanity capable of sustaining a future, not eroded by military-industrial complexes trading on fear, but evolved by nations of angels?

Phyllis W. Curott, JD and HPs, is an attorney, author, Wiccan priestess, and pioneering spiritual teacher of the Euro-indigenous revivals. Described by *New York Magazine* as one of the culture's most intellectually cutting-edge thinkers, Curott is founder of the Temple of Ara, president emerita of the Covenant of the Goddess, and a trustee of the Council for the Parliament of the World's Religions. She is the author of the internationally bestselling memoir *Book of Shadows: A Modern Woman's Journey into the Wisdom of Witchcraft* and *The Magic of the Goddess.*

Thou Art Goddess

The Return of the Divine Feminine

PHYLLIS W. CUROTT, JD AND HPs

The first time I saw the Goddess, She was smiling at me. She had long brown hair, bright brown eyes, and She was wearing an old purple T-shirt under a pair of paint-splattered overalls. That was more than thirty years ago. I was a young Ivy League lawyer in the back of a musty bookstore in New York City, and I was sitting in a circle of women. In the middle of that circle sat an altar—a low, round table filled with fruits and flowers, shells and seeds, and other bits of Nature's brilliance, all of which surrounded a collection of Goddess statues. I was just learning who they were, and each week they changed. This week we had chosen Shakti, the Hindu Goddess of creation; Athena, Greek Goddess of civilization; Bridgid, Celtic Goddess of healing and poetry; Yemaya, the Yoruban Goddess of motherhood; Kuan Yin, Buddhist bodhisattva and Goddess of mercy; the Virgin Mary; and the Venus of Willendorf, who was more than twenty-five thousand years old.

As we did each week, we held hands and created a circle, a sacred space in which we honored the four directions and called upon the Divine Feminine to bless us with Her presence. We sang and danced and then toasted the Goddess as maiden, mother, and crone with wine and fruit juice poured into a large silver bowl and with words spoken from our hearts. The women's spontaneous and profound wisdom made this my favorite moment. We ended by turning to one another and saying, "Thou art Goddess." The words were arcane, the phrase odd and a bit discomfiting. But I said and accepted that blessing with all the sincerity I could muster. Raised in an intellectual, secular family, I didn't believe in God— let alone a Goddess. And I certainly didn't consider myself one! But the effects of participating in that circle were visible, palpable, and shared, and that was why I came back each week. We laughed and listened, consoled and supported, encouraged and inspired one another. We recognized ourselves in the stories and struggles we shared.

Each woman was beautiful in her own unique way because she was lit from within. My heart—and mind—opened to possibilities I'd never considered. I wasn't beginning to believe in the Goddess's existence, I was beginning to experience Her presence. She was in her twenties, Her thirties and forties, and Her sixties. She was white and She was black, skinny and plump, educated and not, a struggling artist, a successful writer, a housewife. It was in their company that I had my first epiphany: *the Goddess is within.* With that realization all my notions about divinity changed.

The second time I saw the Goddess, She was staring back from the mirror I was staring into and Her eyes were shining. I recognized Her because I had seen Her before, shining in the eyes of my sisters. That was my second epiphany: *the Goddess was within me!* With that experience my beliefs about myself began to change. Seeing the Goddess within ourselves meant that we also saw ourselves within the Goddess. She was a mirror reflecting the sacred, precious, and good that we as women shared with Her. The Goddess—by all of Her countless names and in all of Her countless cultural forms—became our guide to the lost parts of ourselves, parts that had been denigrated and suppressed by our culture for thousands of years, but which She had restored and elevated. To see Her in the women around me was to be inspired. To feel Her presence within me was to be empowered.

In that circle I began a journey that continues to this day. I am still discovering the countless ways in which Mother Earth's life-giving powers are shared by women and how each stage of my life reveals the spiritual mysteries reflected in the Moon's monthly cycles—the strength and independence of the Daughter, the fertile and nourishing creativity of the Mother, the wisdom and authority of the Grandmother. I have learned that the wisdom of the heart is as truthful and as necessary as the wisdom of the mind. I have learned to respect and value my body as a flesh-and-blood temple in which the Sacred lives and loves, creates and ages, and discovers Herself.

Together we are creating new and rediscovering ancient ways of encountering, honoring, and learning from the Divine Feminine. To enter into a circle is to invoke Her, not only as symbol but as living embodiment. To participate in circle is to share a universal experience of divinity. Circle is the mythical Holy Grail, the cauldron of rebirth into which our wounded souls enter and from which we emerge revitalized. In circle we are all equal and equally responsible—to ourselves, to one another, to the circle as a whole, and to the holy energy it holds. We give each other the gifts of witnessing and affirming our insights and experiences. Because each of us holds a unique piece of the lost Feminine, our differences are not only respected but appreciated. In circle we are connected and made one by our shared experience of the living Goddess in Her countless manifestations. In circle we learn the most important lesson of all: *the Feminine is sacred.*

Discovering the Divine Feminine has a profound affect on the way women view and value themselves. It changes your life—the choices you make, the work you do, the relationships you have, the values you treasure, the causes you devote yourself to, and the Source you draw on to face the challenges that life inevitably brings you. The Divine Feminine is also a radical change in the realm of religion. To declare that the Sacred is not just masculine but also feminine challenges the most fundamental precept that has dominated Western biblical religion and culture for thousands of years—that the Divine, the ultimate good, is exclusively male, is God the Father and Son. It challenges the belief that men, affirmed in their power by this metaphor of ultimate power, are meant to rule the world and women. Honoring the Goddess doesn't just challenge religious symbolism, language, rituals, or even the roles of women. It challenges the underlying values and the social structures, dynamics, and relationships that grow out of those values. The power unleashed by our recognition that the Feminine is sacred is the power to heal and to change the world in which we live. To change the ultimate measure of reality—the Divine—is to change reality itself.

We long for change, for the feminine side of the Divine. But what is that feminine side? *The Goddess is the missing half of everything.* She is not God's replacement but His partner whose return remedies the isolation of a transcendent God with the partnership of an immanent Goddess. Relationship redeems the "feminine" qualities that our culture needs, and so cooperation can now balance competition, compassion mediate conflict, nurturance temper dominance, connection heal separation. But for women, Goddesses also embody the traditionally "masculine" characteristics of strength, independence, courage, intellectual acumen, and aggressiveness that have been denied to us. The return of the Feminine offers wholeness. She restores the lost parts of ourselves to men as well as to women and to our culture. By achieving balance within, we can restore balance to the world. The Goddess is returning when she is most needed, for we live in a world dangerously out of balance. Wholeness is the key to rediscovering holiness, so Her presence not only challenges, it transforms by healing the wound created by our separation from the sacred—both masculine and feminine—that started when we began to believe that God resided in heaven and that we had been cast out of paradise. It is this great wound that had led us to wound one another and the Earth that sustains us. With Her return, the healing of these wounds has begun.

For me, healing began in a circle with other women, and it was in circle that I received what I believe is the Goddess's greatest gift—a continuously unfolding epiphany: *the Divine dwells in the world with us and within us.* Recognizing that all of Creation is sacred, Mother Nature has served as my greatest spiritual teacher. Like my Euro-indigenous ancestors and in common with indigenous peoples all over the world, I am learning to live in harmony with the Earth. In doing so, I am learning to live in harmony with the Divine as well. But wisdom only has power when it is shared. Although I had earned the title of Priestess in 1983, I became a true Priestess when I began sharing what I had been taught with others. It's a challenge to fulfill a role that's been missing for thousands of years, but it's been an extraordinary experience as a personal, inner journey expanded outward to help create the fastest-growing spiritual movement in the United States, Europe, and Australia.

In 1985, I chose to "come out of the broom closet" as a teacher and an advocate in the courts and the media. In 1998, I was honored by *Jane* magazine as one of the *"Ten Gutsiest Women of the Year,"* along with Hilary Clinton, with the publication of my first memoir, *Book of Shadows*, the story of my discovery of the Divine Feminine. I needed to be gutsy because I was explaining one of the most negative stereotypes in Western culture—the Witch—to the likes of Bill O'Reilly, Anderson Cooper, and the *London Times*. I worked hard to remedy that stereotype, explaining that the word *witch* comes from the old Anglo Saxon term *wicce* (pronounced *witch-a*), meaning a "wise one" or "shaman." Wicca is the modern revival of one of the indigenous traditions of pre-Christian Europe, with practices and values similar to that of Native American and other indigenous traditions.

Why didn't I just abandon the term and call myself a pantheist? Because there's a Witch in every woman. I was determined to challenge the negative stereotype—and the negative stereotypes about women—that grew out of the persecutions of the European Witchcraze. The Witch has been a figure onto which Western culture, and particularly male-dominated religions, have projected their fear of women, our life-giving power, and sexuality. But behind the mask of the hideous hag is the face of the beautiful Goddess, and I knew that the world had nothing to fear. It had only blessings to gain. Countless blessings have come from my refusal to be inhibited by fear. *Book of Shadows* became a best-seller in Italy and Australia, and almost every day someone writes to tell me that my story is her story, that her longings and her experiences have been affirmed. I've written two more books since, also published all over the world, and am working on the fourth. I founded the Temple of Ara, one of the oldest international Wiccan congregations, and I travel the world teaching others how to experience the divinity that dwells within and all around us. I am now a trustee of the Council for the Parliament of the World's Religions, the world's oldest and largest international interfaith organization.

The Goddess has returned. Like a many-faceted jewel dropped into the sea, Her presence is radiating outward in continuously expanding circles. It is we who stand in those circles, wherever we are, by whatever names we have called upon Her, by whatever signs and summonings She has called upon each and everyone of us, and we are responding. I am honored to stand in circle with you, to experience Her wisdom, beauty, power, and grace—and yours. I am grateful to discover new meaning in the words *Thou Art Goddess*.

In my life, I never know what is going to transpire. Seeds of possibilities fly like the milkweed pod bursting open, releasing a thousand white wing wishes on a blustery autumn wind. Storms for these podmates only dare their bold flights to reach further distances. Touching down to earth, these seedroot visions grow even through hard cement cracks or abandoned fields of dreams. Waiting for their bloom, the monarch butterflies find the tender shoots in the sidewalks or empty meadows because life cannot resist itself and there is a hunger for the mother's milk nature gives. There amidst the underbellies of a soft green leaf, a caterpillar knows. She knows. She spins a cocoon streaked with gold more precious than metal, for an oncoming metamorphosis no one can yet see, yet alone believe. You and I are spinning for a future in our hands. We know, that it is time and we are ready, though we may not yet know how.

—ALISA STARKWEATHER, founder of
the Red Tent Movement

Living Our Leadership

Questions

1. How do we create more friendships across demographic boundaries?
2. How can feminine voices of compassion, unity, and hope become more real and compelling than the voices of fear and separation?
3. What does it feel like when we give voice to our strength as women of spirit and faith?
4. Where are the naturally arising opportunities for partnership and synergy?
5. What are the next questions that want to be asked?

Circle Practices

Circles are emerging everywhere. The following are some comments by women who experience circle regularly.

WomenSpirit Circle at Catherine Place

Each Tuesday morning for the past nine years, women gather together at Catherine Place in Tacoma, Washington, for Women-Spirit Circle. Through ritual, inspirational readings, poetry, music, and silence, women explore insights about life and the sacred. In circle, participants are invited into deeper reflection, a renewed sense of their own goodness, and the recognition that each woman possesses the power to create a more just and peaceful world.

On any given Tuesday there may be twelve to twenty-four women. Many are regular attendees; some drop in as they are able. Most arrive a few minutes early for a bit of social time in the kitchen before the group begins. There is fresh coffee and tea available and often snacks. In the meeting room, chairs are arranged in a circle around a low table. The table is the room's focal point, an altar of sorts. It may be draped in a cloth and usually bears at least one candle. It may also hold flowers or other items and images related to the day's theme or the sacred feminine. The day's facilitator calls the circle together. If newcomers are present, as is often the case, the group will begin with a simple introduction, each woman speaking her name in turn. Participants share the group's simple guidelines:

"Every time six women gather in a living room around a candle to speak from their hearts and listen to one another, something happens. An energy is seeded in the universe and spreads out, like ripples in a pond. You can't see where it goes. We are here. We are who we are. Something has shifted in the world. That's all built on the fertile ground of all those fertile conversations, conferences, retreats, and dialogues."

—Participants at a WSF gathering

- This group holds a sacred, safe, confidential space for sharing. What is shared in the circle stays in the circle.
- There is no crosstalk; each woman's sharing stands on its own without comment, question, or problem-solving.
- No one takes a second turn to speak until all have had an opportunity to share; however, no one is obligated to speak; respectful listening is also participation.
- The facilitator offers a meditation or question and invites members of the circle to share their reflections as they feel moved. She may use a poem, an inspirational reading, a piece of music, or an image as a basis for the day's reflections and may or may not include some ritual action. Each week's circle is different.
- The circle meets for about an hour, sometimes going a little over if the sharing warrants it. As the time draws to an end, the facilitator will offer some closing, perhaps brief remarks or another piece of music, and invite the participants to share some sign of peace or blessing as they disperse.

—WomenSpirit Circle at Catherine Place, Tacoma, Washington (www.catherineplace.org)

Circle Tip: How to Start an Open Circle

Open circles are open to all women and girls. At each meeting, circle principles are visible and used. When starting the circle, find two or more women or girls willing to help plan, organize, and facilitate the first circle gathering. Practice circle principles and facilitation on each other, building skills and self-confidence. Find a space that allows for a circle of chairs with a center that will be honored as sacred. This can be a church, library, community center, or home. Advertise your open circle in the local paper and have flyers in public places, so women and girls will know about this wonderful opportunity. Tell Circle Connections (see Resource section) about your circle so we can help you get out the news.

Discuss circle principles at the first gathering and add others if needed, either at the first meeting or along the way. Decide together how often the open circle gatherings are to be held as well as the time, place, and focus. The focus can change depending on the interests of the members. Ask for donations (suggest five dollars) to make the circle sustainable. Use a "talking stick," talk and listen from the heart and without judgment, share the leadership and decisions by consensus. This will empower each woman or girl to contribute to the open circle process.

ANN SMITH, CIRCLE CONNECTIONS
(WWW.CIRCLECONNECTIONS.ORG)

Blessings

Water ceremony. Water is central to the lives of so many women and is one of the issues that connect us globally. This water ceremony can be done with a small circle or a large gathering of three hundred women. Ask every woman to bring a small vial of water from a place that is special to her. Water may be from a vacation to a special place or from a local stream or from her kitchen sink. Place a large bowl at the center of your circle or at the front of the room. At the start of your gathering, have each woman come to the bowl, then speak her name and one sentence about the source of the water as she pours it into the bowl. At the end of the gathering, women come again to the bowl and remove some of the mingled water to take home as a memory of the event.

Anchoring our intentions. Women are asked to write their big dreams and goals on a piece of paper. The group gathers around a fire, and each woman silently places her list into the flames so that the intention can be released into the smoke and intermingled with the dreams of the other women.

How Women Are Leading

Sojourners—Christians for Peace and Justice; www.sojo.net. The mission of this group is to articulate the biblical call to social justice, inspiring hope and building a movement to transform individuals, communities, the church, and the world. the organization includes "God's Politics Blog" and "Faith in Action" campaigns.

Global Women of Faith Network; www.religionsforpeace.org/ initiatives/women/ The organization's mission is to advance the role of religious women in international development, peace-making, postconflict reconstruction; to build the capacity of religious women of faith organizations to engage in peace-building and sustainable development. The network is part of the larger organization known as Religions for Peace.

Leadership Tools

The Global Room for Women; www.globalroomforwomen.com.
The Global Room for Women invites you to step into a warm, inviting virtual living room, "just as you are," to personally meet your global sisters from Central Baghdad, downtown Cairo, rural Kenya, and beyond. Join other amazing women from across North America as we pick up our phones in a live, personal, and interactive teleconference with women from cultures very different from our own. Our global guests share their uplifting personal stories and breakthrough work as we dialogue directly and personally about their lives and share ours. Many come to our calls eager to jump right into the conversations—others come and just listen. Most of us come because we know there is much to learn from our global sisters and discover for ourselves how much we also have in common.

"I have been in a women's sacred circle for the past five years. We gather at every solstice and equinox, to reflect upon the changing seasons and to support one another through the ebb and flow of our lives. We always start with a potluck supper and then move into circle, each lighting a candle and speaking a few words to presence ourselves in the circle. It is a precious part of my life—a safe space that holds me through both my joyful and my challenging moments."

—Kathe Schaaf

In a world filled with sound bites, packaged news, easy stereotypes, and dramatic sensationalism—we often long for places where we can have simple, honest, and real "woman to woman" conversations. At a cellular level we are looking for a place to have important conversations about our path as emerging global women. We know we are about much more than the worldview of the culture in which we live—and the way through to greater understanding of ourselves and what is really going on in the world through the lens of women is to talk with our global sisters! Join us. We are waiting to greet you in our growing global community of women! To learn more, contact Linda Higdon, founder of the Global Room at linda@global-roomforwomen.com.

The Gaiafield Project; www.gaiafield.net. This project links subtle activists for collective healing and social change. Subtle activism is an activity of consciousness or spirit, such as prayer, meditation, or ecstatic dance, intended to support collective healing and social change. Subtle activism grows from the idea that there are many effective ways—some newly emerging, many as old as humanity—to positively influence social change other than overt political action. Subtle activism might include the following:

- Spiritual practices such as prayer, meditation, chant, and sacred movement
- A process of bringing up to consciousness ancient wounds and limiting patterns of thought inherited from our collective history (for example, racism, sexism, heterosexism, and anthropocentrism)
- A global event in which hundreds of thousands of people around the planet unite in silence and prayers for world peace
- Collective deep listening to discern how a group may best serve collective healing or social change

Holding Space

The function of space holder is as real and necessary as any other form of service or activism that assists in healing and transforming self, others, and the world, but our culture does not place much value on such intangible actions. Holding space is, at its essence, feminine. Although every human being is born with the potential to offer this gift to others, women—for a variety of cultural, physical, and spiritual reasons—can more easily access this potential within them. Holding space arises from the energy of yin, the feminine. It requires receptivity and stillness, a willingness to open to surrendering, a

"My women's circle meets every Tuesday afternoon, here in Nevada City, California. We call ourselves Women Awakening and are supporting one another in living our lives from a place of allowing and surrender in order to experience the love and spaciousness that we are and to allow our creativity to flourish."

—Carolyn Anderson

deep listening—both from the heart and from the gut—the womb space, if you will. Holding space requires a loving acceptance and attention without expectations, so that a sense of containment is created that is secure yet spacious enough for what Spirit wants to occur within it.

For quite some time humanity has been driven more by the energy of yang, the more masculine energy expressions of acting and speaking, of moving and deciding. But if we look to nature, we see that both ways are needed. When things are in harmony, there is a balance, a beautiful natural dance of the two. In order for new life to arrive and move into the outer world—whether it be a child, a flower, or a paradigm-shifting idea, it first has to be held in stillness and safety, in patient waiting and unknowing, while it is nourished and given time to evolve. Whether it is the earth cradling a seed in its soil or a lioness carrying a cub in her belly or a person cherishing a dream in his heart, there is a need for the one who is the cradler, the carrier, the cherisher. When we hold space, we open to that oneness, creating a container that embraces inner and outer, spiritual and secular, the ineffable and the tangible.

THE LORD'S PRAYER AS TRANSLATED FROM ORIGINAL ARAMAIC

O cosmic Birther of all radiance and vibration.
Soften the ground of our being and carve out a space
within us where your Presence can abide.

Fill us with your creativity so that we may be
empowered to bear the fruit of your mission.

Let each of our actions bear fruit in accordance with our
desire.

Endow us with the wisdom to produce and share what
each being needs to grow and flourish.

Untie the tangled threads of destiny that bind us, as we
release others from the entanglement of past mistakes.

Do not let us be seduced by that which would divert us from our true purpose, but illuminate the opportunities of the present moment.

For you are the ground and the fruitful vision, the birth, power and fulfillment, as all is gathered and made whole once again.

—ROBERT BARTON AND ANNIE MCGREGOR[3]

Reflecting on the Pattern

(Editors' Note: The following are reflections by the editors of *Women, Spirituality and Transformative Leadership* on the process, content, and feelings stirred by the voices in this book.)

Written in My Bones

KATHE SCHAAF

As I reflect on the pattern of women's wisdom in this book, I am intrigued by the way the stories and the voices of these richly diverse North American women interweave with my own story. I am left even more curious about the holographic nature of our Universe. Although it is vitally important for us to collectively explore big questions and make big commitments in the face of the big challenges that confront our planet, the real transformation seems to happen in the microcosm. I live out my deeply personal story and find myself in a moment having a profound lived experience of my true place in the Divine plan. For just a moment there is clarity amid the chaos; a light goes on and it all makes perfect sense. This book is full of stories about such moments. The tipping point we have all talked about for so long may occur as a vast new constellation of hope made visible as those lights come on in another and another and another of us.

The exact nature of my own light is defined in part by my history: I am a white woman of European descent whose ancestors settled in central Wisconsin when they immigrated from Germany, Holland, and Sweden. I grew up in a city of ten thousand people, a county seat surrounded by flat farm fields and hardwood forest stretching in every direction as far as I could possibly imagine. My family was what is now called a "nuclear family": a mother and father (who are still lovingly and happily married after sixty-four years) and three children (all girls). My father worked in a paper mill for forty-seven years, and my mother went to work part-time when my youngest sister started school. We attended a Wisconsin Synod Lutheran Church, in which I was baptized and where I studied for my confirmation. I left that church behind when I went to college and spent a decade of my life not thinking about spiritual things.

I found my way back to "spirituality" following a crooked path that began with a crisis, moved through various new age explorations and a brief return with my own family to a Lutheran church to anchor my own children in a spiritual life, and eventually landing me in the loving lap of the Sacred Feminine. I began to experience the sacred as it is lived out in the cyclical nature of the seasons and the waning of the moon. I began to crave a spiritual tradition more connected to the Earth and sacred stories told with female pronouns. I began to weave simple ceremonies in circles with other women, using prayers and altars and the four elements of air, water, earth, and fire. I did not have any ancestors to teach me these ways, so I taught myself by watching others and listening to my own inner voices. I borrowed the wisdom of another woman's indigenous grandmother because I could not find a connection to my own.

During this time I first glimpsed my divine assignment as a weaver of the pattern of the women's wisdom, a gatherer of women at the intersection of spirituality and leadership. As I began working with women and women's organizations and sitting in sacred circles, I kept hearing a compelling message repeated by indigenous wisdom keepers and healers: the healing of our world must begin with the Western women. I've been listening to this message for almost a decade, long before the Dalai Lama's now famous pronouncement. I have pondered this message from various vantage points. It makes sense that Western women would have a great resource to offer the world at this time; large numbers of them have economic stability, education, and freedom to a degree that their sisters in other parts of the world could not dream. The post–World War II baby-boom generation is a huge demographic bubble of women who also have the luxury of time as they are coming to the end of both their child-centered years and their traditional careers. Imagine the impact if even 10 percent of those women were to commit some of their creativity, energy, and resources to the global challenge about which they are most passionate.

Yet there is something even deeper and more mysterious beneath these words "the world will be saved by the Western woman." It can be traced directly back to my ancient European ancestors and a broken spiritual lineage that has left me and many of my Western sisters with no access to our original spiritual roots. At one time my ancestors were the indigenous people living on the plains and steppes of northern Europe. Their spiritual lives were Earth-centered, and their wisdom and stories were passed from one generation to the next as oral tradition. The women had special wisdom—how to heal with herbs, how to work with the cycles of the moon, how to midwife the birth and ease the transition to death—which was an important part of the pattern of life for the community. As a daughter, I would have been taught the ways of my grandmothers. I would have learned the skills, and I would have witnessed respect and even reverence for the wisdom of the feminine.

The through-line of my spiritual heritage took a very different turn when Christianity, patriarchy, politics, and economics converged to rain down upon the old religions of Europe. A series of events spanning hundreds of years resulted in successfully severing those spiritual threads. Women took the brunt of this assault. There is great debate about the actual numbers of women killed during the Burning Times (ranging from fifty thousand to nine million), the actual number of years the purge lasted (from the fourteenth to the eighteenth century, with the majority tried between 1550 and 1650), and the actual perpetrators of the violence (was it the Catholic Church or local community courts—or was there a difference in 1600?). However many women died, for however long, and at whose hand—it was enough. It was enough to silence the voice of feminine wisdom, to sever women from their natural spiritual authority, and to leave most of Europe with a God defined and described only as masculine.

I was only vaguely aware of this history for the first fifty years of my life. As I became more awake to the details of the story, a new set of questions began to vibrate within me. Could this story of my ancestors be written in my bones and encoded in my cellular memory? What if this story triggered a sudden fear that would immobilize or sabotage me when I had an exciting opportunity to lead … or be visible … or an opportunity for my voice to be heard … or to form the hint of a real friendship with another woman? How many other women may have the same story written in their bones?

Maybe this is the real frontier for Western women at the intersection of spirituality and leadership—to first individually and then collectively overcome the fear that is written in our bones so that we can reclaim our natural spiritual authority and bring our gifts of loving leadership to this struggling planetary family before it is too late. Maybe this is why—and how—the world could be saved by Western women.

In Transition

KAY LINDAHL

Reflecting on the pattern of what we have read in this book takes me back to December 2009, to Melbourne, Australia. I was standing in a large hallway at the top of the escalators talking to a friend of mine from Chile. Kathe Schaaf signaled that she wanted to talk to me. When my friend left, Kathe turned to me and said, "Kay, we need to talk when we get back home. We have work to do together—to see what is emerging for women of spirit and faith after this Parliament." Part of me knew immediately that she was right. Another part was reminding me that I had promised myself not to take on anything new—I had enough on my plate. So I said something like, "Sure, I'll be glad to talk and support you—maybe as a consultant, but I'm not taking on new projects at this point in my life." Thank goodness Kathe heard this as a *yes*. You know the rest of the story.

The next level of reflection kept leading me to the word *transition*. It seems to me that we are all in a state of transition at this moment in time—from the micro to the macro. For me *transition* means a change—from something or somewhere to a different something or somewhere. It's about movement, a shifting, action. It can be scary, exciting, painful, joyful—the whole range of our emotional repertoire is possible. Some transitions are inevitable; others happen because of the choices we make.

One of the inevitable transitions happens during the birth process. I learned about this when I was studying to be a registered nurse and later had the personal experience of giving birth to five children. We are told that transition is the most difficult phase of labor and delivery. It is that time between—just before the baby is ready to be pushed out. It seems as though the labor is going to go on forever, you are tired, the contractions are intense, and you simply want to give up. Then transition occurs and the next stage begins—and the baby is born. I'll never forget witnessing my first delivery as an observer. It was so clear when the transition stage started and ended. The miracle of seeing the baby take its first breath and the total joy and amazement of the mother as she finally holds her baby in her arms was an experience that stays with me to this day, more than fifty-five years later. You can imagine what it was like when I was the woman giving birth.

I use *transition* as a metaphor in all kinds of situations. Whenever I feel like giving up on something or when I feel stuck, I ask myself, *Is this just a transition? Do I simply need to stick with it a little bit longer to get to the next point?* These questions also work in group settings, when things seem to be at a standstill. I have learned that it isn't possible to force transitions. They happen at their own pace. You may have heard the story of the little child who was watching a butterfly emerge from its cocoon. It was struggling and struggling to get out. Finally the child couldn't stand it anymore and carefully removed the cocoon. Unfortunately, when the butterfly tried to fly, it couldn't and so died. The struggle to emerge is what strengthens the butterfly's wings so they will be ready to support flying. How many times is that true for us in our own struggles?

Transition is also a useful metaphor when looking at the larger picture. Where are we stuck in our community, country, culture, even globally? Reading the stories throughout this collection and reflecting on where we are as women of spirit and faith at this time and in this place lead me to believe that we are in a very particular transition phase. There is uncertainty. There is a sense that something wants to happen, yet we don't know exactly what that means. We know we have choices to make about the way we live our lives. We are not always sure we are making the right choices. We are on the cusp of a transformational shift in the way leadership is perceived. We don't know exactly what that looks like. We are in the midst of massive changes in how we view power, success, what it means to be a woman or a man. There is a lot of chaos when so much change is happening.

One thing I know about chaos is that it is a sign that we are in for transformation of one sort or another. It can be very unsettling. It can lead to deep polarization—those who embrace change and those who are uncomfortable with change. Even for those of us who look forward to change find that when things get tough, we tend to go back to our default drive—the way we know, the familiar. It takes courage to move forward, to stay in action. What I learned from the women throughout the editing of this book is that we are moving forward.

Yes, there is work to do.

Yes, we need to heal our wounds.

Yes, we need to be more intentional about supporting each other.

Yes, we need to claim our voices.

Yes, we need to express ourselves as women of spirit and faith in a world that is hungry for meaning.

Yes, we need to see ourselves as equal partners with men as we move toward balancing power.

Throughout this process I have watched my youngest granddaughter transition from a babe in arms to a walking ten-month-old. First she learned to sit, then crawl, now walk. Each step has reminded me of the inevitability of growth and change. There was no way to impede her progress. Seeing her learn to balance, fall, get up, balance over and over again without thinking she was a failure every time she sat down was a real lesson! She still stumbles and falls from time to time, but she is moving and exploring and so open to life, the falls don't stop her.

My personal journey since that day in Melbourne has been nothing short of extraordinary. I am in my seventies now ("sensational seventies" is my moniker for this decade), and life is even more amazing. My job is to stay centered and open to possibility, which I call divine guidance, and to say *yes* to that guidance. My prayer for all of us is that we continue to surrender to transition, embrace change, and expect miracles.

❖

On Being Advocates, Activists, and Alchemists

Exploring Power on the Way Forward

Kathleen S. Hurty, PhD

The journey through and beyond the Alchemy gathering catalyzed, for many of us, our collective transformational power as women of spirit and faith. How then do we move from personal reflection on the links between leadership and power to an active new worldview of women leaders building communities of compassion and service empowered by the Divine Feminine? What is the power-filled way forward to become alchemists of creative change? I use my own story of struggle in graduate school more than two decades ago to share the difficult journey toward redefining power. I wanted to expand the definition of power by taking into account the experiences of women principals. Some on my academic committee did not understand—*power is power, period,* they said; *you can't expand the definition.* Surprising, I thought, at a major research university. I became angry, felt ignored, defeated, frustrated. I did not know how to communicate the profound excitement I had when my field research among women leaders in the schools clearly showed an exciting array of new power definitions. It seemed as though the limited definition of power had won the day.

It became clear to me that those voices of "powerful" women leading in schools could not, should not, be ignored. So I sought out new mentors who could understand what I was trying to do, who were willing to work with me in the process. My search was for the elements of power these women principals used. I wanted to analyze the concepts drawn from my conversations with them that would differentiate power options, beyond the hierarchical forms most familiar within institutions of the day. I was searching for the kind of power we know exists but do not know how to name. This kind of power, perhaps more common to women's experience and predilection, could bring about a fresh paradigm of connectedness and collaboration, a novel way of working together for the common good. The effect could be transformative!

Elements of this cocreative and coactive power, harvested from the wit and wisdom of women leaders, will lead us into the future. We are catalyzed by connectedness. True collaboration is a profoundly ethical way of working together and has been shown to be effective. The elements of power these women exemplify include the following:[4]

1. Emotional energy
2. Reciprocal talk
3. Pondered mutuality
4. Nurtured growth
5. Collaborative change

These commonsense elements of collective transformational power are not gender limited but are clearly accessible to all leaders choosing to activate change!

This is the power of collaboration, of connectedness, of compromise and compassion. In other words, it is power *with*, not power *over*. The kind of power that was used by these women was a generous, plentiful power. Many people think of power as something to hang on to—a *finite* resource, meaning if I have more, you have less. But these women used power as an *infinite* resource, the kind that draws people together across boundaries for shared effort and takes no credit for singular achievement. This kind of power actually has a long history. It is as old as harems and gossip, midwifery, drumming circles, and quilting groups. It is as contemporary as feminist leadership approaches, women's writing collectives, and collaborative women in executive positions. Naming and claiming this kind of power is one way to join the journey into the future of transformational leadership.

There is a developing paradigm shift around contemporary understandings of power, especially when we look at organizations led by women. In her research and collection of the stories of nonprofit executive women, theological educator Katharine Henderson finds a clear picture of progressive principles of public leadership.

A Profile of Progressive Leadership

Ethic of relationship

- Emphasizes hospitality, nurturing, and interdependent connection.
- Understands justice as a right relationship.

Ethic of inclusiveness

- Values diversity and pluralism, especially including those persons whom society might wish to ignore or reject.
- Prefers a collaborative process.

Belief in the possibility of transformation

- Practices an alchemical understanding of darkness, embracing the rejected cornerstone as a starting place for healing.
- Works along a personal/systemic continuum, believing that individuals and systems alike can change.
- Trusts and emphasizes a grassroots process.

Entrepreneurial spirit

- Feels a sense of agency, convinced that one's actions make a difference in the world.
- Chooses to take risks and work at the margins of social structures, offering fresh patterns of thinking and behavior.

Ethic of seamlessness

- Bridges realms often kept separate, such as public-private, sacred-secular.
- Emphasizes integrity—the coherence between belief and practice in both self and organization.
- Enjoys a sense of vocation—the feeling that one's work sponsors wholeness for both the self and the world at large.

Resistance faith

- Called to alleviate suffering, oppression, and injustice.
- Feels responsibility to resist evil, not simply avoid it.
- Serves as a conscience in the body politic, critiquing mainstream values and structures.
- Relies on inner authority, not necessarily the values mediated by the external authorities, either ecclesial or secular.
- Reclaims radical-root understandings of religious teachings.[5]

Henderson's analysis builds on a deeply reflective understanding of women and power. She calls these women "God's troublemakers" and is of the firm and grounded view that women of spirit and faith will indeed change the world. This is power in the *service without subservience* mode. Power-filled leadership of this sort fits well within my theological understanding, for it draws on a generous, sharable kind of power akin in my faith perspective to the power of the Holy Spirit. It is free-flowing power that grows when used generously rather than hoarded. Power *with* as in "creative coaction with Spirit" is a form of faith-endowed collaboration. It is a remarkable resource for justice and social transformation. Henderson writes: "Being in relationship to an energy called God, as revealed through many different religious traditions, calls us to live together pursuing justice, mercy and peace. These are the organizing principles of a moral social fabric."[6]

Collective transformational power flows from the energy of the Divine Feminine. God as Mother nurtures us, listens to our cries for help and our songs of joy, challenges us to become compassionate advocates for justice, and teaches us the alchemy of shared power. As we form circles of compassion in our own communities, we take on shared commitments to work coactively toward that which nourishes the human family—choosing among the challenges of these times. We may focus on care of the earth, on understanding among diverse cultures and religions, on peace-making in communities, or on strengthening education and health care. Whatever work we choose, we will build on shared wisdom and insights—the creative synergy that brings about powerful collective transformation.

There is a burgeoning movement of women of spirit and faith connecting, acting together, transforming the way power works in the world. It is the start of a new day dawning! We are advocates, activists, and alchemists of a new worldview. We bring our brilliant insights, our driving passion, our cherished commitments into this unboundaried movement we call women of spirit and faith—leading toward a transformed future.

Ever-Evolving Women
of Spirit and Faith
Naming, Doing, and Be-ing

REVEREND GUO CHEEN

Naming

The year was 1968. The nation was divided, bereft, and anguished. In the aftermath of Martin Luther King Jr.'s assassination, an elementary school class in a small Iowa town was deliberately segregated into the blue-eyed and the brown-eyed. The blue-eyed children teased and taunted the brown-eyed children without reprimand. The brown-eyed children could not drink from the water fountain or enjoy recess. All students made to feel superior scored higher on tests that day. Most children made to feel inferior remained on the sidelines, simply relieved that someone else was being picked on rather than them for the time being.

One little girl with freckles and big brown eyes frowned at her teacher's reproach that she was bad because of her eye color and for that she would be shunned by the blue-eyed students. A boy with deep blue eyes "felt happy like a king" as he readily assumed the role of a taunter who freely let out his pent-up anger at any brown-eyed child he wished. Jane Elliott, the authority figure in this classroom, designated the blue-eyed group superior and the brown-eyed inferior (for the first day; the roles switched the next day) as a way of introducing racial discrimination and experiencing walking in the moccasins of another. All the children and teachers who underwent this controversial exercise as described in *A Class Divided* recall how difficult it was to be one of the inferior individuals but recommend that all adults try this drill. Some, however, indicated they would not want their own children to undergo it for fear of psychological damage to young ones.[7]

The lessons I draw from this experiment include the banality of cruelty, schisms, and the Pygmalion effect. As an Asian American Buddhist nun, I am the recipient of (and frequently a rebel against) overt and covert social messaging about my inadequacies and hence apply these lessons to gender, age, class, religion, and other categories, too. It is with this set of lenses that I notice who is missing at the table, including the time I headed for the 2009 Parliament of the World's Religions and observed that the only continent without an active interfaith women's network was North America. Feminist theologians I have met remark on how critical it is to name the feminine face of God and to use and add to the vocabulary of the sacred feminine. For myself, until I heard the stories of young Sikh American Valarie Kaur (included in this volume), I could not identify and properly articulate many of my experiences and the complex emotions surrounding them. Furthermore, other than changing language, it is important to change the authority that slaps on the labels and ask ourselves when we hear any story:

Who is telling the story?

Who is broadcasting the story?

Who is underlining emphases in any fact, fiction, or moral to the story?

Doing

Sometimes it takes a visionary to identify a problem, even a glaringly obvious one. There is genius in someone who recognizes the urgent need for Western women (of all colors and persuasions) to answer the call as spiritual leaders. At the cusp of a humanity's spiritual crisis, women of spirit and faith need to take action on that vision. This requires *doing*, be it via power struggles, politics, or redefining the paths to power. This is partly what our organization Women of Spirit and Faith is about, acting in concert with women, engaging in activities and interactions that encourage power redefined, and making the world (particularly the world of faith and spirit) more balanced and equitable.

Moreover, Women of Spirit and Faith takes an approach that is decidedly about aligning actions with the unfolding of the divine—vision as a force for change rather than an obsession over its realization. As the management guru Peter Senge has put it, "It's not what the vision is, it's what the vision does." He continues, "What happens may not be exactly as you imagined it in your vision, but what happens would otherwise not have happened. You could hold a vision of a genuine perfection in some domain and, although you might never realize that vision, you might also achieve things that would have never been achieved otherwise."[8] Women of Spirit and Faith, for instance, invited twenty-five diverse women leaders to an intimate leadership retreat before the planning of its larger conference. Heated conversations about race and power structures at the retreat raised concerns; however, the organizers heard and acted on that critical need, regarding it as guidance and necessary next steps in the organization's course. At its later and much larger gathering, women from a variety of different backgrounds held hands as they celebrated in song and reveled in each other's unique spiritual journeys. Friendships were made across boundaries, and feedback affirms that many felt seen, heard, and valued. This was an intention that manifested itself in a way that was more fulfilling than any of us could have envisioned.

Be-ing

Women have always been very good at doing, nonstop. In expanding and redefining power and empowerment, women of spirit and faith need to abide in the depth of the Source, ultimately empowering ourselves by fulfilling our spiritual hunger. To me, this requires more awareness, pausing and letting go, including at times the ill-fitting labels. When we are fully steeped in our inherent nature of wisdom and compassion, we are permeated with power, a sacred inner strength and wholeness. Defining *power* in this way and adapting from the principle of interbeing in the Flower Garland Sutra, I offer the following as realizations embodied in a spiritual transformative leader:[9]

1. The empowerment of one *woman of spirit and faith* embodies, consists of, and constitutes empowerment for many others.
2. Power in one woman of spirit and faith does not, and does not have to, negate the power of another. The whole is greater than the sum of its parts with regard to the empowerment of women of spirit and faith.
3. A balance of many roles in different aspects of her life—whether as a mother and daughter at home, a spiritual leader and beneficiary in the community, or an executive and subordinate at work—some of which can seem inconsistent or at least varied, yet all are congruent at the soul level.

4. Versatility, flexibility, and a willingness to play whether she is leading from out front, supporting from behind, or in a circle with others.

5. The circumstances she faces and the characteristics of those circumstances are all divine and about the divine.

6. At the heart and depth of her is an expansive and hindrance-free peace.

7. Intimate knowledge of power and experiences of power. She acknowledges that the power is in us, the power is with us.

8. Her personal transformation where grace meets power is increasingly visible and palpable across dimensions of time and space. Her spiritual transformation makes an impact in another part of the globe and into the future readily. Furthermore, she leaves an imprint in the consciousness of all connected beings and our collective consciousness past, present, and future.

8.5 Transformations occur as she brings out the sacred in each being, starting with herself.

An empowered woman of spirit and faith is like a candle—when one is lit, countless flames light up the world around her; her world reflects her, infinitely. A deep sense of interdependence likened to that of Indra's Net—each pearl's sheen reflects and multiplies the radiance of other pearls—informs her naming, doing, and being.

May I soon see you in me and you see me in you.

Transformative Leadership

Kathe Schaaf, Kay Lindahl, Kathleen S. Hurty, PhD, Reverend Guo Cheen

As we come to the end of this journey, it seems a good time to pause for a moment and reflect on this topic of women, spirituality, and transformative leadership. We have heard the stories, voices, and experiences of richly diverse women who are living their spiritual leadership in the world; each voice is distinct and yet there are threads that connect them all into a powerful and compelling pattern. What have we learned about new models of leadership grounded in feminine principles and lived in the world with grace and power? What is being asked of you as an individual woman looking for ways to make a meaningful contribution at this time in your life? How do women begin to collectively step into the opportunities before us now in the most powerful way and with the most impact? How do we find our way forward, together, for the greater good?

Once again, we do not need to have all the answers to these questions. All we need is curiosity, some safe spaces to have deeper conversations with others, and the capacity to listen with our hearts open. Answers take root in such rich soil, and we find ourselves launched into exciting new frontiers of leadership led by spirit and fueled by our own passions. What does transformative leadership look like? Throughout this collection you have witnessed personal examples of leadership in action and seen glimpses of fresh models for collective action. We offer one final example of how women and women-led organizations are defining and living new models of leadership.

One Organization's Experiment in Collaborative Leadership

Women of Spirit and Faith is organized using a unique model of collaborative leadership. Our core circle of four women has had an active and generative first year, which included hosting two successful gatherings for more than 180 North American women spiritual leaders. We have received our designation as a 501(c)(3) nonprofit corporation, written several successful grant proposals, developed organizational relationships with more than twenty networking partners, launched a Young Leaders Council, and been offered a book contract—all without a traditional organizational chart, any paid staff, or Robert's Rules of Order.

How do we work together, sharing leadership and responsibilities? How do we make decisions and generate outcomes? Our process relies on several important feminine principles:

- Our most fundamental core principle is that we are all invited and encouraged to *lead*. Each contributes according to her own gifts, talents, resources, and availability. Each is invited to do what she does best, and then we collectively watch for how those individual offerings fit together into a cohesive whole greater than the sum of its parts. One of us functions as the weaver of the group—convening calls, tracking the details of projects, serving as a communication and administration hub. Another brings a valuable expertise in grant writing and administration. One of us is much more adept at Internet technology and takes the lead on social media, blogs, and online networking. One of us is a master listener, who has taught us all how to listen better to one another, to women everywhere, and to our individual and collective divine guidance.

> "Believe in your own leadership as a precious gift where grace meets power."
> —Participant at a WSF gathering

- We open every conference call and meeting with a prayer, asking for divine guidance, and offering ourselves in service.
- We follow the flow of grace as it shows up moment to moment.
- We sometimes take a pause, waiting and listening for ideas, opportunities, and invitations to show up as clues about our next steps.
- When we get a "no," we understand that we are somehow headed in the wrong direction and it is a good time to look for other ideas.
- We make every attempt to be honest and loving in our interactions. We do have challenging experiences, times when we face conflict and strong differences of opinion. We have found it works best to speak our truth in the moment and to stay with the conversation all the way through to an emotional resolution. Being attentive to a healthy process is actually more important than any outcome.
- We live in different cities many miles apart, so we rely upon conference calls to do much of our work together. We use the same circle principles on the phone that we do in person—and we make a commitment to meeting in person as often as

possible. There is no substitute for the hugs, laughter, and deep conversation that happen when we are together.

- We trust our intuition and witness that it is even stronger when we are together than when we are apart.
- We expect that there will be an ebb and flow to the pattern of our individual participation. It's a fact of life for women that health, family, and community will call us away from our work occasionally; we know that each of us will have times when we have to step back from our responsibilities to take care of these commitments. If one of us misses a call or meeting, the others are empowered to move ahead for the good of the organization.
- We have had the experience several times that Women of Spirit and Faith has grown exponentially in a short period of time and that our entire reality has shifted—very much like a ball of warm yeasty dough rising so fast that it has broken the bowl. We notice our first reaction often is a wish to patch that bowl back together with superglue and squeeze the dough back in. Then we exhale and realize what a waste of time and precious energy that would be! Such times may call for a pause to reflect and then a flurry of activity to create a new bigger space that welcomes women's gifts and offerings.
- We express gratitude and appreciation to one another and to Spirit. We celebrate joyfully our abundance.

Engaging with Women of Spirit and Faith

The intent of our organization, Women of Spirit and Faith (WSF), is to invite the many brilliant threads of women's spiritual leadership into relationship and to support emerging transformations. Here are some of the current threads and initiatives.

The Young Leaders Council of WSF

Young women are a vital part of the emerging pattern of global spiritual leadership. This is an excellent time to support and nurture the leadership of young women in seminaries and universities, starting young families and launching careers, in feminist organizations and faith-based communities. At a time when the "stained-glass ceiling" hampers full participation of women in religious communities all over the globe, when women make up only 16 percent of elected officials in the Congress of the United States, and when women struggle to bring their feminine leadership qualities into hierarchal organizations, it is essential to lift up, encourage, and learn from the next generation of feminists, religious pluralist theologians, thought-leaders, and grassroots activists.[10] The Young Leaders Council of the WSF creates unique events and projects to build connection and nurture the leadership of young women. For more information, contact Alisa Roadcup (alisa.roadcup@mac.com).

The Mentoring Project

As we've listened to women of all ages and from diverse backgrounds, many share a yearning for mentoring. One of our Young Leaders expressed it this way: "I want to take all of the good instincts in me, all of the parts of me that haven't been totally twisted by the past thirty years, and give them space and support to grow. But … I need someone to model it for me. Sure, I could make it up as I go along, and I suppose much of what I will do will be just muddling along—after all, no generation ever copies the last one exactly—but what I have learned in the last year is how much easier that can be when I can watch others who are also walking the path and have covered more ground than I have."

WSF's Mentoring Project offers opportunities for a sharing of experience and a way to support each other as we come out into the world. Previously defined primarily as a one-way exchange from elder to younger, WSF sees women looking for a mutual exchange of wisdom and support. Seasoned leaders have just as much to gain from their relationships with young women. This mutual exchange of wisdom and support can occur in a variety of creative ways: in mentoring circles or in one-on-one intergenerational pairs of elder and younger or as pairs of peers with shared passions. For more information, contact Laura Paskell-Brown (laurapb@gmail.com).

Local WSF Circles

We believe in the value of coming together with other women in circles. You are invited to create a local WSF circle and join us in our exploration of the questions at the intersection of spirituality and women's leadership. The WSF website (www.womenofspiritandfaith.org) offers information about how to start your own circle and how to connect with other circles. For more information, contact Kay Lindahl (thelisteningcenter@yahoo.com).

Parliament of the World's Religions 2014

Women of Spirit and Faith was born at the 2009 Parliament of the World's Religions in Melbourne, Australia. We are very excited about the opportunities to make women's leadership visible at the 2014 Parliament in Brussels. We will be launching several new initiatives to build the stream of feminine leadership headed for Brussels. For more information, contact Kathe Schaaf (katheschaaf@cox.net).

WSF in Canada

A new initiative to engage and connect Canadian women was born at "The Alchemy of Our Spiritual Leadership: Women Redefining Power" in 2011. This emerging pattern of women is welcome to all. Learn more about how to get engaged at www.womenofspiritandfaith.org, or contact Louise Mangan (mangan.louise@gmail.com).

CLOSING BLESSING

Once again we call upon the Ancestors of Turtle Island, upon all the Sacred Directions, Father Sky, and Mother Earth. Creator, God, we humbly ask you for strength and courage to speak up against injustice, greed, and the destruction of our sacred water, air, and earth. We pray that all women respectfully guide the men, standing side by side, balancing the energies of compassion, generosity, and love. We pray that all nations join together in unity and peace. We ask for help to remember to be true human beings, to live in goodness for humanity and all living things. Please guide our decisions and actions to help heal our Earth Mother so that peace and love will await our next generations. May you bless us so that we will always choose to think through our hearts.

Pilamaya Tunkasila, Wakan Tanka. Mitakuye Oyasin,

To all my relations, may you walk in the Light of the Great Spirit.
—RACHELLE FIGUEROA, Sundancer and founder,
the Morning Star Foundation

RESOURCES AND NETWORKS

This is not a complete list but a glimpse of the wealth of resources available to help you explore the rich field of women, spirituality, and transformative leadership. New organizations are forming constantly, and existing ones are shifting. This list includes interfaith organizations, women's organizations, networks for young leaders, seminaries, educational organizations, and so on.

Circle and Dialogue Resources

Circle Connections
www.circleconnections.com

The mission of Circle Connections is to foster the empowerment and connection of women and girls to start, sustain, and unite circles that are dedicated to take action for the greater good.

Conversation Café
www.conversationcafe.org

At Conversation Cafés, people learn together how to create a culture of conversation—which is a culture of intelligence, peace, and political awareness.

Millionth Circle
www.millionthcircle.org

This organization seeks to seed and nurture circles, wherever possible, in order to cultivate equality, sustainable livelihoods, preservation of the earth, and peace for all; to bring the circle process into United Nations–accredited nongovernmental organizations and the Fifth United Nations World Conference on Women; and to connect circles so they may know themselves as a part of a larger movement to shift consciousness in the world.

PeerSpirit

www.peerspirit.com

PeerSpirit offers a bounty of resources, including the gift of down-loadable PDF circle guidelines on their website in multiple languages.

Public Conversations Project

www.publicconversations.org

This project seeks to prevent or transform conflict driven by deep differences in identity, beliefs, or values.

World Café

www.theworldcafe.com

World Café Conversations are an intentional way to create a living network of conversation around questions that matter. A Café Conversation is a creative process for leading collaborative dialogue, sharing knowledge, and creating possibilities for action in groups of all sizes.

Environment/Ecology

Bioneers—Women's Leadership

www.bioneers.org

Bioneers are social and scientific innovators from all walks of life and disciplines who have peered deep into the heart of living systems to understand how nature operates, and to mimic "nature's operating instructions" to serve human ends without harming the web of life. One focus of their work is women's leadership.

The Forum on Religion and Ecology at Yale

www.fore.research.yale.edu

The Forum is engaged in exploring religious worldviews, texts, and ethics in order to broaden understanding of the complex nature of current environmental concerns.

Pachamama Alliance

www.pachamama.org

This alliance works to empower indigenous people of the Amazon rain forest to preserve their lands and culture and, using insights gained from that work, to educate and inspire individuals everywhere to bring forth a thriving, just, and sustainable world.

Women's Earth Alliance (WEA)

www.womensearthalliance.org

Women's Earth Alliance partners with community-based organizations globally to create local solutions to issues of water, food, land, and climate change by providing women with trainings, resources, and advocacy support.

Interfaith Organizations

Council for a Parliament of the World's Religions

www.parliamentofreligions.org

The Council for a Parliament of the World's Religions was created to cultivate harmony among the world's religious and spiritual communities and to foster their engagement with the world and its guiding institutions to achieve a just, peaceful, and sustainable world. Women of Spirit and Faith was born at the 2009 Parliament of the World's Religions in Melbourne, Australia.

Global Peace Initiative of Women (GPIW)

www.gpiw.org

The Global Peace Initiative of Women was founded to help awaken and mobilize spiritual energies in places of great need with the goal of aiding in healing and unifying the world community.

Groundswell

www.groundswell-movement.org

Groundswell fuels a movement for justice that transcends partisan politics. They generate open-source social action campaigns that unite people from all walks of life around shared moral imperatives. A rising generation is hungry for a multifaith movement that's not just about a single issue or political party, but a shared moral vision for a better world.

Interfaith Center at the Presidio

www.interfaith-presidio.org

Never has the need for healthy cross-culture relationships been greater. The Interfaith Center at the Presidio has historical commitment to healing and peace-making within, between, and among religious and spiritual traditions. The center's mission is to welcome, serve, and celebrate the diverse faith traditions and spiritual wisdom of the Bay Area.

Interspiritual Centre of Vancouver

www.interspiritualcentre.org

Interspiritual Centre of Vancouver believes the time has come to bring our traditions and communities together to share one house, just as we all share this very earth. They are building a shared sacred space in Vancouver, British Columbia. More than ten different traditions are working harmoniously together to make this vision a reality.

North American Interfaith Network (NAIN)

www.nain.org

North American Interfaith Network aims to build bridges of interfaith understanding, cooperation, and service. The network was envisioned by a group of leaders from existing interfaith councils in the United States and Canada from 1985–1987. In 1990, a constitution for the network was approved and they were incorporated as a nonprofit organization in New York. NAIN continues to sponsor conferences, now familiarly called "Connects," and also networks member interfaith organizations via their website and online newsletter, *NAINews*.

Odyssey Networks

www.odysseynetworks.org

Odyssey Networks is the nation's largest multifaith coalition dedicated to promoting tolerance, peace, and social justice through the production and distribution of media. Odyssey's membership includes more than sixty faith groups and organizations. A list of member faith groups and organizations is available in the member section on the website. Odyssey Networks is a service of the National Interfaith Cable Coalition, established in 1987.

Patheos

www.patheos.com

Founded in 2008, Patheos.com is a destination for engaging in the global dialogue about religion and spirituality and for exploring the world's beliefs. Patheos offers credible and balanced information and resources about religion, bringing together the public, academia, and the faith leaders in a single environment for insight into questions, issues, and discussions. Patheos is designed to serve as a resource for those looking to participate in productive, moderated discussions on some of today's most talked about and debated topics.

The Pluralism Project at Harvard University

www.pluralism.org

This project was designed to help Americans engage with the realities of religious diversity through research, outreach, and the active dissemination of resources.

Prayables

www.prayables.com

This free online prayer community offers women short prayers that reflect women's stories. They are relevant to the times and honor all faith perspectives. Prayables gives women a way to bring more meaning to their lives and a space to simply take time for themselves. The website offers a new way to deal with everyday issues, global concerns, and spirituality. Women can also help others through prayer and build stronger relationships.

Temple of Understanding

www.templeofunderstanding.org

Founded in 1960 by a pioneering visionary, Juliet Hollister, the Temple of Understanding educates youth and adults both cross-culturally and interreligiously for global citizenship and peaceful coexistence. The Temple advocates for acceptance and respect for religious pluralism by the world's governing bodies and actively promotes justice and tolerance.

United Religious Initiative (URI)—North American Affiliate

www.urinorthamerica.org

The purpose of the United Religions Initiative is to promote enduring daily interfaith cooperation, to end religiously motivated violence, and to create cultures of peace, justice, and healing for the Earth and all living beings.

Leadership and Partnership Organizations

Berkana Institute

www.berkana.org

The Berkana Institute works in partnership with a rich diversity of people around the world who strengthen their communities by working with the wisdom and wealth already present in their people, traditions, and environment. As pioneers, the institute does not deny or flee from the global crisis; rather, it responds by moving courageously into the future now, experimenting with many different solutions.

Center for Partnership Studies (CPS)

www.partnershipway.org

Founded by Dr. Riane Eisler and Dr. David Loye in 1987, CPS has worked with thousands of individuals and organizations to change consciousness, promote positive personal action, encourage social advocacy, and influence policy. They offer online leadership training for women's empowerment and real wealth.

Spiritual Directors International (SDI)

www.sdiworld.org

Spiritual Directors International is a global resource both for seekers and for people who offer spiritual companionship. SDI serves a broad spectrum: from seekers who have little to no background in any spirituality to those who want to find specialized spiritual directors in a specific tradition (for example, Benedictine, Buddhist, Franciscan, Ignatian, Jewish). SDI supports a diverse multifaith learning community through educational programs and publications, including a peer-reviewed journal, *Presence: An International Journal of Spiritual Direction.*

Seminaries and Educational Organizations

Auburn Theological Seminary

www.auburnseminary.org

Auburn Theological Seminary is an institute for religious leadership that faces the challenges of our fragmented, complex, and violent times. The seminary envisions religion as a catalyst and resource for a new world—one in which difference is celebrated, abundance is shared, and people are hopeful, working for a future that is better than today's.

Awakening Truth

awakeningtruth.org

This nonprofit is run by volunteers to support a Bhikkhuni training monastery for Buddhist nuns, bringing ancient teachings into the modern world.

Chaplaincy Institute

www.chaplaincyinstitute.org

The Chaplaincy Institute is an interfaith seminary, re-visioning theological education to serve the pluralistic world.

Office of Church Relations of Chapman University

www.chapman.edu/ChurchRelations

The Office of Church Relations stewards the institution's rich heritage as a church-related school, in covenant with its founding denomination, the Christian Church (Disciples of Christ).

Women's Organizations

DreamWeather Foundation

www.dreamweather.org

The DreamWeather Foundation offers workshops, retreats, and conferences throughout the United States that provide time for women to gather, to share dreams and meditation, and to listen to the guidance of the heart.

Earth Child Institute

www.earthchildinstitute.org

The Earth Child Institute is an international not-for-profit, nongovernmental organization working in consultative status with the United Nations and UNICEF. The institute is dedicated to the development and implementation of multicultural, interdisciplinary educational programs that are designed to integrate holistic and indigenous ways of teaching and learning into the context of the modern world.

Fifth World Conference on Women (5WCW)

www.5wcw.org

A call to action in support of a United Nations sponsored 5th World Conference on Women.

Gather the Women

www.gatherthewomen.org

Linked globally by the group's interactive website, Gather the Women invites women to demonstrate their courage to risk leaving old conformities by joining with millions of others throughout the world to celebrate women's true worth, to express shared concern for the human family, and to create and support actions that will enable humanity to live together in a balanced, harmonious, and peaceful world.

Global Room for Women

www.globalroomforwomen.com

The Global Room for Women's mission is to provide a virtual space where women from different cultures come together for dialogue and understanding, where impoverishment gives way to empowerment, and where every woman is awakened to the other. This awakening benefits children, men, the earth, and all beings.

Morning Star Foundation

www.themorningstarfoundation.org

The Morning Star Foundation is committed to creating public awareness for the protection and preservation of all indigenous nations on Mother Earth. The primary purpose of the foundation is to protect and support "Traditional" Elders, sacred sites, sacred burial grounds, and sacred ceremony.

Mothers Acting Up

www.mothersactingup.org

Mothers Acting Up inspires, educates, and engages mothers—a gigantic force to be reckoned with—to prioritize children in corporate and public policies. The organization believes that when mothers lead, generations of global citizens will follow.

North American Women of Faith Network

www.religionsforpeace.org/initiatives/women/northamerica.html

The purpose of this network is to advance the role of religious women in international development, peace-making, and postconflict reconstruction. It is part of the Global Women of Faith Network of the larger organization known as Religions for Peace.

Peace X Peace

www.peacexpeace.org

This is a global network that links women's groups inside the United States with women's groups outside the United States by areas of mutual concern. Circles work locally on all aspects of community building—from financial equity to prevention of abuse to inclusive governments to truth in media and more.

The Red Shoes

www.theredshoes.org

This Louisiana nonprofit organization endeavors to empower the dreams and spirit of women by deepening spiritual awareness. The group provides opportunities for spiritual transformation within a supportive community.

The Sophia Institute

www.thesophiainstitute.org

The institute provides leading-edge programs taught by the world's foremost thinkers and teachers that foster wisdom, wholeness, oneness, sustainability, peace, and the integration of the sacred feminine for the transformation of self and society.

The Spiritual and Religious Alliance for Hope (SARAH)

www.sarah4hope.org

Based in Southern California, SARAH is composed of interfaith women committed to making a difference in their communities.

UN Women

www.unwomen.org

UN Women is a United Nations organization dedicated to gender equality and the empowerment of women. A global champion for women and girls, UN Women was established to accelerate progress on meeting their needs worldwide.

WATER (Women's Alliance for Theology, Ethics and Ritual)

www.waterwomensalliance.org

An international community of justice-seeking people who promote the use of feminist values to make religious and social change.

WISDOM (Women's Interfaith Solutions for Dialogue and Outreach in Metro Detroit)

www.interfaithwisdom.org

This group has been helping women of different faiths and cultures build bridges of understanding in Metro Detroit since 2006.

Women-Church Convergence

www.women-churchconvergence.org

A coalition of autonomous Catholic-rooted organizations and groups working for recognition and empowerment of women in church and society.

Women of Wisdom (WOW)

www.womenofwisdom.org

The Women of Wisdom Foundation is a national women's organization based in Seattle, Washington, providing diverse and innovative programs that offer women opportunities for personal growth and transformation. WOW promotes women's spirituality, creativity, and wholeness, empowers women's voices, and acknowledges women's contributions to the world, honoring the Divine Feminine in all. Women's events include a range of mind, body, and spirit topics for a full healing experience.

Women's Perspective on Money and Spirituality

www.womensperspective.org

Women's Perspective provides transformational education for women seeking to understand their spiritual and economic power. Whether a woman's funds are significant or minimal, Women's Perspective can help bring a woman's financial life into alignment with her core values.

Women Transcending Boundaries

www.wtb.org

This Syracuse, New York–based group has been bringing women together since 9/11.

Women's Organizations, Faith Based

Anglican Women's Empowerment (AWE)

www.anglicanwomensempowerment.org

AWE is a membership movement of Episcopal/Anglican women and girls with a broad diversity of backgrounds, interests, and skills. The organization works for gender equity and social justice around the world.

Church Women United

churchwomen.org/denominations.html

Founded in 1941, Church Women United is a racially, culturally, theologically inclusive Christian women's movement, celebrating unity in diversity and working for a world of peace and justice. Denominational members include:

African Methodist Episcopal Church (AME)
Women's Missionary Society
www.wms-amec.org

African Methodist Episcopal Zion Church (AMEZ)
Women's Home and Overseas Missionary Society
www.whoms.org

American Baptist Churches in the USA (ABC)
American Baptist Women and Girls
www.abwministries.org

Christian Church: Disciples of Christ (CCDC)
Disciples Women
www.discipleshomemissions.org/pagesDW-CWU

Christian Methodist Episcopal Church (CMEC)
Women's Missionary Council
www.c-m-e.org/core/womensmissionarycouncil.htm.

Church of God (COG)
Christian Women's Connection
www.womenofthechurchofgod.org

Church of the New Jerusalem—Swedenborgian (CNJ)
Alliance of New Church Women
womensalliance.blogspot.com/

Community of Christ (COC)
Women's Ministries Commission
www.cofchrist.org

Cumberland Presbyterian Church (CPC)
Women's Ministry of the Cumberland Presbyterian Church
www.ministrycouncil.cumberland.org/womensministry

The Episcopal Church (EC)
Episcopal Church Women
www. ecwnational.org/twentytwelve

The Evangelical Lutheran Church in America (ELCA)
Women of the ELCA
www.womenoftheelca.org

International Council of Community Churches (ICCC)
Women's Christian Fellowship
www.icccusa.com

The Mar Thoma Church (MTC)
Mar Thoma Women's Auxiliary (Sevika Sangham)
www.MarThomasWomensAuxiliary.org

The Mennonite Church (MC)
Mennonite Women
www.mennonitewomenusa.org

National Baptist Convention of America (NBCAM)
NBCA Women's Auxillaries
www.nbca-inc.com

National Baptist Convention, USA (NBCUSA)
NBCUSA Women's Auxiliary
www.nationalbaptist.com/departments/womans-auxiliary/index.html

Presbyterian Church USA (PCUSA)
Presbyterian Women
gamc.pcusa.org/ministries/pw

Progressive National Baptist Convention (PNBC)
www.pnbc.org

Reformed Church in America (RCA)
Reformed Church Women's Ministries
www.rca.org

Religious Society of Friends (RSF)
Unity Society of Friends Women
www.usfwi.org/index.html

United Church of Christ (UCC)
United Church of Christ Women
www.ucc.org/women

United Methodist Church (UMC)
United Methodist Women
gbgm-umc.org/umw

Episcopal Women Gathering

www.circleconnections.com/circles-connections/
episcopal-women-gathering

The mission of this group is to foster the empowerment and connection of women and girls to start, sustain, and unite circles dedicated to taking action for the greater good.

Islamic Networks Group (ING)

www.ing.org

Islamic Networks Group is a nonprofit, educational organization based in the San Francisco Bay Area with affiliates throughout the United States. Founded in 1993, ING promotes interfaith dialogue and education about world religions. Using trained and certified speakers, ING delivers thousands of presentations and other educational programs annually in schools, colleges and universities, law enforcement agencies, corporations, health-care facilities, and community organizations. ING reaches hundreds of groups and tens of thousands of individuals a year at the local grassroots level, thereby building bridges among people of all faiths and none.

Sakyadhita: The International Association of Buddhist Women

www.sakyadhita.org

Since 1987, Sakyadhita has been working to benefit Buddhist women around the world.

Saranaloka Foundation

www.saranaloka.org

This foundation supports western Theravada Buddhist nuns in the forest tradition.

Sojourners: Christians for Peace and Justice

www.sojo.net

The mission of this group is to articulate the biblical call to social justice, inspiring hope and building a movement to transform individuals, communities, the church, and the world.

Jewish Women's Organizations

Jewish Orthodox Feminist Alliance (JOFA)

www.jofa.org

JOFA is a grassroots nonprofit organization established in 1997 to educate and advocate for women's increased participation in Orthodox Jewish life and to create a community for women and men dedicated to such change.

National Council of Jewish Women (NCJW)

www.ncjw.org

The National Council of Jewish Women defines itself as a grassroots organization of volunteers and advocates who turn progressive ideals into action. Inspired by Jewish values, NCJW strives for social justice by improving the quality of life for women, children, and families and by safeguarding individual rights and freedoms.

Women's League for Conservative Judaism (WLCJ)

www.wlcj.org

Women's League for Conservative Judaism supports its individual members, six hundred sisterhoods and synagogue women's groups through innovative programming materials designed to educate and activate members of every age, customized training services, regional networking opportunities with like-minded women, and leadership development to ensure an exciting tomorrow. WLCJ is the voice of the women of the Conservative Movement, representing its membership at a wide array of national, international, religious, and social action organizations.

Women of Reform Judaism (WRJ)

www.womenofreformjudaism.org

Established in 1913, Women of Reform Judaism now represents more than 65,000 women in nearly five hundred women's groups in North America and around the world. With a mission to ensure the future of Reform Judaism, WRJ works to educate and train future sisterhood and congregational leadership about membership, fundraising, leadership skills, advocacy for social justice, and innovative and spiritual programming. It provides financial support to rabbinic and cantorial students at Hebrew Union College-Jewish Institute of Religion, to the youth programs of the Reform Movement, and to programs benefiting women and children in Israel, the former Soviet Union, and around the world.

Muslim Women's Organizations

Canadian Council of Muslim Women (CCMW)

www.ccmw.com

Canadian Council of Muslim Women believes that Muslim women must develop their Muslim identity while being a part of and making a positive contribution to Canadian society and that they must provide positive role models for Muslim youth

Women's Islamic Initiative in Spirituality and Equality (WISE)

www.wisemuslimwomen.org

The Women's Islamic Initiative in Spirituality and Equality is a global program, social network, and grassroots social justice movement led by Muslim women. WISE is empowering Muslim women to fully participate in their communities and nations and amplifying their collective voices.

Young Leaders

Interfaith Youth Core (IFYC)

www.ifyc.org

IFYC's work is based on three guiding ideas that draw from relevant social science data and research: (1) appreciative knowledge of diverse religious traditions and philosophical perspectives; (2) meaningful encounters between people of different faiths and philosophical backgrounds; and (3) common action projects between people of different backgrounds.

REVEAL

www.revealconference.org

REVEAL empowers and advances the next generation of feminine spirituality. The nonprofit believes that when women claim the authentic voice of their souls, they are empowered to change themselves and the world around them.

State of Formation

www.stateofformation.org

State of Formation is a forum for up-and-coming religious thinkers to draw upon the learning that is occurring in their academic and community work, to reflect on the pressing questions of a religiously pluralistic society, and to challenge existing religious definitions.

ACKNOWLEDGMENTS

We have been inspired by so many women on the path to this book. As we learn more about our ancestors and foremothers, we are awed by their example as courageous pioneers on behalf of women's spiritual leadership. We honor and respect the mother-work of thousands of women and hundreds of organizations stepping up to serve humanity at this time. We have learned much from you and look forward to many collaborative efforts in the future.

We have been awakened and nurtured by the depth of wisdom expressed whenever we have gathered in circle with other women. The Young Leaders are teaching us every day with their vitality and keen insights. Every woman who spoke at one of our Women of Spirit and Faith events and every woman who contributed to the fabric of this book has revealed something new about the incredible wholeness at the intersection of women's leadership and spirituality. We are deeply grateful for all of them.

We especially would like to acknowledge Emily Wichland, vice president of Editorial and Production at SkyLight Paths Publishing. This book would not be in your hands without her vision, encouragement, and support. She has guided us through the process with grace, patience, and a big heart. Thank you. We would also like to thank other members of the SkyLight Paths team for their involvement in this book: Tim Holtz, director of Design and Production, for designing the interior, typesetting, and overseeing the overall production development of this book; and Heather Pelham, book designer and production coordinator, for designing the book jacket.

In addition we want to specifically acknowledge each of the twenty-six women who shared their lives with us through their essays. We learned so much from them. We thank them for their wisdom and for the gift of their time in the face of very full schedules.

It is important to note that this book reflects our multiple understandings of that wondrous mystery undergirding our life in community, called by many names: God, Spirit, Creator, Divine Feminine, Higher Power, or by any other sacred words. The book itself is a miracle of divine grace and for this we are profoundly grateful.

Finally we wish to acknowledge our families and friends, who not only put up with the many hours we spent focused on this book, but also became our cheerleaders, supporting us all the way—and reminding us of our bigger vision when we got caught up in the "doingness" of editing a book. We are blessed to have you in our lives.

About the Artists: Charlotte Backman and David Rankin

Charlotte Backman

www.mandalavisions.com

Mandala (pronounced *mund*-dah-la) is the Sanskrit word for *circle*, the most basic form of sacred geometry. Circular forms—combined with spirals, squares, triangles, and crosses—form a symbolic language found throughout the world. These images have been used as tools for spiritual contemplation, healing, and transformation. They represent integration, eternity, and wholeness in both Eastern and Western cultures. Painting mandalas is a spiritual practice for artist Charlotte Backman. Of mandalas she has said, "I am inspired to create them both as an expression and an invitation to the viewer to experience a connection to the Divine. Within their geometrical frameworks lie infinite possibilities of form, color, shape, and texture. Mandalas are visual reminders of universal spiritual truths: everything is connected, and everything is integral to the whole. Their beauty and balance evoke a sense of peace and harmony."

David Rankine

www.davidrankineart.com

David Rankine has graciously allowed WSF to use his art as our logo. Born and raised in Willowdale, Ontario, and educated at York University, Rankine has been exploring through his art, music, and writing the nature of sacredness and creativity. For the past twenty-five years, his visual art has been at the forefront of the Celtic art revival. His interest in the sacred art of his own Celtic background has expanded into a interest in the sacred art of many cultures and faiths, especially that of Hinduism, Judaism, Buddhism, and Islam. Rankine also lectures on sacred art and geometry. He has recently extended his exploration of sacred art and sacred sound into the healing modalities, creating a healing method that incorporates Reiki, music, and sacred geometry. He lives and works in Simcoe County, Ontario.

NOTES

Introduction

1. John Shea, *Stories of God* (Dublin: Mercier Press, 1989), 29.
2. Margaret Wheatley, *Turning to One Another*, 2nd ed. (San Francisco: Berrett-Koehler Publishers, 2009), 142.
3. Frances Hesselbein, *Hesselbein on Leadership* (San Francisco: Jossey-Bass, 2002), 3.
4. Sharon G. Hadary, "What's Holding Back Women Entrepreneurs?" *Wall Street Journal*, May 17, 2010.
5. Sheryl Gay Stohlberg, "When It Comes to Scandal, Girls Won't Be Boys," *New York Times*, June 11, 2011.
6. Mary Daly, *Beyond God the Father: Toward a Philosophy of Women's Liberation* (Boston: Beacon Press, 1973), 19.
7. Jeanette Clancy, *God Is Not Three Guys in the Sky: Cherishing Christianity Without Its Exclusive Claims* (Edina, MN: Beaver Pond Press, 2007).
8. Kathe Schaaf, *Some Things I Know to Be True*, self-published, 2006.

Exploration I: How Do I Express Being an Empowered Woman of Spirit and Faith?

1. Nancy Bieber, *Decision Making and Spiritual Discernment: The Sacred Art of Finding Your Way* (Woodstock, VT.: SkyLight Paths Publishing, 2011), 12.
2. Albert Einstein, *The Human Side: New Glimpses from His Archives*, ed. Helen Dukas and Banesh Hoffman (Princeton: Princeton University Press, 1981), 33.
3. Luciano de Crescenzo, "Thus Spake Bellavista, " *Magill Book Reviews* (Ipswich, MA: Salem Press, 1989), 15.
4. Stephen Mitchell, *The Enlightened Mind: An Anthology of Sacred Prose* (New York: HarperPerennial, 1991), 41.
5. Daniel Landinsky, *I Heard God Laughing: Poems of Hope and Joy, Renderings of Hafiz* (New York: Penguin, 2006), 26.
6. www.beliefnet.com/Prayers/Multifaith/Guidance/Lead-Me-To-Peace.aspx#ixzz1ZIAJdHdo

Exploration II: How Do My Spiritual Values Inform Me about Living with the Challenges and Blessings of Diversity?

1. Frank Newport, "More Than 9 in 10 Americans Continue to Believe in God," *Gallup.Com: Daily News, Polls, Public Opinion on Government, Politics, Economics, Management*, www.gallup.com/poll/147887/Americans-Continue-Believe-God.aspx (accessed June 5, 2011).

2. Baha'u'llah, *The Arabic Hidden Words* (Wilmette, IL: Baha'i Publishing Trust, 1994), 68.
3. Isabel Fraser Chamberlain, *Abdu'l-Baha on Divine Philosophy* (Boston: Tudor Press, 2007), 83.
4. Abdu'l-Baha, *Foundations of World Unity* (Wilmette, IL: Baha'i Publishing Trust, 1955), 29–30.
5. Abdu'l-Baha, *Baha'i Prayers* (Wilmette, IL: Baha'i Publishing Trust, 1982), 150.
6. Landmark Forum is a program of Landmark Education Corporation, which focuses on transformational work for better self-understanding, self-growth, and development. See www.landmarkeducation.com.
7. Most generally defined, the Anglican Communion consists of those churches throughout the world that recognize the leadership of the see (the official *seat* or *throne* of a bishop) of Canterbury in England.
8. The Episcopal Church exists not only in the United States, but also in Honduras, Taiwan, Haiti, the Dominican Republic, Ecuador, Columbia, Venezuela, and parts of Europe.
9. President Barack Obama's full statement can be found at http://www.whitehouse.gov/the-press-office/2011/01/27/statement-president-killing-david-kato.
10. The full transcript of President Obama's remarks can be found at http://www.whitehouse.gov/the-press-office/2011/06/29/remarks-president-reception-observing-lgbt-pride-month.
11. Ibid.
12. Jean Janzen, based on the writings of Julian of Norwich, 1991.
13. Jan L. Richardson, *In Wisdom's Path: Discovering the Sacred in Every Season* (Cleveland: Pilgrim Press, 2000), 116. A new edition was published in 2011 by Wanton Gospeller Press, Orlando, FL.

Exploration III: How Do We Stand for the Greatness of Each Other?

1. Evelyn Underhill, *The School of Charity* (New York: Morehouse Publishing, 1991), 19–20.
2. V. F. Cordova, "Doing Native American Philosophy," in *From Our Eyes: Learning From Indigenous Peoples*, eds. S. Meara and D. A. West (Toronto: Garamond Press, 1996), 14.
3. Gregory Cajete, *Look to the Mountain: An Ecology of Indigenous Education* (Durango, CO: Kivaki Press, 1994).
4. Dawn T. Maracle, "A Story Untold: Contextual Oral Narratives of Mohawk Women from Point Anne" (Master's thesis, OISE/University of Toronto, 2000).
5. North American Indian Travelling College, *Traditional Teachings* (Cornwall Island, Ont., 1984), 3.
6. Llewellyn Vaughan-Lee, *The Return of the Feminine and the World Soul* (Inverness, CA: The Golden Sufi Center, 2009).
7. Margaret Wolff, *In Sweet Company* (Hoboken, NJ: John Wiley & Sons, 2006), ix.
8. Judy Chicago, www.judychicago.com, 1979.
9. Patricia Lynn Reilly, "Imagine a Woman," www.imagineawoman.com, 1995.
10. Dawna Markova, *I Will Not Die an Unlived Life: Reclaiming Purpose and Passion* (Newburyport, MA: Conari Press, 2000), 1.

Exploration IV: How Do We Catalyze Our Collective Transformational Power as Women of Spirit and Faith?

1. Judy Brown, *A Leader's Guide to Reflective Practice* (Bloomington, IN: Trafford Publishing, 2006).
2. Tutu, Desmond, *No Future Without Forgiveness* (New York: Doubleday, 1999), 31.
3. Robert Barton and Annie McGregor, *Theatre in Your Life* (Boston: Wadsworth Publishing, 2008), 33.
4. Kathleen S. Hurty, "Women in the Principal's Office: Perspectives on Leadership and Power," PhD diss. (Berkeley, CA: University of California Microfilms, 1985).
5. Katharine Henderson, *God's Troublemakers: How Women of Faith are Changing the World* (New York: Continuum, 2006), 37–38.
6. Ibid., 21.
7. William Peters, *A Class Divided* (New York: Ballantine, 1971).
8. Peter Senge, "What the Vision Does," http://www.ijourney.org/?tid=669PeterSenge.
9. Thomas Cleary, *The Flower Sutra Scripture* (Boston: Shambhala, 1987).
10. Kate Linthicum, "When It's Time to Run for Office, Fewer Women Stand Up," *Los Angeles Times*, May 23, 2011.

Credits

Grateful acknowledgment is given for permission to use the following: Pp. 17–18, "Willingness," excerpted from *Decision Making and Spiritual Discernment: The Sacred Art of Finding Your Way* © 2010 by Nancy L. Bieber (Woodstock, VT: SkyLight Paths Publishing). Permission granted by SkyLight Paths Publishing, P.O. Box 237, Woodstock, VT 05091 www.skylightpaths.com. P. 51, "Circles," by Hafiz, from the Penguin publication, *I Heard God Laughing: Renderings of Hafiz* © 1996 and 2006 by Daniel Ladinsky and used with his permission. P. 113, "Mothering God," by Jean Janzen, based on the writings of Julian of Norwich, © 1991 by Jean Janzen. P. 117, "Creating God," by Jan L. Richardson, from *In Wisdom's Path: Discovering the Sacred in Every Season*. Original edition published by The Pilgrim Press, Cleveland, Ohio, 2000. New edition published by Wanton Gospeller Press, Orlando, Florida, 2011. P. 139, "Profound Mystery," from *The School of Charity: Meditations on the Christian Creed*, © 1991 Morehouse Publishing. Pp. 167–168, "In Sweet Company," by Margaret Wolff © 2006 (Hoboken, NJ: John Wiley & Sons), reprinted with permission of John Wiley & Sons, Inc. P. 170, "Merger Poem, by Judy Chicago, © 1979 by Judy Chicago, www.judychicago.com. Pp. 175–176, "Imagine a Woman I," © 1995 by Patricia Lynn Reilly, www.imagineawoman.com. P. 183, "I Will Not Die an Unlived Life," by Dawna Markova, excerpted from *I Will Not Die an Unlived Life* by Dawna Markova © 2000, used with permission of Conari Press, an imprint of Red Wheel/Weiser, Newburyport, MA. www.redwheelweiser.com, 1-800-423-7087. Pp. 185–186, "Fire," by Judy Brown, excerpted from *A Leader's Guide to Reflective Practice* © 2006 by Judy Sorum Brown (Bloomington, IN: Trafford Publishing 2006). Pp. 232–233, from *God's Troublemakers: How Women of Faith Are Changing the World* © 2006 by Katharine Henderson (New York: Continuum, 2006), reprinted with permission from the Continuum International Publishing Group.

SELECTED BIBLIOGRAPHY

Anderson, Carolyn, and Katharine Roske. *The Co-Creators Handbook*. Nevada City, CA: Global Family, 2008.

Anderson, Sherry Ruth, and Patricia Hopkins. *The Feminine Face of God: The Unfolding of the Sacred in Women*. New York: Bantam Books, 1991.

Baldwin, Christina. *Calling the Circle: The First and Future Culture*. Bantam: New York, 1998.

Beckett, Wendy. *Sister Wendy's Book of Meditations*. New York: DK Publishing, 1998.

Bishop, Anne. *Becoming an Ally: Breaking the Cycle of Oppression in People*. London: Zed Books, 2002.

Bolen, Jean. *Crones Don't Whine: Concentrated Wisdom for Juicy Women*. Boston: Conari Press, 2003.

———. *Crossing to Avalon*. San Francisco: HarperSanFrancisco, 1994.

———. *Goddesses in Every Woman: A New Psychology of Women*. San Francisco: Harper and Row, 1994.

———. *Goddesses in Older Women: Archetypes in Women over Fifty*. San Francisco: Harper, 2002.

———. *Like a Tree: How Trees, Women, and Tree People Can Save the Planet*. San Francisco: Conari Press, 2011.

———. *The Millionth Circle*. Berkeley, CA: Conari Press, 1999.

———. *Urgent Message from Mother: Gather the Women, Save the World*. Boston: Conari Press, 2005.

Bourgeault, Cynthia. *Centering Prayer and Inner Awakening*. Cambridge, MA: Cowley Publications, 2004.

———. *The Meaning of Mary Magdalene: Discovering the Woman at the Heart of Christianity*. Boston: Shambhala, 2010.

Brussat, Frederic, and Mary Ann. *Spiritual Literacy: Reading the Sacred in Everyday Life*. New York: Touchstone, 1998.

Buchanan, Constance. *Choosing to Lead: Women and the Crisis of American Values*. Boston: Beacon Press. 1996.

Caiazza, Amy. *The Ties That Bind: Women's Public Vision for Politics, Religion, and Civil Society*. Washington, DC: Institute for Women's Policy Research. 2005.

Caplan, Mariana. *Eyes Wide Open: Cultivating Discernment on the Spiritual Path*. Louisville, CO: Sounds True, 2009.

Chittister, Joan. *Called to Question: A Spiritual Memoir*. Lanham, MD: Sheed & Ward, 2009.

———. *The Friendship of Women: The Hidden Tradition of the Bible*. New York: BlueBridge, 2006.

———. *The Gift of Years: Growing Older Gracefully*. New York: BlueBridge, 2008.

———. *God's Tender Mercy: Reflections on Forgiveness*. New London, CT: Twenty-third Publications, 2010.

———. *Listen with the Heart: Sacred Moments in Everyday Life*. Lanham, MD: Sheed & Ward, 2003.

———. *The Monastery of the Heart: An Invitation to a Meaningful Life*. Katonah, NY: BlueBridge, 2011.

———. *Scarred by Struggle, Transformed by Hope*. Grand Rapids, MI: William B. Eerdmans, 2005.

——— and Rowan Williams, *Uncommon Gratitude*. Collegeville, MN: Liturgical Press, 2010.

Clancy, Jeanette. *God Is Not Three Guys in the Sky: Cherishing Christianity without Its Exclusive Claims*. Edina, MN: Beaver Pond Press. 2007.

Coughlin, Linda, Ellen Wingard, and Keith Hollihan, eds. *Enlightened Power: How Women Are Transforming the Practice of Leadership*. San Francisco: Jossey-Bass, 2005.

Curott, Phyllis. *Book of Shadows: A Modern Woman's Journey into the Wisdom of Witchcraft and the Magic of the Goddess*. New York: Broadway Books, 1998.

Eagly, Alice H., and Linda L. Carli. *Through the Labyrinth: The Truth about How Women Become Leaders*. Cambridge, MA: Harvard Business School Press, 2007.

Ehrenreich, Barbara, and Dierdre English. *For Her Own Good: Two Centuries of the Experts' Advice to Women*. New York: Anchor Books, 2005.

Eisler, Riane. *The Chalice and the Blade: Our History, Our Future*. Cambridge, MA: Harper & Row, 1987.

———. *The Real Wealth of Nations: Creating a Caring Economics*. San Francisco: Berrett-Koehler Publishers, 2007.

———, and David Loye. *The Partnership Way: New Tools for Living and Learning*. San Francisco: Harper & Row, 1990.

Estes, Clarissa Pinkola. *Women Who Run with the Wolves*. New York: Ballantine Books, 1992.

Everist, Norma Cook, and Craig L. Neesan. *Transforming Leadership: New Vision for a Church in Mission*. Minneapolis: Fortress Press. 2008.

Fiedler, Maureen. *Breaking through the Stained Glass Ceiling: Women Religious Leaders in Their Own Words*. New York: Seabury Books, 2010.

Flinders, Carol Lee. *At the Root of This Longing: Reconciling a Spiritual Hunger and a Feminist Thirst*. San Francisco: HarperSanFrancisco, 1998.

———. *Enduring Grace: Living Portraits of Seven Women Mystics*. San Francisco: HarperSanFrancisco, 1993.

———. *Enduring Lives: Portraits of Women in Faith and Action*. New York: Tarcher/Penguin, 2006.

————. *Rebalancing the World: Why Women Belong and Men Compete and How to Restore the Ancient Equilibrium.* San Francisco: HarperSanFrancisco, 2003.

Freeman, Sue J. M., Susan C. Bourque, and Christine M. Shelton, eds. *Women on Power: Leadership Redefined.* Boston: Northeastern University Press, 2001.

Galland, China. *The Bond between Women: A Journey of Fierce Compassion.* New York: Riverhead Books, 1998.

————. *Love Cemetery: Unburying the Secret History of Slaves.* New York: HarperOne, 2007.

Goleman, Daniel, Richard Boyatzis, and Annie McKee. *Primal Leadership: Realizing the Power of Emotional Intelligence.* Boston: Harvard Business School Press, 2002.

Gross, Rita. *Buddhism after Patriarchy: A Feminist History, Analysis, and Reconstruction of Buddhism.* New York: State University of New York, 1993.

Guiterrez Baldoquin, Hilda. *Dharma, Color, and Culture: New Voices in Western Buddhism.* Berkeley: Parallax Press, 2004.

Hart, Hilary. *The Unknown She: Eight Faces of an Emerging Consciousness.* Inverness, CA: The Golden Sufi Center, 2003.

Henderson, Katharine Rhodes. *God's Troublemakers: How Women of Faith Are Changing the World.* New York: Continuum International Publishing Group, 2006.

Hesselbein, Frances, and Marshall Goldsmith, eds. *The Leader of the Future.* 2nd edition. San Francisco: Jossey-Bass, 2006.

Hobgood, Mary Elizabeth. *Dismantling Privilege: An Ethics of Accountability.* Cleveland, OH: Pilgrim Press, 2009.

Holmes, Barbara. *Race and the Cosmos: An Invitation to View the World Differently.* Harrisburg, PA: Trinity Press International, 2002.

Hunt, Helen LaKelly. *Faith and Feminism: A Holy Alliance.* New York: Atria Books, 2004.

Hurty, Kathleen S. "Women Principals—Leading with Power." In *Women Leading in Education.* Edited by Diane M. Dunlap and Patricia A. Schmuck. Albany: State University of New York Press. 1995.

Johnson, Elizabeth A. *She Who Is: The Mystery of God in Feminist Theological Discourse.* New York: Crossroad, 1992.

Kanyoro, Musimbi. *In Search of a Round Table: Gender, Theology, and Church Leadership.* Geneva: WCC Lutheran World Federation, 1977.

————. *Introducing Feminist Cultural Hermeneutics: An African Perspective.* London: Sheffield Academic Press, Continuum Books, 2002.

————, and Wendy Robins. *The Power We Celebrate: Women's Stories of Faith and Power.* Geneva: WCC Publications, 1992.

Keepin, Will, and Cynthia Brix. *Women Healing Women: A Model of Hope for Oppressed Women Everywhere.* Prescott, AZ: Hohm Press, 2009.

Kidd, Sue Monk. *The Dance of the Dissident Daughter.* San Francisco: HarperSanFrancisco, 2002.

————. *Traveling with Pomegranates: A Mother-Daughter Story.* With Ann Kidd Taylor. New York: Viking, 2009.

LaMott, Anne. *Plan B: Further Thoughts on Faith.* New York: Riverhead Books, 2005.

———. *Traveling Mercies*. New York: Anchor Books, 2000.

Lesher, A. Jean, ed. *Pathways to Peace: Interreligious Readings and Reflections*. Cambridge, MA: Cowley Publications, 2005.

———. *Prayers for the Common Good*. Cleveland, OH: Pilgrim Press, 1998.

Lindahl, Kay. *How Does God Listen?* Woodstock, VT: SkyLight Paths Publishing, 2005.

———. *Practicing the Sacred Art of Listening*. Woodstock, VT: SkyLight Paths Publishing, 2003.

———. *The Sacred Art of Listening*. Woodstock, VT: SkyLight Paths Publishing, 2002.

Mackenzie, Vicki. *Cave in the Snow: A Western Woman's Quest for Enlightenment*. London: Bloomsbury Publishing, 1999.

Malachi, Tau. *St. Mary Magdalene: The Gnostic Tradition of the Holy Bride*. Woodbury, MN: Llewellyn Publications, 2006.

Manuel, Earthlyn. *Black Angel Cards: A Soul Revival Guide for Black Women*. San Francisco: Harper San Francisco, 1999.

———*Seeking Enchantment: A Spiritual Journey of Healing from Oppression*. San Francisco: Kasai River Press, 2002.

Martin, Courtney E. *Do It Anyway: The New Generation of Activists*. Boston: Beacon Press, 2010.

———, and J. Courtney Sullivan. *Click: When We Knew We Were Feminists*. Berkeley: Seal Press, 2010.

Maser, Shari. *Blessingways: A Guide to Mother-Centered Baby Showers Celebrating Pregnancy, Birth, and Motherhood*. Ann Arbor, MI: Moondance, 2004.

McGowan, Kathleen. *The Expected One: Book One of the Magdalene Line*. New York: Simon & Schuster, 2006.

Merritt, Carol Howard. *Reframing Hope: Vital Ministry in a New Generation*. Herndon, VA: Alban Institute, 2010.

Norton, Joan. *The Mary Magdalene Within*. New York: iUniverse, 2005.

Palmo, Ani Tenzin. *Reflections on a Mountain Lake: Teachings on Practical Buddhism*. New York: Snow Lion Publications, 2004.

Porter, Jeanne L. *Leading Lessons: Insights on Leadership from Women of the Bible*. Minneapolis: Augsburg Books, 2005.

Porter, Tom, and Lesley Forreste. *And Grandma Said—Iroquois Teachings: As Passed Down through the Oral Tradition*. Philadelphia: Xlibris Corporation, 2008.

Powell, Robert. *The Sophia Teachings: The Emergence of the Divine Feminine in Our Time*. Great Barrington, MA: Lindisfame Books, 2007.

Redmont, Jane. *When in Doubt, Sing: Prayer in Daily Life*. New York: HarperCollins Publishers, 1999.

Remen, Rachel Naomi. *Kitchen Table Wisdom: Stories That Heal*. New York: Riverhead Books, 1996.

Rene, Lucia. *Unplugging the Patriarchy: A Mystical Journey into the Heart of a New Age*. Tulsa, OK: Crown Chakra Publishing, 2009.

Robinson, Rita Marie. *Ordinary Women Extraordinary Wisdom: The Feminine Face of Awakening*. Winchester, UK: O Books, 2007.

Ruether, Rosemary Radford, ed. *Gender, Ethnicity, Religion: Views from the Other Side.* Minneapolis: Fortress Press, 2002.

———. *Goddesses and the Divine Feminine: A Western Religious History.* Berkeley: University of California Press, 2005.

Russell, Letty, Kwok Pui-lan, Ada Maria Isasi-Diaz, and Katie Geneva Cannon. *Inheriting Our Mothers' Gardens: Feminist Theology in Third World Perspective.* Louisville, KY: Westminster Press, 1988.

Schaefer, Carol. *Grandmothers Counsel the World: Women Elders Offer Their Vision for Our Planet.* Boston: Trumpeter, 2006.

Schori, Katharine Jefferts. *The Heartbeat of God: Finding the Sacred in the Middle of Everything.* Woodstock, VT: SkyLight Paths Publishing, 2011.

———. *A Wing and a Prayer: A Message of Faith and Hope.* Harrisburg, PA: Morehouse Publishers, 2007.

Scott, Anne. *Women, Wisdom and Dreams: The Light of the Feminine Soul.* Freestone, CA: Nicasio Press, 2008.

Scott, Susan L. *Stories in My Neighbor's Faith: Narratives from World Religions in Canada.* Etibicoke, Ontario: United Church Publishing House, 1999.

Simons, Nina, and Anneke Campbell. *Moonrise: The Power of Women Leading from the Heart.* Rochester, VT: Park Street Press, 2010.

Skog, Susan, ed. *Embracing Our Essence: Spiritual Conversations with Prominent Women.* Deerfield Beach, FL: Health Communications, 1995.

Spretnak, Charlene. *Resurgence of the Real: Body, Nature, and Place in a Hypermodern World.* Reading, MA: Addison-Wesley, 1997.

Starbird, Margaret. *The Goddess in the Gospels: Reclaiming the Sacred Feminine.* Santa Fe, NM: Bear & Co, 1998.

———. *The Woman with the Alabaster Jar: Mary Magdalen and the Holy Grail.* Santa Fe, NM: Bear & Co, 1993.

Suh, Sharon A. *Being Buddhist in a Christian World: Gender and Community in a Korean American Temple.* Seattle: University of Washington Press, 2004.

Taylor, Barbara Brown. *An Altar in the World: A Geography of Faith.* New York: HarperOne, 2009.

———. *When God Is Silent.* Cambridge, MA: Cowley Publications, 1998.

Terry, Lynda, *The Eleven Intentions: Invoking the Sacred Feminine as a Pathway to Inner Peace.* Santa Rosa, CA: L. Terry, 2005.

Tisdale, Sallie. *Women of the Way: Discovering 2,500 Years of Buddhist Wisdom.* Chicago: HarperOne, 2006.

Toms, Justine Willis. *Small Pleasures: Finding Grace in a Chaotic World.* Charlottesville, VA: Hampton Roads Publishing, 2008.

Townes, Emilie M. *In a Blaze of Glory: Womanist Spirituality As Social Witness.* Nashville, TN: Abingdon Press, 1995.

Tsomo, Karma Lekshe. *Buddhism through American Women's Eyes.* New York: Snow Lion Publications, 1995.

———. *Buddhist Women across Cultures.* New York: State University New York, 1999.

———. *Buddhist Women and Social Justice.* New York: State University New York, 2004.

————. *Innovative Buddhist Women: Swimming against the Stream.* New York: Routledge Press, 2000.

————. *Into the Jaws of Yama, Lord of Death: Buddhism, Bioethics, and Death.* New York: State University New York, 2006.

————. *Sakyadhita: Daughters of the Buddha.* Ithaca, NY: Snow Lion Publications, 1988.

————. *Sisters in Solitude: Two Traditions of Ethics for Buddhist Women.* New York: State University New York, 1996.

United Church of Canada, *Faith in My Neighbor: World Religions in Canada: An Introduction.* Toronto: United Church Publishing House, 1994.

Vaughan-Lee, Llewellyn. *The Return of the Feminine and the World Soul.* Inverness, CA: The Golden Sufi Center, 2009.

Walsh, Diana. *Trustworthy Leadership: Can We Be the Leaders We Need Our Students To Become?* Kalamazoo, MI: Fetzer Institute, 2006.

Welch, Sharon D. *Sweet Dreams in America: Making Ethics and Spirituality Work.* New York: Routledge, 1999.

West, Melissa Gayle. *Exploring the Labyrinth: A Guide for Healing and Spiritual Growth.* New York: Broadway Books, 2000.

Williamson, Marianne. *A Woman's Worth.* London: Rider, 1994.

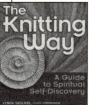
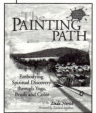
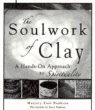

Judaism / Christianity / Islam / Interfaith

Christians & Jews—Faith to Faith: Tragic History, Promising Present, Fragile Future *by Rabbi James Rudin*
A probing examination of Christian-Jewish relations that looks at the major issues facing both faith communities. 6 x 9, 288 pp, HC, 978-1-58023-432-0 **$24.99***

Getting to the Heart of Interfaith
The Eye-Opening, Hope-Filled Friendship of a Pastor, a Rabbi and a Sheikh
by Pastor Don Mackenzie, Rabbi Ted Falcon and Imam Jamal Rahman
Offers many insights and encouragements for individuals and groups who want to tap into the promise of interfaith dialogue. 6 x 9, 192 pp, Quality PB, 978-1-59473-263-8 **$16.99**

Hearing the Call across Traditions: Readings on Faith and Service
Edited by Adam Davis; Foreword by Eboo Patel
Explores the connections between faith, service and social justice through the prose, verse and sacred texts of the world's great faith traditions.
6 x 9, 352 pp, Quality PB, 978-1-59473-303-1 **$18.99**; HC, 978-1-59473-264-5 **$29.99**

How to Do Good & Avoid Evil: A Global Ethic from the Sources of Judaism
by Hans Küng and Rabbi Walter Homolka; Translated by Rev. Dr. John Bowden
6 x 9, 224 pp, HC, 978-1-59473-255-3 **$19.99**

Blessed Relief: What Christians Can Learn from Buddhists about Suffering
by Gordon Peerman 6 x 9, 208 pp, Quality PB, 978-1-59473-252-2 **$16.99**

The Changing Christian World: A Brief Introduction for Jews
by Rabbi Leonard A. Schoolman 5½ x 8½, 176 pp, Quality PB, 978-1-58023-344-6 **$16.99***

Christians & Jews in Dialogue: Learning in the Presence of the Other *by Mary C. Boys and Sara S. Lee; Foreword by Dorothy C. Bass* 6 x 9, 240 pp, Quality PB, 978-1-59473-254-6 **$18.99**

Disaster Spiritual Care: Practical Clergy Responses to Community, Regional and National Tragedy *Edited by Rabbi Stephen B. Roberts, BCJC, and Rev. Willard W.C. Ashley, Sr., DMin, DH*
6 x 9, 384 pp, HC, 978-1-59473-240-9 **$40.00**

InterActive Faith: The Essential Interreligious Community-Building Handbook
Edited by Rev. Bud Heckman with Rori Picker Neiss; Foreword by Rev. Dirk Ficca
6 x 9, 304 pp, Quality PB, 978-1-59473-273-7 **$16.99**; HC, 978-1-59473-237-9 **$29.99**

The Jewish Approach to God: A Brief Introduction for Christians
by Rabbi Neil Gillman, PhD 5½ x 8½, 192 pp, Quality PB, 978-1-58023-190-9 **$16.95***

The Jewish Approach to Repairing the World (*Tikkun Olam*): A Brief Introduction for Christians *by Rabbi Elliot N. Dorff, PhD, with Rev. Cory Willson*
5½ x 8½, 256 pp, Quality PB, 978-1-58023-349-1 **$16.99***

The Jewish Connection to Israel, the Promised Land: A Brief Introduction for Christians *by Rabbi Eugene Korn, PhD* 5½ x 8½, 192 pp, Quality PB, 978-1-58023-318-7 **$14.99***

Jewish Holidays: A Brief Introduction for Christians *by Rabbi Kerry M. Olitzky and Rabbi Daniel Judson* 5½ x 8½, 176 pp, Quality PB, 978-1-58023-302-6 **$16.99***

Jewish Ritual: A Brief Introduction for Christians
by Rabbi Kerry M. Olitzky and Rabbi Daniel Judson 5½ x 8½, 144 pp, Quality PB, 978-1-58023-210-4 **$14.99***

Jewish Spirituality: A Brief Introduction for Christians *by Rabbi Lawrence Kushner*
5½ x 8½, 112 pp, Quality PB, 978-1-58023-150-3 **$12.95***

A Jewish Understanding of the New Testament *by Rabbi Samuel Sandmel; New preface by Rabbi David Sandmel* 5½ x 8½, 368 pp, Quality PB, 978-1-59473-048-1 **$19.99***

Modern Jews Engage the New Testament: Enhancing Jewish Well-Being in a Christian Environment *by Rabbi Michael J. Cook, PhD* 6 x 9, 416 pp, HC, 978-1-58023-313-2 **$29.99***

Talking about God: Exploring the Meaning of Religious Life with Kierkegaard, Buber, Tillich and Heschel *by Daniel F. Polish, PhD* 6 x 9, 160 pp, Quality PB, 978-1-59473-272-0 **$16.99**

We Jews and Jesus: Exploring Theological Differences for Mutual Understanding
by Rabbi Samuel Sandmel; New preface by Rabbi David Sandmel
6 x 9, 192 pp, Quality PB, 978-1-59473-208-9 **$16.99**

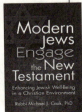

Who Are the *Real* Chosen People? The Meaning of Chosenness in Judaism, Christianity and Islam *by Reuven Firestone, PhD*
6 x 9, 176 pp, Quality PB, 978-1-59473-290-4 **$16.99**; HC, 978-1-59473-248-5 **$21.99**

* A book from Jewish Lights, SkyLight Paths' sister imprint

Spirituality

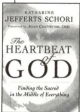

The Heartbeat of God: Finding the Sacred in the Middle of Everything
by Katharine Jefferts Schori; Foreword by Joan Chittister, OSB
Explores our connections to other people, to other nations and with the environment through the lens of faith. 6 x 9, 240 pp, HC, 978-1-59473-292-8 **$21.99**

A Dangerous Dozen: Twelve Christians Who Threatened the Status Quo but Taught Us to Live Like Jesus
by the Rev. Canon C. K. Robertson, PhD; Foreword by Archbishop Desmond Tutu
Profiles twelve visionary men and women who challenged society and showed the world a different way of living. 6 x 9, 208 pp, Quality PB, 978-1-59473-298-0 **$16.99**

Decision Making & Spiritual Discernment: The Sacred Art of Finding Your Way *by Nancy L Bieber*
Presents three essential aspects of Spirit-led decision making: willingness, attentiveness and responsiveness. 5½ x 8½, 208 pp, Quality PB, 978-1-59473-289-8 **$16.99**

Laugh Your Way to Grace: Reclaiming the Spiritual Power of Humor
by Rev. Susan Sparks A powerful, humorous case for laughter as a spiritual, healing path. 6 x 9, 176 pp, Quality PB, 978-1-59473-280-5 **$16.99**

Living into Hope: A Call to Spiritual Action for Such a Time as This
by Rev. Dr. Joan Brown Campbell; Foreword by Karen Armstrong
A visionary minister speaks out on the pressing issues that face us today, offering inspiration and challenge. 6 x 9, 208 pp, HC, 978-1-59473-283-6 **$21.99**

Claiming Earth as Common Ground: The Ecological Crisis through the Lens of Faith
by Andrea Cohen-Kiener; Foreword by Rev. Sally Bingham
6 x 9, 192 pp, Quality PB, 978-1-59473-261-4 **$16.99**

Bread, Body, Spirit: Finding the Sacred in Food
Edited and with Introductions by Alice Peck 6 x 9, 224 pp, Quality PB, 978-1-59473-242-3 **$19.99**

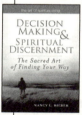

Creating a Spiritual Retirement: A Guide to the Unseen Possibilities in Our Lives
by Molly Srode 6 x 9, 208 pp, b/w photos, Quality PB, 978-1-59473-050-4 **$14.99**

Creative Aging: Rethinking Retirement and Non-Retirement in a Changing World
by Marjory Zoet Bankson 6 x 9, 160 pp, Quality PB, 978-1-59473-281-2 **$16.99**

Keeping Spiritual Balance as We Grow Older: More than 65 Creative Ways to Use Purpose, Prayer, and the Power of Spirit to Build a Meaningful Retirement
by Molly and Bernie Srode 8 x 8, 224 pp, Quality PB, 978-1-59473-042-9 **$16.99**

Hearing the Call across Traditions: Readings on Faith and Service
Edited by Adam Davis; Foreword by Eboo Patel
6 x 9, 352 pp, Quality PB, 978-1-59473-303-1 **$18.99**; HC, 978-1-59473-264-5 **$29.99**

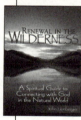

Honoring Motherhood: Prayers, Ceremonies & Blessings
Edited and with Introductions by Lynn L Caruso 5 x 7¼, 272 pp, HC, 978-1-59473-239-3 **$19.99**

Journeys of Simplicity: Traveling Light with Thomas Merton, Bashō, Edward Abbey, Annie Dillard & Others *by Philip Harnden*
5 x 7¼, 144 pp, Quality PB, 978-1-59473-181-5 **$12.99**; 128 pp, HC, 978-1-893361-76-8 **$16.95**

The Losses of Our Lives: The Sacred Gifts of Renewal in Everyday Loss
by Dr. Nancy Copeland-Payton 6 x 9, 192 pp, HC, 978-1-59473-271-3 **$19.99**

Renewal in the Wilderness: A Spiritual Guide to Connecting with God in the Natural World *by John Lionberger*
6 x 9, 176 pp, b/w photos, Quality PB, 978-1-59473-219-5 **$16.99**

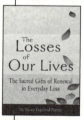

Soul Fire: Accessing Your Creativity
by Thomas Ryan, CSP 6 x 9, 160 pp, Quality PB, 978-1-59473-243-0 **$16.99**

A Spirituality for Brokenness: Discovering Your Deepest Self in Difficult Times
by Terry Taylor 6 x 9, 176 pp, Quality PB, 978-1-59473-229-4 **$16.99**

A Walk with Four Spiritual Guides: Krishna, Buddha, Jesus, and Ramakrishna
by Andrew Harvey 5½ x 8½, 192 pp, b/w photos & illus., Quality PB, 978-1-59473-138-9 **$15.99**

The Workplace and Spirituality: New Perspectives on Research and Practice
Edited by Dr. Joan Marques, Dr. Satinder Dhiman and Dr. Richard King
6 x 9, 256 pp, HC, 978-1-59473-260-7 **$29.99**

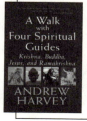

Spiritual Practice

Fly Fishing—The Sacred Art: Casting a Fly as a Spiritual Practice
by Rabbi Eric Eisenkramer and Rev. Michael Attas, MD
Illuminates what fly fishing can teach you about reflection, awe and wonder; the benefits of solitude; the blessing of community and the search for the Divine.
5½ x 8½, 192 pp (est), Quality PB, 978-1-59473-299-7 **$16.99**

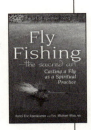

Lectio Divina—The Sacred Art: Transforming Words & Images into Heart-Centered Prayer *by Christine Valters Paintner, PhD*
Expands the practice of sacred reading beyond scriptural texts and makes it accessible in contemporary life. 5½ x 8½, 240 pp, Quality PB, 978-1-59473-300-0 **$16.99**

Haiku—The Sacred Art: A Spiritual Practice in Three Lines
by Margaret D. McGee 5½ x 8½, 192 pp, Quality PB, 978-1-59473-269-0 **$16.99**

Dance—The Sacred Art: The Joy of Movement as a Spiritual Practice
by Cynthia Winton-Henry 5½ x 8½, 224 pp, Quality PB, 978-1-59473-268-3 **$16.99**

Spiritual Adventures in the Snow: Skiing & Snowboarding as Renewal for Your Soul *by Dr. Marcia McFee and Rev. Karen Foster; Foreword by Paul Arthur*
5½ x 8½, 208 pp, Quality PB, 978-1-59473-270-6 **$16.99**

Divining the Body: Reclaim the Holiness of Your Physical Self *by Jan Phillips*
8 x 8, 256 pp, Quality PB, 978-1-59473-080-1 **$16.99**

Everyday Herbs in Spiritual Life: A Guide to Many Practices
by Michael J. Caduto; Foreword by Rosemary Gladstar
7 x 9, 208 pp, 20+ b/w illus., Quality PB, 978-1-59473-174-7 **$16.99**

Giving—The Sacred Art: Creating a Lifestyle of Generosity
by Lauren Tyler Wright 5½ x 8½, 208 pp, Quality PB, 978-1-59473-224-9 **$16.99**

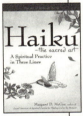

Hospitality—The Sacred Art: Discovering the Hidden Spiritual Power of Invitation and Welcome *by Rev. Nanette Sawyer; Foreword by Rev. Dirk Ficca*
5½ x 8½, 208 pp, Quality PB, 978-1-59473-228-7 **$16.99**

Labyrinths from the Outside In: Walking to Spiritual Insight—A Beginner's Guide
by Donna Schaper and Carole Ann Camp
6 x 9, 208 pp, b/w illus. and photos, Quality PB, 978-1-893361-18-8 **$16.95**

Practicing the Sacred Art of Listening: A Guide to Enrich Your Relationships and Kindle Your Spiritual Life *by Kay Lindahl* 8 x 8, 176 pp, Quality PB, 978-1-893361-85-0 **$16.95**

Recovery—The Sacred Art: The Twelve Steps as Spiritual Practice *by Rami Shapiro; Foreword by Joan Borysenko, PhD* 5½ x 8½, 240 pp, Quality PB, 978-1-59473-259-1 **$16.99**

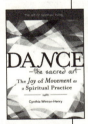

Running—The Sacred Art: Preparing to Practice *by Dr. Warren A. Kay; Foreword by Kristin Armstrong* 5½ x 8½, 160 pp, Quality PB, 978-1-59473-227-0 **$16.99**

The Sacred Art of Chant: Preparing to Practice
by Ana Hernández 5½ x 8½, 192 pp, Quality PB, 978-1-59473-036-8 **$15.99**

The Sacred Art of Fasting: Preparing to Practice
by Thomas Ryan, CSP 5½ x 8½, 192 pp, Quality PB, 978-1-59473-078-8 **$15.99**

The Sacred Art of Forgiveness: Forgiving Ourselves and Others through God's Grace
by Marcia Ford 8 x 8, 176 pp, Quality PB, 978-1-59473-175-4 **$18.99**

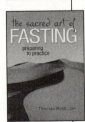

The Sacred Art of Listening: Forty Reflections for Cultivating a Spiritual Practice
by Kay Lindahl; Illus. by Amy Schnapper 8 x 8, 160 pp, b/w illus., Quality PB, 978-1-893361-44-7 **$16.99**

The Sacred Art of Lovingkindness: Preparing to Practice
by Rabbi Rami Shapiro; Foreword by Marcia Ford 5½ x 8½, 176 pp, Quality PB, 978-1-59473-151-8 **$16.99**

Sacred Attention: A Spiritual Practice for Finding God in the Moment
by Margaret D. McGee 6 x 9, 144 pp, Quality PB, 978-1-59473-291-1 **$16.99**

Soul Fire: Accessing Your Creativity
by Thomas Ryan, CSP 6 x 9, 160 pp, Quality PB, 978-1-59473-243-0 **$16.99**

Thanking & Blessing—The Sacred Art: Spiritual Vitality through Gratefulness
by Jay Marshall, PhD; Foreword by Philip Gulley 5½ x 8½, 176 pp, Quality PB, 978-1-59473-231-7
$16.99

Prayer / Meditation

Sacred Attention: A Spiritual Practice for Finding God in the Moment
by Margaret D. McGee
Framed on the Christian liturgical year, this inspiring guide explores ways to develop a practice of attention as a means of talking—and listening—to God.
6 x 9, 144 pp, Quality PB, 978-1-59473-291-1 **$16.99**

Women of Color Pray: Voices of Strength, Faith, Healing, Hope and Courage
Edited and with Introductions by Christal M. Jackson
Through these prayers, poetry, lyrics, meditations and affirmations, you will share in the strong and undeniable connection women of color share with God.
5 x 7¼, 208 pp, Quality PB, 978-1-59473-077-1 **$15.99**

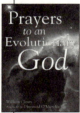

Secrets of Prayer: A Multifaith Guide to Creating Personal Prayer in Your Life   *by Nancy Corcoran, CSJ*
This compelling, multifaith guidebook offers you companionship and encouragement on the journey to a healthy prayer life. 6 x 9, 160 pp, Quality PB, 978-1-59473-215-7 **$16.99**

Prayers to an Evolutionary God
by William Cleary; Afterword by Diarmuid O'Murchu
Inspired by the spiritual and scientific teachings of Diarmuid O'Murchu and Teilhard de Chardin, reveals that religion and science can be combined to create an expanding view of the universe—an evolutionary faith.
6 x 9, 208 pp, HC, 978-1-59473-006-1 **$21.99**

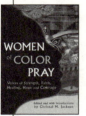

The Art of Public Prayer, 2nd Edition: Not for Clergy Only
by Lawrence A. Hoffman, PhD 6 x 9, 288 pp, Quality PB, 978-1-893361-06-5 **$19.99**

A Heart of Stillness: A Complete Guide to Learning the Art of Meditation
by David A. Cooper 5½ x 8½, 272 pp, Quality PB, 978-1-893361-03-4 **$18.99**

Meditation without Gurus: A Guide to the Heart of Practice
by Clark Strand 5½ x 8½, 192 pp, Quality PB, 978-1-893361-93-5 **$16.95**

Praying with Our Hands: 21 Practices of Embodied Prayer from the World's Spiritual Traditions   *by Jon M. Sweeney; Photos by Jennifer J. Wilson; Foreword by Mother Tessa Bielecki; Afterword by Taitetsu Unno, PhD*
8 x 8, 96 pp, 22 duotone photos, Quality PB, 978-1-893361-16-4 **$16.95**

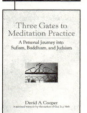

Three Gates to Meditation Practice: A Personal Journey into Sufism, Buddhism, and Judaism   *by David A. Cooper* 5½ x 8½, 240 pp, Quality PB, 978-1-893361-22-5 **$16.95**

Prayer / M. Basil Pennington, OCSO

Finding Grace at the Center, 3rd Edition: The Beginning of Centering Prayer   *with Thomas Keating, OCSO, and Thomas E. Clarke, SJ; Foreword by Rev. Cynthia Bourgeault, PhD* A practical guide to a simple and beautiful form of meditative prayer. 5 x 7¼, 128 pp, Quality PB, 978-1-59473-182-2 **$12.99**

The Monks of Mount Athos: A Western Monk's Extraordinary Spiritual Journey on Eastern Holy Ground   *Foreword by Archimandrite Dionysios*
Explores the landscape, monastic communities and food of Athos.
6 x 9, 352 pp, Quality PB, 978-1-893361-78-2 **$18.95**

Psalms: A Spiritual Commentary   *Illus. by Phillip Ratner*
Reflections on some of the most beloved passages from the Bible's most widely read book.   6 x 9, 176 pp, 24 full-page b/w illus., Quality PB, 978-1-59473-234-8 **$16.99**

The Song of Songs: A Spiritual Commentary   *Illus. by Phillip Ratner*
Explore the Bible's most challenging mystical text.
6 x 9, 160 pp, 14 full-page b/w illus., Quality PB, 978-1-59473-235-5 **$16.99**
HC, 978-1-59473-004-7 **$19.99**

Women's Interest

Spiritually Healthy Divorce: Navigating Disruption with Insight & Hope
by Carolyne Call
A spiritual map to help you move through the twists and turns of divorce.
6 x 9, 224 pp, Quality PB, 978-1-59473-288-1 **$16.99**

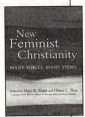

New Feminist Christianity: Many Voices, Many Views
Edited by Mary E. Hunt and Diann L. Neu
Insights from ministers and theologians, activists and leaders, artists and liturgists
who are shaping the future. Taken together, their voices offer a starting point for
building new models of religious life and worship.
6 x 9, 384 pp, HC, 978-1-59473-285-0 **$24.99**

New Jewish Feminism: Probing the Past, Forging the Future
Edited by Rabbi Elyse Goldstein; Foreword by Anita Diamant
Looks at the growth and accomplishments of Jewish feminism and what they mean
for Jewish women today and tomorrow. Features the voices of women from every
area of Jewish life, addressing the important issues that concern Jewish women.
6 x 9, 480 pp, Quality PB, 978-1-58023-448-1 **$19.99**; HC, 978-1-58023-359-0 **$24.99***

Bread, Body, Spirit: Finding the Sacred in Food
Edited and with Introductions by Alice Peck
6 x 9, 224 pp, Quality PB, 978-1-59473-242-3 **$19.99**

Dance—The Sacred Art: The Joy of Movement as a Spiritual Practice
by Cynthia Winton-Henry 5½ x 8½, 224 pp, Quality PB, 978-1-59473-268-3 **$16.99**

Daughters of the Desert: Stories of Remarkable Women from Christian, Jewish and
Muslim Traditions
by Claire Rudolf Murphy, Meghan Nuttall Sayres, Mary Cronk Farrell, Sarah Conover and Betsy Wharton
5½ x 8½, 192 pp, Illus., Quality PB, 978-1-59473-106-8 **$14.99** Inc. reader's discussion guide

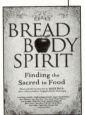

The Divine Feminine in Biblical Wisdom Literature
Selections Annotated & Explained
Translation & Annotation by Rabbi Rami Shapiro; Foreword by Rev. Cynthia Bourgeault, PhD
5½ x 8½, 240 pp, Quality PB, 978-1-59473-109-9 **$16.99**

Divining the Body: Reclaim the Holiness of Your Physical Self
by Jan Phillips 8 x 8, 256 pp, Quality PB, 978-1-59473-080-1 **$16.99**

Honoring Motherhood: Prayers, Ceremonies & Blessings
Edited and with Introductions by Lynn L. Caruso 5 x 7¼, 272 pp, HC, 978-1-59473-239-3 **$19.99**

Next to Godliness: Finding the Sacred in Housekeeping
Edited by Alice Peck 6 x 9, 224 pp, Quality PB, 978-1-59473-214-0 **$19.99**

ReVisions: Seeing Torah through a Feminist Lens
by Rabbi Elyse Goldstein 5½ x 8½, 224 pp, Quality PB, 978-1-58023-117-6 **$16.95***

The Triumph of Eve & Other Subversive Bible Tales
by Matt Biers-Ariel 5½ x 8½, 192 pp, Quality PB, 978-1-59473-176-1 **$14.99**

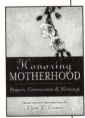

White Fire: A Portrait of Women Spiritual Leaders in America
by Malka Drucker; Photos by Gay Block 7 x 10, 320 pp, b/w photos, HC, 978-1-893361-64-5 **$24.95**

Woman Spirit Awakening in Nature
Growing Into the Fullness of Who You Are
by Nancy Barrett Chickerneo, PhD; Foreword by Eileen Fisher
8 x 8, 224 pp, b/w illus., Quality PB, 978-1-59473-250-8 **$16.99**

Women of Color Pray: Voices of Strength, Faith, Healing, Hope and Courage
Edited and with Introductions by Christal M. Jackson
5 x 7¼, 208 pp, Quality PB, 978-1-59473-077-1 **$15.99**

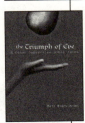

The Women's Torah Commentary: New Insights from Women Rabbis on the 54
Weekly Torah Portions *Edited by Rabbi Elyse Goldstein*
6 x 9, 496 pp, Quality PB, 978-1-58023-370-5 **$19.99**; HC, 978-1-58023-076-6 **$34.95***

---

* A book from Jewish Lights, SkyLight Paths' sister imprint

About SKYLIGHT PATHS Publishing

SkyLight Paths Publishing is creating a place where people of different spiritual traditions come together for challenge and inspiration, a place where we can help each other understand the mystery that lies at the heart of our existence.

Through spirituality, our religious beliefs are increasingly becoming a part of our lives—rather than *apart* from our lives. While many of us may be more interested than ever in spiritual growth, we may be less firmly planted in traditional religion. Yet, we do want to deepen our relationship to the sacred, to learn from our own as well as from other faith traditions, and to practice in new ways.

SkyLight Paths sees both believers and seekers as a community that increasingly transcends traditional boundaries of religion and denomination—people wanting to learn from each other, *walking together, finding the way.*

For your information and convenience, at the back of this book we have provided a list of other SkyLight Paths books you might find interesting and useful. They cover the following subjects:

Buddhism / Zen	Global Spiritual	Monasticism
Catholicism	Perspectives	Mysticism
Children's Books	Gnosticism	Poetry
Christianity	Hinduism /	Prayer
Comparative	Vedanta	Religious Etiquette
Religion	Inspiration	Retirement
Current Events	Islam / Sufism	Spiritual Biography
Earth-Based	Judaism	Spiritual Direction
Spirituality	Kabbalah	Spirituality
Enneagram	Meditation	Women's Interest
	Midrash Fiction	Worship

Or phone, fax, mail or e-mail to: SKYLIGHT PATHS Publishing
Sunset Farm Offices, Route 4 • P.O. Box 237 • Woodstock, Vermont 05091
Tel: (802) 457-4000 • Fax: (802) 457-4004 • www.skylightpaths.com
Credit card orders: (800) 962-4544 (8:30AM–5:30PM ET Monday–Friday)
Generous discounts on quantity orders. SATISFACTION GUARANTEED. Prices subject to change.